T0283455

ENGINEERED
in India

Enjoy reading
Best wishes

[signature]

ADVANCE PRAISE FOR THE BOOK

'Mohan's autobiography is a heart-warming success story of an indomitable young man who has risen from modest beginnings to become one of India's first-generation IT billionaires through sheer determination and hard work. He is one of the pioneers of the Indian IT industry, and his remarkable life is worthy of emulation'—Prof. Raj Reddy, winner of the ACM A.M. Turing Award (Nobel Prize in computing)

'It is instructive that Mohan recognized his purpose early in life and got into the habit of asking himself at every turn—Does this support my dream? He firmly stood by his convictions and chose trajectories that aligned with his purpose, leading to the launch of Cyient, which today is a billion-dollar multinational. Even more inspiring, Mohan has demonstrated that entrepreneurship is not just about profit-making but also about giving back to society. *Engineered in India* faithfully captures Mohan's journey and contains some of the finest business lessons'—Anand Mahindra, chairman, Mahindra Group

'I have known Mohan for over thirty years now. This book brings the distilled wisdom from his experiences and successes as an entrepreneur, a happy family man, an angel investor and a generous philanthropist. It brings out the DNA of his personality—leadership, courage, determination, honesty, integrity, simplicity, conviviality and concern for the less fortunate. Business leaders would benefit much from this book'—N. Narayana Murthy, co-founder, Infosys Limited

'India's demographic dividend, being a young country in an ageing world, is the greatest opportunity to cement its rise. The dividend, however, will realize its potential only if we equip and enable the hundreds of millions of students and working adults with entrepreneurial skills to create jobs and participate in the economy. *Engineered in India* brilliantly scripts Mohan's steadfastness of purpose in motivating the nation's youth to entrepreneurship through his experiences of building a successful multinational from India. This evocative memoir is surfeit with entrepreneurial wisdom that an aspiring youngster will find indispensable to translate their dream into reality!'—Nandan Nilekani, chairman and co-founder, Infosys, and founding chairman, UIDAI (Aadhaar)

'Digitalization and innovation are accelerating the transitioning of the old economy into a more open and dynamic entrepreneurial ecosystem. *Engineered in India* is replete with Mohan's experiences of experimenting with risk-taking and continuous reinvention to perpetuate innovation, the foundation for knowledge-intensive new economy. While nurturing the collaborative spirit, his stewardship of industry bodies such as NASSCOM and CII also demonstrated that an entrepreneur's vision must go beyond the enterprise. This memoir makes a delightful read for every management enthusiast'—Kris Gopalakrishnan, co-founder, Infosys, and chairman, Axilor Ventures

'Dr Mohan Reddy has accomplished more than most, building one of the successful ER&D firms. And as the founder director of T-Hub and chairman of IIT Hyderabad, he left his mark in creating a vibrant innovation and entrepreneurship culture in Hyderabad. *Engineered in India* puts all his achievements in perspective. By narrating not only facts but giving glimpses of his state of mind during difficult and sensitive situations, he helps the readers understand the importance and economics of strong convictions and even stronger values. By sharing his unfiltered past, Mohan Reddy encourages today's entrepreneurs to see a limitless future'—K.T. Rama Rao, cabinet minister for information technology, electronics and communications, and industries and commerce departments, Government of Telangana

'*Engineered in India* is an amalgamation of innovation, differentiation, entrepreneurial spirit, and the foresight that goes into building people and enterprises. Today, India's technology landscape has transcended boundaries, created records and emerged as the world's third-largest start-up ecosystem. Our pioneering initiatives such as Digital India, Start-up India, etc., coupled with the unparalleled contribution of companies such as Cyient, have made India a formidable technology ecosystem. I am confident this book will prove to be a truly motivational and hard-hitting read for all those who continue to redefine the boundaries of innovation'—Amitabh Kant, CEO, NITI Aayog

'B.V.R. Mohan Reddy is one of those rare pioneers who translated his engineering passion into creating an entirely new industry sector. Mohan Reddy has been deeply involved in CII and held several leadership positions over the years. His extensive knowledge, management expertise and solution-oriented approach have guided CII's work and we greatly value his support over the years. This book would resonate with those who are passionate about promoting innovation, entrepreneurship and in creating the right mindset required for making India a thriving entrepreneurial hub'—Chandrajit Banerjee, director general, CII

'Today's India, as a global technology powerhouse, was fostered by determined evangelists like Mohan Reddy. Cyient's evolution mirrors not only the journey of India's economic liberalization and its coming of age but also the origins and growth of ER&D sector, which is now a $36 billion sector. As Indian technology companies continue to create solutions at scale, the next crop of business leaders is poised to transform India into a global hub of unicorns. This book will hopefully become the "North Star" for every entrepreneur to dream, evangelize uncharted opportunities, experiment, fail and bounce back, create world-class organizations and, more importantly, contribute back to the country. The story of Cyient's journey is an absolute must-read'—Debjani Ghosh, president, NASSCOM

'Mohan Reddy is an iconic changemaker who checks every box that characterizes entrepreneurship. Mohan wears multiple hats and yet gives his fullest to every role he takes. The most striking aspect about him is that despite all that he achieved in his incredible journey, he is humble and remains incessantly hungry to learn. *Engineered in India* will take Mohan's legacy beyond Cyient and commit his entrepreneurial journey for posterity'—Sangita Reddy, joint managing director, Apollo Hospitals, and former president, FICCI

'At a time when most Indians who were able to study at a prestigious US university were taken by the American dream, Mohan chose to return home, launch Cyient and groom it to be one of the top engineering service providers worldwide. In my two decades of association with Mohan, I found him to be one of the most ethical people I worked with. Mohan's success has never been motivated by money or recognition. He always focused on creating opportunity, building things that are sustainable, bringing education to people in need and making the world a better place. I find it truly inspirational to see a friend achieve great success by doing all the right things, the right way, for all the best motivations'—Paul Adams, former president, Pratt & Whitney

'Mohan Reddy is, beyond doubt, an exceptional entrepreneur. He is one of the few people who combine growing a company to great success with constantly giving back to society. This makes him unique! Reading the book, one gets fascinated by the fact that Mohan makes everything sound logical and evident, while we all know that achieving the results he achieved is far from trivial. While there's no such thing as a manual to become a good entrepreneur, *Engineered in India* gives evidence-based advice for youngsters aspiring to become an entrepreneur and for seasoned entrepreneurs to further grow their capabilities'—Alain de Taeye, member of the management board, TomTom

'*Engineered in India* is not just a memoir of a highly successful entrepreneur but much beyond. It provides deep insights into various facets of organization-building. Mohan has discussed in detail the concept of PPT—People, Process and Tools—and how he balanced them dynamically as the organization evolved. Yet another interesting aspect is his focus on constant learning and always asking "what's the lesson" from each misstep. I strongly recommend *Engineered in India* to both serious learners and inquisitive explorers of management. The style and the very many anecdotes make the reading enjoyable and relaxing'— Kavil Ramachandran, professor of entrepreneurship (practice), Indian School of Business

'*Engineered in India* is an authentic account of a first-generation entrepreneur who navigated his way to global acclaim. The birth of an enterprise is undoubtedly a deliberate act, as Mohan says, one that he was preparing for right while at the campuses of IIT Kanpur and University of Michigan. Blooming within the diverse cultures of Shriram, MICO, HCL and OMC Computers, he decided to ride the software services tide by launching Infotech. What is striking is its transformation into Cyient edifice as a credible brand. Mohan Reddy continues his odyssey, now focusing on technology start-ups and education. This book is a must-read for the younger generation'—Dr K. Radhakrishnan, former chairman, Space Commission, and chairperson, Board of Governors, IIT Kanpur and IIT Ropar

'The Government of India launched several programmes and initiatives such as Digital India, Start-up India and Aatma Nirbhar Bharat to provide opportunities and empower start-ups. However, for the start-ups to be successful, start-up enablers, the spirit of enquiry, design thinking, innovation, incubation and funding ecosystem are critical. In *Engineered in India*, Mohan Reddy whittles his life's experience and guidance to existing and potential start-ups to help enrich their knowledge and accelerate their entrepreneurial journey. I strongly recommend *Engineered in India*'—Prof. Anil D. Sahasrabudhe, chairman, All India Council for Technical Education

'*Engineered in India* is an amazing story of entrepreneurship, courage and humility, a rare combination. But there is an additional hero in this book that entrepreneurs usually do not talk about: the spouse. Mohan's spouse, Suchi, is the anchor, support and balance required to transform a dream into reality. While many entrepreneurs make money, money was not the single target for Mohan. When he made money and could rest and enjoy life, he changed the spotlight on to infusing entrepreneurial spirit in the younger generation to make India and the world a better place to live in'—Dov Moran, inventor of the USB flash drive, and managing partner, Grove Ventures, an Israeli venture capital fund

'Mohan's uncanny ability to see opportunities where others don't, seizing them and meticulously converting them into long-term business have helped Cyient reach a pole position in the engineering services space. He is a unique mix of high aspiration, humility and prudence, which also defines the culture of Cyient. Mohan's work has been a great influence on me and I consider him a mentor and guide. Like every interesting story, Mohan's life is not one that is linear but a roller coaster of successes and challenges, which he skilfully captured in *Engineered in India*. It's a compelling read, not just for entrepreneurs and business leaders, but for everyone'—G.V. Prasad, co-chairman and managing director, Dr Reddy's Laboratories

'Mohan's storytelling skills make this a compelling read, and his journey paves a path that seems pragmatic and easy to follow. An important lesson to learn from Mohan's approach is the criticality of choosing a path less trodden. It is easier to become a "category leader" if you start out being a "category creator", as his life journey so ably demonstrates. This book is mandatory reading if you are a budding entrepreneur or aspiring to become one'—Rajendra S. Pawar, chairman and co-founder, NIIT Group

'It is a rare and significant achievement to be an innovator multiple times in a lifetime. What my friend and industry colleague Mohan has achieved in this regard is exemplary. He demonstrated that true success comes from a spirit of continuous innovation interspersed with bursts of radical innovation. The companies he nurtured and built, most recently Cyient, are role models for many entrepreneurs and even larger businesses to come together and create a significant segment of the 200-billion-dollar global technology industry from India that we are all proud to belong to. This book is a must-read, and I look forward keenly to my copy'—Dr Ganesh Natarajan, chairman, 5F World, Honeywell Automation India, Lighthouse Communities

ENGINEERED
in India

From Dreams to Billion-Dollar CYIENT

B.V.R.
MOHAN
REDDY

BUSINESS

An imprint of Penguin Random House

PENGUIN BUSINESS

USA | Canada | UK | Ireland | Australia
New Zealand | India | South Africa | China

Penguin Business is part of the Penguin Random House group of companies
whose addresses can be found at global.penguinrandomhouse.com

Published by Penguin Random House India Pvt. Ltd
4th Floor, Capital Tower 1, MG Road,
Gurugram 122 002, Haryana, India

Penguin
Random House
India

First published in Penguin Business by Penguin Random House India 2022

ISBN 9780670097340

Typeset in Adobe Caslon Pro by Manipal Digital Systems, Manipal
Printed at Thomson Press India Ltd, New Delhi

www.penguin.co.in

To my parents, Nagi Reddy and Ratna Kumari,
for all the sacrifices they made for their four children

My wife, Sucharitha,
one of the finest human beings to walk the earth

Our children, Krishna and Vaishnavi,
for all the joy they bring to our lives

A special thanks to my colleague BhanuRekha. She has put in painstaking efforts in recording and transcribing my journey, validating and strengthening facts further through research and interviewing several colleagues, family, friends and customers. Bhanu's passion for perfection, ability to distil complex thoughts and ideas into simple writing, robust vocabulary, continuous intrigue for more stories and countless hours of hard work have enhanced the presentation of this book.

Contents

Foreword by Nirmala Sitharaman

The Indian economy, under the leadership of Prime Minister Shri Narendra Modi, has covered giant strides in the areas of financial inclusion, digital economy, infrastructure growth, and development of new and existing businesses. India now has the fastest-growing major economy in the world. A large part of this growth has been driven by the entrepreneurial spirit intrinsic to India's character.

Today, India has the third-largest start-up ecosystem in the world and has witnessed a manifold increase in the number of unicorns. The country is now home to at least 100 unicorns, with a new unicorn on average being created every ten days. It is this innovative and enterprising drive that the Modi government has been nurturing in its endeavour to forge a New India.

A staunch believer in India's growth opportunity, B.V.R. Mohan Reddy gave up greener pastures elsewhere and embarked on an entrepreneurial journey over three decades ago in the then nascent information technology sector. He first blazed a trail in computer-aided design (CAD) and computer-aided manufacturing, and then in engineering services, becoming a cornerstone for technology-led manufacturing and engineering and research and development (ER&D) services in the country.

Engineered in India faithfully chronicles this journey and enumerates how catalysts like Mohan Reddy can be able partners in nation-building. As India marches towards an *amrit kaal* of shared prosperity and growth, entrepreneurial stories such as these will inspire countless enterprising youths to strive and create their own unicorns.

Nirmala Sitharaman,
Minister of Finance and
Corporate Affairs, Government of India

Foreword by M.M. Murugappan

I first met Mohan in August 1976 on the streets of Ann Arbor in the United States of America. We were graduate students at the University of Michigan—he at the Department of Industrial and Operations Engineering and I at the Department of Chemical Engineering. Little did I know that it was the beginning of an enduring friendship which would mean so much to each of us as we traversed our respective paths through academics, professional pursuits and entrepreneurship.

The story of Mohan sacrificing family togetherness around the birth of his son Krishna to study at the University of Michigan, his steadfast commitment to the motherland and his determination to be an entrepreneur in India was, to me, the most inspiring. This was at a time when youngsters educated in American universities sought opportunities in the US and preferred those over returning to India. Even I, who wished to test the possibility of working in America despite a family business to return to, chose the latter, thanks to Mohan and my late father. Incidentally, my father once told me that Mohan was the finest young man he had ever met.

There are many inspiring autobiographies of successful entrepreneurs, but *Engineered in India* stands out in many ways. It is a passionate saga of professionalism and entrepreneurship built on the bedrock of a farsighted vision and sound values rooted in our culture and heritage. Yet, one that recognizes the need for change and continuously adapts to it while building a global business. It is the story of firm conviction in entrepreneurial risk and extraordinary character that built enduring institutional partnerships while nurturing strong personal relationships. Mohan has done all of this admirably and has chosen to share his experiences, spanning both successes and failures, with great humility.

Mohan's drive for excellence as a trainee engineer, a manager and a business leader, acknowledgement of the value of great mentors and emphasis on continuous learning are indeed object lessons for all of us. More importantly, his relentless and diligent pursuit of goals despite road blocks or a change of stance through introspection is worth emulating. While recognizing the fortuitous events that opened new business opportunities, he also acknowledges his mistakes, enumerates how he corrected them with sage advice, and eventually won the trust of customers and colleagues.

The company and its subsidiaries progressed worldwide on the foundation of well-thought-out strategies, prudent mergers and acquisitions, and international leadership. In parallel, the company institutionalized the value of serving all stakeholders with integrity, dignity and discipline. This is the mantra of Cyient, run by a capable team and inspired by a great leader. In doing so, Mohan has instilled in many an associate in the company the importance of serving the customer as a team with a view to incorporating sustainability across various facets of the business. Choosing board members for their skills, giving them the space to evolve and influencing them to work alongside an efficient management team are the hallmarks of Cyient's culture. This, together with good governance and a clear succession plan at every stage based on experience and competence, has brought robustness to the business.

I have had the privilege of witnessing all of this and was humbled when Mohan and the board invited me to succeed him. Entrepreneurs do not often let go of the companies they built from the ground up, but Mohan had planned his transition, too, with grace and gratitude. Thus, this book will serve as an essential guide to starting up, scaling, bringing growth and sustaining a global business.

At the core of Mohan's achievements have been a supportive family, good friends and well-wishers. He speaks about each of them in a touching tone, explaining how they played an essential role in his journey. Today, Mohan spends significant time pursuing his mission of supporting school education through philanthropy and reforming higher education through policy interventions. Simultaneously, he engages with start-ups and mentors young entrepreneurs. He says they keep him youthful, agile and current.

Though titled *Engineered in India*, this book will inspire readers across all walks of life, not just in India but around the world. This is Mohan's contribution to humanity to make the world a better place to live in with sincerity of purpose.

M.M. Murugappan,
former executive chairman,
Murugappa Group

Preface

This book owes its existence to a moment of truth that most people of my age are faced with: that the old order must yield to the new and that it is in the fitness of things that it should be so. This epiphany struck me when I had turned sixty. Cyient (Infotech was rebranded as Cyient in 2014) had been on a growth drive, was outperforming market expectations, and had an accomplished executive team committed to the long-term sustainability of the company.

To allow the company that I had built from the ground up to take off into the next phase of growth, I needed to choose my successor and gradually cut loose. To my mind, the time had come to take on alternative roles and contribute to nation-building.

I decided to pursue my ardour for entrepreneurship, but in a new avatar: mentoring entrepreneurs and fostering start-ups. My early encounters with some of the young business founders were an eye-opener. Consider these:

Start-up one: Takes cardiac diagnostics to remote locations and allows doctors hundreds of miles away to monitor patients. Replaces large, cumbersome equipment with easy-to-use, small, handheld device that relays critical patient information and artificial intelligence-based analytics in real-time to healthcare providers.

The hitch—the product falls short of delivering the promised functionality repeatedly; substantial changes to product leads to cost and time overruns; operates sub-optimally with a questionable business model.

Start-up two: A pioneer in geothermal cooling technology. Develops a natural and sustainable way to cool buildings and reduce power consumption by 60 per cent. Large, addressable market, a WWF Climate Solver Partner, recognized for innovation and sustainable technology. The hitch—fumbles in implementation and faces the ire of customers; hires wrong people and creates unhealthy culture; mis-assesses the entry barriers and underestimates the looming competition.

Start-up three: Sees a clear opportunity in managing frontline workers and helps them perform their jobs in a better, faster, cheaper and safer manner. Creates a platform that fuels innovation and collaboration, helps customers increase revenues and margins. Scales the company and builds a leadership team. The hitch—lacks a sharp go-to-market strategy; frequent churn in the team leads to unwarranted delays; takes too long to customize and roll out the platform.

These start-up founders are passionate about addressing business challenges and solving society's problems with cutting-edge technology solutions. They are committed, resourceful and inspired to do more and be more. Yet, to translate their fervour into a scalable top-line, they needed guidance in many areas—team, talent, technology, fundraising, sales engine, valuation, partnerships, and short- and long-term strategy, to name a few. I encountered several such experiences as I began taking budding entrepreneurs under my wing.

I was already speaking at engineering colleges, B-schools and start-up events, sharing my entrepreneurial experiments and experiences. I enjoyed sitting through start-up pitches, listening to brilliant ideas and fielding questions to gauge the depth of the entrepreneur's conviction in their product/service. Aware that, unlike my generation, these next-gen entrepreneurs are typically very young and lack experience, I encouraged them to ask questions and was open to assisting them with mentorship, finances and market connections. I even joined the boards of a few of them as an independent director.

By this time, I was deeply convinced that if India was to reap the demographic dividend a young working-class population bestows on it, the nation needed to create enough jobs year after year. Else, the country was poised to face a demographic disaster with unmanageable levels of unemployment. Entrepreneurship, especially technology-based private enterprise, was the perfect engine for job creation, as it would boost innovation and allow India to become *atmanirbhar* (self-sufficient) Bharat and stand tall in a knowledge-intensive global economy. Entrepreneurship was my calling too, so I zealously dived into the activity and engaged with several start-ups over the years.

It was at around this time that the realization dawned on me that, despite my best efforts, I was only able to coach a small set of people—youth with whom I could interact physically during meetings or budding entrepreneurs who approached me for counsel. I kept asking myself: how could I tutor these youngsters to understand entrepreneurship in greater detail and depth? How could I reach out and motivate the millions of capable people out there to turn to entrepreneurship?

I decided it was best to draw from the theory of effectuation (in entrepreneurship) and capture my experiences in a memoir. When COVID-19 hurtled the world into lockdown, it gave me time to pause, reflect and write about how I engineered my passion to build a successful and sustainable company from India, and *Engineered in India* was born. Only in hindsight did I realize this was as much a need to rediscover myself as it was a desire to commit my story for posterity.

In Part One, this memoir traces the background, the setting up, scaling, growth and expansion phases of Cyient, giving experiential evidence of what it takes to ideate, scale, grow and expand an enterprise beyond a country's borders and build a billion-dollar business. In Part Two, I address significant attributes of a successful, sustainable company: customer centricity, quality and process orientation, strategy, finance management, crisis management, people development and institution-building, against the backdrop of Cyient.

Simultaneously, I try to address the intangible and subtle dimensions of being an entrepreneur; the need for a higher vision coupled with operational acumen, grit and persistence, the ability to take risks and connect the dots, communicate and network, empathy, flexibility and lifelong learning.

In short, *Engineered in India* allows readers to understand what to expect from an entrepreneurial journey, and see human truths and the tools they can use to make sense of their experiments.

I wish the aspiring youth of this nation venture to turn their entrepreneurial ambition into an enduring triumph. And if this book helps them in living their dreams in any small measure, I will count this effort worthwhile.

PART ONE

1

Entrepreneur in the Making

It all began when I was seven and spotted a steam engine chugging along the railway line coughing up wisps of white smoke. I was floored. Nanna (father) was on his daily run—driving my siblings and me to school—a ritual that was often peppered with the thrill of watching him take his hands off the steering wheel to light his cigarette. But on this occasion, our car had stopped at the railway crossing to await a passing train, Nanna told us. And, suddenly, there it was—this huge, mammoth object that caught my eye. My father's heroics suddenly faced serious competition from the world of machines, as I watched the engine effortlessly lug an endless chain of bogies. One, two, three, four . . . I was fiercely glad that I knew my numbers.

And thereby hangs the tale of the beginning of my lifelong love affair with mathematics and machines.

At eight, my fascination for steam engines and trains was superseded by roadrollers. 'Magic!' I thought as they trundled around town rolling massive amounts of weight, laying new roads or repairing those in bad shape.

Curious, I wanted to know the ins and outs of its 'magic' and pestered Nanna with a volley of questions till he explained the mechanics of roadrollers in simple and easy terms. I quickly made up my mind to become a roadroller engineer. With all the conceit of the very young, from then on, I informed everyone ad nauseum that I was going to become a road-roller engineer when I grew up. The thought stayed with me, and although I didn't quite remain true to my early pronouncements, I did become an engineer—a mechanical engineer.

I was a curious child with an enormous appetite for reading and learning, and participated in every science debate and elocution in school. As a young adult, machines, especially internal combustion engines, became my ruling passion. New technologies that made efficient engines enthralled me to the extent that even my undergraduate project was devoted to the intricacies of internal combustion (IC) engines.

I took my ardour for machines to the next level by pursuing an MTech at IITK (Indian Institute of Technology, Kanpur), a premier institute for engineering then and now. Industrial engineering was the most sought-after field in the early 1970s and I opted for it. The course and my thesis on 'Assembly line balancing using heuristics' had given me a fair idea of machine production on shop floors, efficiency, optimization, etc.

Throughout the engineering course, the inevitable questions whirled in my mind. 'What is my path? What can I do out of the ordinary to distinguish myself? How can I contribute to society?' It was at around this time that I started toying with the idea of becoming an entrepreneur. I was fascinated with internal combustion engines but I certainly did not envisage doing any research on them. I just had an inner knowing that my play ought to be at the intersection of technology and business.

Companies of that era—the early 1970s—were primarily brick-and-mortar entities and required significant capital. Worse still, work experience was de rigueur for wannabe entrepreneurs who dared to dream of setting up their own shops.

Fresh out of IIT in 1974, I had neither the capital nor the experience. Expecting support from my family was unfair. My family didn't have the money to fund my dreams even if they were so inclined. I came from a middle-class background where education was our primary God, a secure job our mandated path and entrepreneurship unheard of. There were no traces of any business acumen on either side of my ancestry. My paternal grandfather was a farmer. My mother's father was a revenue inspector in British India and Nanna was a police officer. My path was clear. I had to forge my own destiny and invest my youth and capacity into it; it was the only way open to me to gather the necessary knowledge to understand the industry better and gain a deeper perspective of the opportunity landscape.

My purpose set, from then on, I saw every situation, challenge, opportunity and person I encountered as a prospect that would take me closer to my destination. I spent the first eighteen years of my professional life training myself to become an entrepreneur, proactively taking on challenges and delivering results irrespective of the roles that I took on. I believe these were essential years of experience that went on to become the foundation for my eventual entrepreneurial journey.

I landed my first job as senior management trainee with Shriram Refrigeration, a DCM Group company, in Balanagar, Hyderabad. In the 1970s, it was a dream job for a graduating engineer. I was tasked with running the operations of the diesel engine assembly on the shop floor.

Straight out of college, I started managing a team of 300 shop-floor workers, largely skilled, and a few semi-skilled, comprising assembly line operators, painters and packers. I put the knowledge and skills I gained during my Masters to good use on the shop floor. Coupled with my innate discipline and ability to organize work, running the assembly shop turned out to be a breeze.

I acted as though it was my shop. Call it youthful passion, but if we did not produce the targeted twenty-five diesel engines per shift, seventy-five engines per day and 450 engines a week, I self-flagellated and felt I did not deserve my salary. I did everything possible to meet the target. I was short on experience but high on curiosity, and my hunger to learn was a bottomless pit. A compulsive planner, I chalked out detailed production plans and cleared all bottlenecks so that we could meet our targets.

And that's when I developed a healthy respect for Murphy's law on best-laid plans. Despite the planning, meeting targets was not without hiccups. It was a world without computers and those were the days when bills of material (BOMs) were made on paper. My practice was to send a BOM required for the following week to the store manager on a Sunday morning. Monday being a holiday in the Balanagar industrial area of Hyderabad, it was the best way to ensure that everything was in place for the work week ahead. This was when I encountered my first snag. At about 3 p.m., the store manager sent the BOM back to me to apprise me that certain parts were not available at the store. No inventory alerts had come to me ahead of time—either out of ignorance of the production schedule or due to lack of communication from the purchasing department.

'You should have given us advance warning,' I told the individual concerned, feeling thoroughly aggrieved.

He was not open to suggestions. 'How was I to know how much you were going to produce?' He retorted.

'You should have known from the monthly plan,' I said with icy politeness. 'Now we're going to run short of materials.'

'How was I to know? I'm not in the purchase department, I'm the storekeeper. Go and yell at the purchase guys. Why didn't they procure the material for you?'

I gave up, defeated. It was obvious that I was heading nowhere in this particular wrangle. I was in a bind and the only way out was to take matters in my own hand. I would have to keep a microscopic eye on details and plan even more meticulously.

Decision made, I started pre-empting nasty surprises from the stores and purchase departments by travelling fairly often—at least once a month—to Kolhapur. It was the only way to avert delays and ensure that components could be sourced at a moment's notice. I would take the Sunday evening train to Pune, board the unreserved compartment, get off on Monday morning in Pune and take a bus to Kolhapur. After collecting the required parts throughout the day, I would board the train, again in an unreserved compartment, deboard on Tuesday morning in Hyderabad and head straight to the factory to deliver the components. I made sure the assembly line did not come to a standstill when production resumed on Tuesday morning. This continued till we got the procedures in place and the folks in the purchase and stores departments to communicate with us better.

Irrespective of who I was reporting to on paper, I was mainly answerable to N.J. Rao, a tech-savvy senior manager in charge of operations. But the last word in the company belonged to Lala Charat Ramji, chairman of Shriram Refrigeration. He was master of all he surveyed and the ultimate arbitrator on how things ran—and they mostly ran on his whims and fancies.

A disciplinarian and stickler for detail, he would come from Delhi for a review at least once a month. We would get a fax notice on Thursday morning, with the advance intelligence that he would be paying us a visit the following Tuesday. By afternoon, an agenda of fourteen items Lalaji wished to review would arrive. A flurry of activity would kick in. Cleanliness became all important; production came to a grinding halt. Everyone scurried around preparing the agenda items. Two of his executive assistants (EAs)—EA commercial and EA technical—would arrive by the following morning to supervise anything and everything. The minutest details would be looked into—such as spacing between lines in documents—Lalaji had been most unhappy with the double spacing on his previous visit! Anxious discussions would ensue over the colour of ribbons on files—Lalaji had taken a strong dislike to the green ribbons that bound our files, so let's get some blue ones. Whoever drew the short straw would be immediately dispatched to the best shop in Balanagar to procure the said ribbons; next on the list of to-dos would be the all-crucial hierarchy of signatures on the agenda. Seniority-wise, should the signatures begin from left to right or right to left—the things that went under scrutiny were mind-boggling.

Lalaji would duly arrive in Hyderabad at the appointed time on the promised Tuesday morning. He would walk around the facility and pull up everyone in his inimical style. Small of frame, with a pronounced nose and of wheatish complexion, he was well-versed with technology. Hailing from a family that had been in industry for two generations, he was educated, sophisticated and usually gave perfect suggestions to the team. But there were times when he got his priorities mixed up and indulged in operational details that led to hasty decisions and unwanted outcomes.

To be fair to him, he was wonderful to his management trainees and regarded us as the future mainstays of the company. He allowed us to take ownership of our tasks and achieve our targets. I might have been a trainee, but he made me believe that the responsibility and capability to manage the production of diesel engines as per plan was mine, cent per cent. He was not as kind to his senior personnel.

Reviewing people's performance was one of his favourite pastimes. While he gave people a great deal of latitude to learn on the job, his expectations regarding efficiency and turnaround time involved in completing tasks were often unrealistic. We, the management trainees, were the apples of his eye, but some executives became the unwitting targets of his ire. A case in point was our quality manager. Lalaji loved to vent at him for reasons unknown.

'Let's have a review,' he announced one day and turned a gimlet eye on the quality manager.

'Lalaji,' Rao intervened hastily. 'Mohan Reddy is sitting here. He's a trainee in the company.'

I cringed at that point, wishing I could evaporate.

Lalaji took no notice. 'Bhai, Rao,' he said. 'You'll never learn. How many times have I told you that management trainees are the pillars of this company? They are the future. You are too hierarchy-driven! You'll need to do something about it.'

Having disposed of Rao's objections in this rough-and-ready fashion, he continued, 'Rao, which organ in the body is not of much use?'

Poor Rao! He averted his eye and mumbled, 'Appendix.'

'That's right!' said Lalaji, with a glint in his eye. 'Our quality manager is like an appendix. You know what we do with the appendix, don't you? If it troubles you, you cut it and throw it away.'

Young, naive and new to the niceties of working life, the idealist in me was thoroughly unnerved as I warily watched the unfolding scene with a bleak eye. Lalaji was fond of me. He gave me enormous freedom, promotions and hikes at every review (sometimes within three months). He inculcated the entrepreneurial spirit in me like he did with a few others all through his regime. At the same time, I was learning how not to operate a business and manage people; there was also a growing realization within me that this was the kind of business I could not see myself working in for the rest of my career. I contemplated quitting but my principles would not allow me to jump ship at a moment's notice. Instead, I focused on my work and started mapping out how I could head to the US for higher education.

The American Dream

In the US, the Immigration and Nationality Act of 1965, also known as the Hart-Cellar Act, had removed the de facto discrimination against Asians, Southern and Eastern Europeans and other ethnic groups immigrating into the country. It had altered the demographic mix of the country dramatically, encouraging many Indians to move to the US in search of higher education and gainful employment in the subsequent decades.

I was quite keen on getting the best-in-class education, and my determination to work towards it had grown firmer after I had joined Shriram. I was both determined and captivated by the idea of studying in an American university. I simultaneously yearned to see the West. I had heard and read so much about the dramatic technological progress in the western world that I wanted to witness it personally by being part of an American university. By this time, I also understood that in addition to education, I needed to develop lateral thinking, understand different cultures and nurture diversity of thought. I did not want to remain the proverbial frog in the well. I secured a masters' seat at the University of Michigan in 1976, and dispatched my resignation to Lalaji after being awarded a Rotary Foundation fellowship.

He called me to Delhi, another favoured pastime.

'So, you're leaving your father and heading for the US,' he observed disapprovingly as soon as I stepped into his office.

'Lalaji, I've always dreamt of getting a better education,' I said, keeping my calm. 'I've managed to get a seat in a good university and I've got a fellowship to support my studies. Not too many people get such opportunities.'

He did not look too impressed. 'I want to pursue my dream,' I told him, in what I hoped was a firm voice.

'Hmm, so you're determined to leave us,' he said. 'You should stay.'

'I'll complete my masters and come back,' I assured him.

'Sign a bond that you'll return to us,' he said, unmoved. 'Take a salary.'

'I can't do that,' I told him. 'You'll have to take my word for it. You can keep me on your rolls, it'll help me in my provident fund. But I don't want your salary and I don't wish to sign a bond.'

'Alright,' he said. And there the matter ended, much to my immense relief.

The situation at home was even more fraught. When I broke the news to my father he almost fell apart and I saw tears rolling down his cheeks, for the first time in my life. I was appalled.

'Why are you so upset?' I asked him.

'You are disowning the family and taking off for the US. Suchi (Sucharitha, my wife) is pregnant with your first child. I am not keeping good health. How can you abandon us in such a situation?'

My father was the first person from his village to graduate in the late 1940s. My mother was a homemaker. We were four siblings. In my eyes, as far as I could remember, my father had been my hero. A tall and broad-shouldered man, he had trudged about in his starched uniform with state emblems on his shoulder flaps all his working life. He was an honest, courageous and spirited officer affiliated to the Special Police. If there was one thing I could never reconcile to, it was the sad fact that in his long government service from 1947 till his retirement in 1974, he had received just one promotion. He joined as an assistant commandant and retired as commandant, despite all the good work that he put in.

I reckoned he was disappointed with himself for not making it big in life. Within six months of his retirement at fifty-five, he suffered a massive heart attack and developed other complications that went undiagnosed until much later. Unfortunately for my family, these events disturbed his frame of mind. I was quite mindful of the fact and sensitive to his needs.

I tried to reassure him. 'Nanna, I'm not abandoning you or the family. Studying in the US is my dream and I will go. Please be brave. I promise I'll come back.'

'You'll never come back,' he shot back, unconvinced.

There was little I could do to ease his apprehensions except reiterate that I would be back.

I left for the US on 27 August 1976 and the very next day, my son Krishna was born. I lived in a studio apartment on the North Campus in Michigan, missing my wife and child, regretting that I would not be there to see him reach his early milestones.

Since Suchi could not travel to the US with a small baby on her hands, my only option was to finish the course as quickly as I could and get back home. I did eighteen credits per semester (people typically did ten to twelve credits per semester) and completed the thirty-six credits required to gain the degree in less than a year. People said I was killing myself, but I did not care. I was pining for my wife and child and wanted to get back to them as quickly as possible. I would gaze at their photographs endlessly when not thrusting them on my friend M.M. Murugappan and burdening him with my mounting nostalgia. To my mind, the additional burden was well worth the cause.

I completed my MS in Industrial and Operations Management from the University of Michigan in 1977. One of the courses I pursued was small business management under the tutelage of visionary educator Prof LaRue Hosmer at the Ross School of Entrepreneurship. The course introduced me to the operational and strategic problems of small business firms and detailed the ways to manage every aspect of a small business—marketing and sales, people, operations, money—and how to survive in an economy dominated by larger companies. Taking this course was the best thing I did in Michigan as it would be essential to have all these skills when the time came to run my own business.

In those days, about 99 per cent of the Indians who went to the US for a higher education chose to stay back after completing their courses; they found jobs, and became American citizens over time. However, I bucked the trend and came back to India. It's a decision which gives me immense satisfaction to this day. I honoured the promise I made to my father. While this was my primary reason for coming back, at the same time I believed that India had much to offer by way of opportunities for engineers like me.

I also kept my word to Lalaji and resumed work at Shriram. I was back at the diesel engine assembly shop cranking out seventy-five engines every day. Shriram had a compressor assembly shop as well, which was more complex, bigger and produced 300–400 compressors each day; they were used to manufacture air conditioners and refrigerators.

A few weeks after I had rejoined the company, Lalaji summoned me to Delhi. When I met him, to my utter astonishment, he said, 'I will give you three months. Learn everything about the compressor assembly shop.'

I was even more taken aback when he indicated that he wanted me to replace the senior manager who was heading the compressor assembly shop—a competent professional and a person whom I held in high esteem.

My stay in the US had changed my outlook towards life. The liberal values, inclusive culture and egalitarian approach to life I witnessed in the States had made a significant impression on me. I could not think of building my career at the cost of someone else's job. I came back to Hyderabad, gave it a good deal of thought and sent in my resignation.

Lalaji summoned me to Delhi, yet again.

'*Yeh kya kar rahe ho* (What do you think you're doing)?'

'Lalaji, computers fascinate me. I've been working on them since my MTech. My stay in America has made me realize that the world is opening up to their enormous potential and every industry is embracing computers. I wish to work with them.'

'So, install them here,' he said, reasonably.

We had a long chat. But I stood my ground and he eventually let me go. His brand of feudalism just did not appeal to me. Moreover, by then I was dead sure that I wanted to align my career with the computer industry, though I was not very certain where my craft lay.

Enter the World of Computers @ MICO Bosch

Moving out of Shriram, I joined Motor Industries Company Ltd or MICO (subsequently MICO Bosch and now Robert Bosch) in their computers department, which was popularly referred to as the electronic data processing department (EDP). I joined as EDP Systems Analyst, designed their systems and wrote software programs.

I was au fait with higher-level programming languages such as FORTRAN and BASIC. I had written a 2000-line program in FORTRAN for my MTech thesis on assembly line balancing using heuristic methods. However, at MICO, I had to program in Autocoder, a primitive, lower-level language meant for machine-level coding. It was like writing the machine language itself. I was surprised as it was a bit of a comedown, but could not find any reason to crib just because I faced the onerous task of learning a lower-level programming language! My outlook was simple. I had accepted the job at hand and I was determined to succeed. Every evening, I carried Autocoder manuals home and crammed the language. In about three months into my new role, people thought I was close to being an expert. I believe knowledge is a lifelong pursuit and learning something new is not difficult as long as you are driven by curiosity.

After Shriram, MICO was a 180-degree somersault for me. A German company, it was extremely process-driven, quite unlike Shriram, which was people-centric. Every activity/task was structured, documented, communicated and adhered to the last dot. I used to joke that even a washroom visit had a time-stamp and managers possessed complete information on the intervals one spent there.

At MICO, I worked with an interesting boss, Vinod Krishna. He had a large painting in his cabin which was an unusual sight on an office wall. It depicted the organized bullock cart races that were so much a part of the traditional celebrations of Pongal (Sankranti) in south Indian villages. During these races, each cart is typically pulled by two bulls with the cart-driver sitting in front and two people standing by the side as guides. When the carts approach the finishing line, drivers grab the tail of each bullock and bite down hard to make them run faster. This was the scene the painting in Vinod Krishna's cabin depicted and I was quite intrigued by its message.

Embodying the spirit of the painting, Vinod Krishna had an enormous capacity to drive people. Meticulous about processes, he was quite stoic as a person. He arrived sharp at 7.45 a.m. at the office each day. Everything was official about him and he had two secretaries supporting him to uphold the flag of officialdom. All discussions in meetings were typed out and neatly documented in triplicate; one for his office, one for his secretary's office and the third for the individual who had attended the meeting. Those were the days when offices ran on Remingtons and carbon paper and harried secretaries scurried around taking dictations in Pitman's shorthand.

I was not particularly well-acquainted with him in the initial days. All I knew was that Vinod Krishna had fought with the divisional manager Vikram Talwar over my selection. Vikram thought I did not have sufficient experience and was not equipped to lead the team. Against Vikram's best judgment, Vinod hired me.

One day at the computer centre, while I was engaged in a passionate discussion with a senior colleague about programming, Vinod Krishna stood quietly behind us and listened to our conversation for fifteen minutes. After this, my stars changed and I became his blue-eyed boy. Whenever there was a spot of any troubleshooting to be done at the office, he would say, 'Call Mohan Reddy upstairs.'

MICO was an entrepreneurial lesson for me, one that was not quite evident at the time. Entrepreneurs do not simply waltz into entrepreneurship and become overnight stars. I learnt to appreciate and view all my experiences as good learnings. They made me adaptable and helped me perceive opportunities in places where there appeared to be none. Since it was a management position, I learned teamwork, delegation, time management and resource-allocation— skills a startup entrepreneur would require from the word go.

My position at MICO prepped me for an entrepreneurial leap far better than any textbook or coursework ever could. Often, the lessons were subtle as nobody explained explicitly how things worked, but I saw that as long as I was receptive enough, learning was exponential. The more proactive I was in learning from experiences and integrating them into my personality and work style, the more well-rounded I became.

At MICO, we ran a large project on incentive calculation, working out the variable pay of individuals based on their productivity. The production planning department had been handling this task manually until then. We computerized it, and I was in-charge of the project. We had 9000 workers on the shop floor and we processed all 9000 records over one weekend, once in two weeks on an IBM 1401!

At one point, we had to release twenty-one people from the production planning department—redundancies on account of computerization. Vinod Krishna did not let us sleep till the twenty-first person had exited the said department. MICO's work culture and Vinod Krishna's aggressive management style were highly educational and would stay with me for the rest of my career. For several years, I would cite him as a leader who walked the talk. When he left MICO, he said the only person he wanted to take with him was Mohan Reddy. He had taken up a job at Wheels India in Durgapur and asked me to join him. But Durgapur as a career option did not appeal to me very much, so I politely declined his offer. I had my sights set on becoming an entrepreneur, and I wanted to opt for roles that would enrich my experience and enable me to become one. After spending two-and-a-half years at MICO, I started exploring other opportunities.

One of the larger projects I handled at MICO was installing microprocessor-based computers in regional offices. I evaluated computer models available in the market, prepared the capital budget, detailed the cost-benefit analysis and got the project approved. This was when I started interacting with several people at Hindustan Computers Limited (HCL), Shiv Nadar and Arjun Malhotra, co-founders of HCL, among them.

Cracking Sales at HCL

In an informal conversation, Arjun Malhotra asked me if I would be interested in taking up a sales role at HCL. The offer surprised me, but I took it up nevertheless. After learning operations at Shriram and systems management at MICO, sales and marketing were the skills I needed to augment my learning and make it holistic before my big leap. So, I made a conscious choice to venture into sales in 1980. In retrospect, I believe it was the right move. At the time, HCL was celebrating its fifth anniversary. It designed and launched India's first 8C microcomputer and later a 16-bit processor-based computer, becoming one of India's pioneers in the computer manufacturing industry.

The culture at HCL, a homegrown and new-age technology enterprise, was yet another cultural switch for me. Everyone worked with one singular objective—the 'will to win and will to succeed'.

I discussed my designation with Shiv Nadar.

'The Company Law Board permits only one person to hold the title of managing director. Other than that, you can choose any title you want. I will define your role and output, give you a budget to perform, and appraise you purely on what you deliver. The rest is your choice,' Shiv told me with staggering generosity.

I started as the sales manager of the combined state of Andhra Pradesh and had an eight-member team. I was clueless about customer-facing sales processes. Being an introvert, I was good at building relationships one-on-one, but had never been given to garrulity, nor had I ever charmed a group of people to buy into my thinking or product until then. But I had to change with the demands of my role, and I was desirous to do so.

I put my best foot forward and landed my first order from Hindustan Machine Tools (HMT). I was jubilant. As per the terms, the customer had to pay 25 per cent in advance. So, I insisted on getting it. HMT said public-sector companies did not make any advance payments. While this mutual prodding was going on, HMT suddenly asked me to provide a bank guarantee. I was up in arms! I could not understand why I needed to give a guarantee for taking money. Luckily, before things went south, Arjun Malhotra quietly stepped in and patiently explained to me that we had to cough up a bank guarantee for public-sector companies. 'It's the norm, you know,' he added.

My ignorance was obvious, but I saw no reason to confirm it and he was too polite to belabour the point.

He sat me down and set about educating me on the ABCs of customer relationships. I was a quick learner. I examined the nuances of a sales process right from prospecting to closing a sale and coupled it with proactive follow-ups. I groomed myself in the art of sales so well that I often surprised myself.

Typically, sales people adopted four strategies to sell technology products in the 1980s. One set believed they knew everything, including their product, customer behaviour and customer needs. They would aggressively push their company's products or services with an assurance that they could solve all customer challenges. In many instances, this caused grief to both parties.

A good feature of HCL, which is true to a great extent to this day, is that it makes sales personnel believe that they are the best. Graduates, fresh out of college, handsome and with good communication skills, cleverly swept past receptionists, fearlessly barged into offices of senior executives, convinced them about the benefits of using computers and emerged triumphant with purchase orders. Such aggressive selling used to perplex me.

HCL sold computers in amazing ways. More than training, the mindset shift it brought, that everything was possible and the perennial optimism that ruled the roost, were invaluable assets for the company. Even today, it is one of the best firms in India and I respect its marketing and aggressive selling.

The second set believed they had a complete understanding of their product. Instead of approaching potential customers proactively, this conservative clique responded only to those prospective buyers who made inquiry calls. After initial information sharing, they visited their prospects, educated them about the product, made a sales pitch and closed the deal. In many instances, the executive's perception that every possible prospect knew about his company did not hold true, and consequently such executives underperformed constantly.

A third group sold computers through networking and cultivated friends at 'high places', such as decision-makers in government and private sectors. These relationships were not strictly transactional, took time to build and provided upfront value without expectations of any kind in the immediate term. The sales professional sought to earn a return favour and clinched a commercial deal at an appropriate time, later on. It was a tall order, for one can never make friends with all prospects. I did not consider it a good strategy as it completely ignored what a salesperson was selling to the prospect—a solution to his or her problem.

The first step to close a sales deal successfully is to respect a prospect's understanding of his or her business. Instead of treating the product as a commodity, I found it important to research a prospect's needs upfront before starting the outreach conversation. Next, putting forward a solution and explaining how it would add value to his or her business is the key to closing the deal. This fourth strategy created a win-win situation and turned prospects into happy, loyal customers.

I evolved my philosophy around selling by integrating the best elements from all four strategies. We had an excellent product. People called us after reading newspaper advertisements. I encouraged my team to respond to calls actively, visit prospective customers and turn leads into orders. In the first few sales calls, I understood that people were not particularly interested in the technical specifications of the hardware and software. They wanted solutions to tackle the trial balance and P&L (profit and loss) statements of their business as quickly as possible after closing their books every month instead of waiting endlessly for accountants to prepare their reports manually.

I used to tell my team, 'Don't make random claims about the product. Understand the product and its capabilities thoroughly. Invest your energies in building relationships at the right decision-making levels, develop a familiarity with their business challenges, pitch the right solution, demonstrate how you can solve their problems and how your solution can improve their organizational efficiency.'

We slowly brought this cultural shift into the group. Not just by advocating it to my team, but by following the strategy in letter and spirit, myself. I leveraged the traits that were intrinsic to me, such as empathy, analytical capabilities and introverted nature and linked them to the Confucian adage I believed in—nine thoughts to one word—and went on to improve the sales results dramatically.

Although I was not in marketing, my desire to learn how a company acted to attract customers and maintain relationships impelled me to take an interest in it. I became actively involved in HCL's market development activity for its 8C/2 microcomputer. A combination of well-thought-out product positioning, attractive price point, bill discounting scheme with IDBI, and full-page advertisements generated a huge pipeline of prospects leading to record sales. It was a great learning experience.

HCL was a flat organization, and though he was not my reporting manager, I interacted with Arjun Malhotra routinely. Arjun stood at 6 feet in his socks and was a 200 lb hunk, with an attitude as soft as silk. He had the gift of making every senior or junior executive working with him feel as though he/she was his peer. Blessed with a brilliant mind, he could handle any tricky sales situation and would always look for solutions. It was from Arjun that I learned to never give up. I learnt to keep my motivation high till we signed the order or the customer released a PO (Purchase Order). And, in some instances, even after the order was lost, I worked on getting the contract opened again.

The aspiring entrepreneur that I was, I considered sales and marketing as important, if not more than the product/service itself. My sales experience certainly prompted me to build relationships; it taught me how to be self-motivated and ingenious in achieving targets; and it trained me to rely on teamwork. More importantly, I learnt how to handle rejections. I may have started with a set of assumptions, but each rejection ruled out one or more of them and forced me to persist. Tenacity is an extremely valuable trait as a sale rarely happens on first contact. Also, a part of my compensation was linked to the targets. In a sense, my livelihood and ability to provide a comfortable life for my family depended on my success, quarter on quarter—which was likely the case for any entrepreneur.

Three impulses helped me transform into an outperforming salesperson—the need for excellence, a persuasive mindset and achievement motivation. The zeal to excel made a big difference in the outcome of every task leading to success. Though I had no formal training in sales, I consciously nurtured my ability to sell. Once I was convinced of the positive impact an idea, a product or a service could create for a larger group, I persuaded them to buy into my vision, join my team, invest in our company or purchase our products.

Achievement motivation acted as a virtuous cycle, always encouraging me to take on the next challenge.

My appetite for continuous learning helped me build on the initial successes. I analysed every sales success and understood the best and worst parts of the experience, inculcating the habit of never repeating a mistake, and playing on what worked best. I evolved strategies to continuously improve the sales leads, order sizes and shorten the sales cycles. At MICO, I developed solutions for the company, while at HCL, I used my ability to develop solutions to convince the customer to buy them.

For two consecutive years, I became HCL's best sales manager. I was promoted to regional manager in Mumbai to oversee sales of the west zone. This was a larger responsibility in a different geography but the role was largely selling. It left me cold.

'Time to go,' I thought.

I convinced the HCL leadership that I was evaluating entrepreneurial opportunities and exited the company double-quick! I had spent two-and-a-half years at HCL and felt sure I was armed with sufficiently varied experiences on all fronts. I was ready to become an entrepreneur, or so I thought.

2

Thinking like an Entrepreneur, Acting like a CEO

The notion of setting up a personal computer manufacturing company fascinated me. I was continuously researching for a viable start-up idea and this was immensely appealing because it presented a chance to participate in nation-building through import substitution and create much-needed employment in the country. I tentatively floated the idea amongst my friends. Their response was not very encouraging.

A common reaction was surprise: 'You want to become *a computer manufacturer?*'

I would manfully admit that I did.

A touch of scepticism accompanied the next salvo. 'I hope you're aware that you'll need a licence to manufacture computers?'

I felt exasperated. Didn't they realize that I had been working in a computer manufacturing firm for the past couple of years? Of course I knew I would need a licence. I said as much, taking great care to mask my irritation.

Still unconvinced, they tried to dissuade me. 'You do realize that we're under a licence raj, don't you?'

I meekly confessed that I did. The conversation would inevitably end in two ways. The pessimists would invariably pronounce that 'you'll never get a licence' while the more tactful amongst my advisers would predict that 'it'll take you at least three years to get a hold of a licence'.

On one thing, however, there was complete unanimity. Everyone agreed that my plans would be delayed endlessly! I did not quite blame them. Labour unions were up in arms against computers, viewing them as job-hogs. The most difficult challenge was getting government permissions to manufacture computers. As the saying went in those days, 'the toughest challenge was not designing or manufacturing computers but getting a licence to produce them.'

While I may have sympathized with the purity of motive that drove all these naysayers to cast a collective wet blanket on my burgeoning aspirations, I was not deterred. Perversely, it only firmed up my resolve and I began to regard the task of getting a permit as a challenge. It was now incumbent upon me to prove them wrong.

I worked out the details ahead of time, made three trips to Delhi and got my license issued by the Government of India in two months flat!

It involved making a beeline at an institution known as the Director General of Technology Development (DGTD) and dragging my heels while I waited to meet the Director General, a gentleman named Balraj Bhanot. It was an unpleasant experience. There used to be two chairs just outside his room for the unfortunates, one of which was permanently occupied by a chain-smoking peon, who would puff away at his foul-smelling bidis (tendu leaf) without a pause. The second chair was a piteous looking broken-down item that boasted only three highly precarious looking legs. This summed up the arrangements for the dubious comfort of visitors who had dared to enter DGTD's august environs. Imagine inhaling noxious smoke while simultaneously balancing on a three-legged chair with the support of a grimy wall and waiting to be called by the big man. This, I deduced, was the first trial to test one's hardiness of spirit.

Fortunately, once the waiting period was over, matters took on a rosier hue. Balraj was a nice man. He liked my proposal and took it to the Inter-Ministerial Standing Committee (IMSC) and had it approved in record time. It took me a couple of visits to the DGTD office to get my licence. (Subsequently, I visited him a number of times during my stint at OMC, especially when we had to import components and peripherals.)

But how had I reached here? What prompted me to get a computer manufacturing licence? There were several contributory factors.

The personal computer industry—one of the dynamic segments of the electronics industry in the 1970s both in terms of growth and creation of new industry organization models—offered global opportunities for pioneers such as Altair, Apple and IBM. Decisions made by these MNCs had a ripple effect not just on the rest of the computer industry but also on other sectors, including contract manufacturing, electronic components production, distribution, logistics service and support across the world.[1]

In the Asia-Pacific, production facilities were concentrated in Southeast Asia, particularly Singapore and Taiwan. MNCs from the US and other countries set up computer hardware production, especially disk drives, in Singapore. In Taiwan, the government-funded R&D efforts to develop BIOS (Basic Input/Output System) firmware and licensed it for free to local companies. This bore fruit and enabled large-scale manufacturing of motherboards. Taiwan soon became the prime destination for motherboards worldwide.

Over time, labour-intensive activities relocated to low-wage locations such as Thailand, Malaysia and China. Companies in Singapore and Taiwan coordinated production at these sites while executing the more sophisticated manufacturing processes at home.

In India, the government flung the doors open to domestic private-sector participation in the computer industry with the Minicomputer Policy in 1978, announcing the norms to obtain industrial licenses to manufacture computers.[2] The move came after IBM, which had been refurbishing the used 1401 computers and supplying them till then in India, turned down a request from the government to take an Indian partner and manufacture IBM 360-series computers in the country. IBM promptly shut shop in India. Its departure from the Indian market and the policy announcement was timely as a number of private entrepreneurs were ready to occupy the space it had left. Also, the move came at a time when the computer industry was undergoing a tectonic shift from mainframes to mini-computers and microprocessor-based systems.

Though the policy opened the hitherto greenfield computer industry to technocrats, it did not entirely free it from the 'license-permit raj'. Elaborate bureaucratic processes and red-tape led to indefinite delays in obtaining manufacturing licences. To corner the market quickly, HCL, one of the first companies to foray into the computer market, forged a joint venture with Uttar Pradesh Electronics Corporation Ltd, which had the licence to manufacture computers. It designed and launched India's first 8C microcomputer in 1978.

DCM Data Products, ORG Systems, International Data Machines (IDM), PSI Data Systems, Wipro Systems, Patni Computers, and Zenith Computers joined the PC manufacturing race. However, companies could not take advantage of the policy change fully because of high import duties on components and capital goods, restrictions on import of technology and caps on industrial capacities. To meet the demand for computers in the country, entrepreneur-driven companies had no option but to develop their own design capabilities. They designed their systems from scratch using imported microprocessors, support chips, peripherals, and local components.[3] These companies designed motherboards and device drivers, built bespoke operating systems (OS), wrote compilers from scratch and, in some cases, customized UNIX OS to suit their hardware, and developed application programs. But once the government relaxed the policy, motherboards became freely assembled in India and PCs became popular, companies shifted to disk operating systems (DOS), licensing them from Microsoft.

From 1978 to 1984, India witnessed considerable local design and development of computer hardware systems and application software by private entrepreneurs. Thanks to the competition, prices went south. After selling computers at HCL and witnessing the industry's growth in India, I believed computer manufacturing was a good business proposition with a huge addressable market in the country.

In 1982, personal computers were just being introduced in India. The technology was new and exciting. Computers had become a compelling purchase, especially for organizations of any size. I went about my research and developed a project report working out the technical, financial, managerial, production, marketing and sales aspects of manufacturing personal computers (PCs). The opportunity was significant and rapidly growing, and I had all the prospects of becoming an early bird. I began convincing family and friends that computer manufacturing was a good business proposition and started exploring partnerships to launch the business.

I met executives at the Andhra Pradesh Electronics Development Corporation Ltd (APEDC), as it was active in developing electronics units in the state through investments in assisted and joint ventures (JVs). In the absence of private venture capital funds or angel networks in the pre-liberalization era, forging JVs with government entities such as APEDC was vital for a start-up to take off. Having the government as an equity partner reduced the risk for an entrepreneur, improved his credibility and enhanced market access as government agencies were the largest buyers at the time. I presented my business case to the APEDC board. When I got back home, I received a call from Jayabharath Reddy, the chairman. Our families knew each other, and he was a well-wisher.

'Mohan,' he said. 'I wanted to have a word with you.'

'Sure,' I said, encouragingly. 'Go ahead.'

'You're a very bright guy, you know what selling is, and you know how to run a business. But I have some serious apprehensions about your proposal, even though I like it. I don't think you have the right technology with you. The motherboard you have won't last too long and I don't think you have enough money either. You'll probably end up borrowing. I know you're very devoted to your project, but without technology, I don't see your start-up going too far and if you're thinking of borrowing, my advice is to refrain.'

I listened to him keenly and when there were no arguments coming forth from me, he continued. 'I like your concept and I also like you. So, here's my proposition. We have recently approved a proposal to partner a computer manufacturing venture. The proposal was made by Dr Raj Reddy. He's a famous computer scientist. He's going to bring in the technology from the US. The Tatas, through Voltas, are coming in as his local partner, and APEDC is entering as his joint venture partner. The structuring that's been agreed to is that Raj will have 30 per cent ownership in the new entity, Tatas (through Voltas) will hold 30 per cent, and APEDC will own 20 per cent. We're also allowing employees, including you if you choose to join us, to participate in the remaining 20 per cent, and I'll make you our No. 1 employee.'

I was extremely enthusiastic about launching my start-up. I had done the market research and built a business plan. In my eagerness, I may have let a few biases creep into my plan that confirmed or supported my beliefs and market understanding. This might have made me overlook the finer details. Despite the long hours and effort that had gone into crafting my plan, what I believed was a viable business proposition did not seem to cut the ice with APEDC, which was sceptical.

Perhaps it was good to infuse some objectivity into the project right in the beginning. These moments of doubt provided me with an opportunity to recalibrate my beliefs. I took a rational approach to Jayabharath Reddy's feedback and began refining my proposal. I simultaneously started considering his proposition seriously.

I met Dr Raj Reddy. Raj, an amazing computer scientist with a brilliant mind, was the first person of Asian origin to win the ACM A.M. Turing Award (considered the Nobel Prize in computing, in 1994) for his pioneering work in artificial intelligence. Raj was also the first computer science PhD (subsequently faculty) in speech recognition from Stanford University in the early 1960s and had founded the Robotics Institute at the Carnegie Mellon University.

He went on to help build several technical institutes in India, such as IIIT Hyderabad and the Rajiv Gandhi University of Knowledge Technologies (to cater to the educational needs of low-income, talented rural youth). He was honoured with the Padma Bhushan in 2001. He could wax eloquently on driverless cars way back in the 1980s. He ideates brilliantly, is rational, exudes optimism and speaks softly.

A man of slight build with not much hair on his head, he is a wizard as a communicator. Raj, despite being an American citizen, was deeply committed to Indian interests. I was impressed with Raj's vision and also had full confidence in Tata's business acumen and values.

I introspected and realized that a start-up was not just limited to powerful ambition and a game-changing idea. I admittedly had an aspiration, a viable business idea and a scalable opportunity with a substantial addressable market. However, getting the concept right and imagining possibilities was the easy part. The project needed technology access, it was capital intensive and required good financial muscle. I acknowledged that my pockets were not deep enough and that the start-up ecosystem and venture capital funding in the country in the early 1980s was in its infancy.

I saw merit in Jayabharath Reddy's proposition and quietly deferred my dreams. I decided to join the venture. OMC Computers was born. I became part of the leadership team and thereafter its president and managing director in quick succession. I was thirty-one at the time.

I reported to A.H. Tobaccowala, the non-executive chairman of the board. He came with a CV that was impressive enough to scare anyone. A brilliant man, hardly 5 feet 4 inches tall, he had been director on the board of Tata Sons and very dear to J.R.D. Tata. Tobi, as he was popularly called, was a chartered accountant by profession who could see technology inside out, thanks to his experience and ever-burning curiosity. He was a good leader, blessed with a beneficence that I would later come to appreciate. He was also a visionary. The management gave me sufficient freedom within their guardrails and tight financial controls to execute what they expected for the company.

The Omega 58000 Is Born

The word 'workstation' came into existence in the early 1980s. We call personal computers alternately as workstations today, but at that point a workstation was a purpose-built machine. Workstations offered higher performance than mainstream personal computers in terms of CPU (used Motorola 68000 16/32-bit processors as opposed to the Intel 8-bit processors), had a graphics processing unit, a large memory and multitasking capability. They were optimized for visualizing and manipulating different types of complex graphics data and carrying out CPU-intensive analyses, engineering simulation, animation, and rendering of images and mathematical plots.[4] Workstations were equipped with Ethernet to network other computers to form a LAN, with protocols to facilitate smooth data sharing within the network at faster rates (10 MBPS). Working in teams is critical for the continuous exchange of models, analysis and data files in engineering design work and workstations are the perfect fit for such complex activity.

SUN Microsystems (started as a student project at Stanford University[5]) and Apollo Computer Inc were the leading players in the workstation market in the US in the early 1980s. They had a field day fighting fiercely for the top position in the workstation market. The two machines, however, were vastly different. While Apollo was a closed machine with its own OS called Aegis, SUN's workstation had an open architecture and worked on UNIX.

PERQ, conceived by the alumni of Carnegie Mellon University (CMU), was another significant player. Raj, who was working at CMU at the time, had co-founded PERQ. He wanted to bring the PERQ workstation to India through OMC and position it as a mini-computer. His premise was that it had an extremely powerful CPU. Also, there were no multi-user mini-computers manufactured in India and it presented a good market opportunity for PERQ.

I believed that a multi-processing machine should have strong I/O power for business/commercial applications and not necessarily a powerful multi-processing CPU. I contended that PERQ did not have the I/O capability to work like a mini-computer and that it was a single user-networked OS (POS) though capable of multitasking. I was clear and firm that we needed to position the PERQ system as an engineering workstation to support computer-aided design (CAD) and computer-aided manufacturing (CAM) and not as a mini-computer. I convinced Raj that we should introduce CAD/CAM/CAE into the country. Raj agreed to the positioning.

There is no denying that the positioning was excellent and gave OMC a competitive advantage for years. Many companies followed our lead. In subsequent years, Wipro saw a similar opportunity and tied up with Sun Microsystems. HCL, too, exploited the favorable circumstances and partnered with Apollo Computers.

At the point of time we planned to bring PERQ to India, it was a typical graphics workstation and not a CAD/CAM/CAE machine in the true sense. It was being made robust for the commercial environment (as opposed to the academic environment). Once we agreed on the positioning, we put in a substantial amount of effort to make it ready for market. We also felt its proprietary, single-user operating system—POS or PERQ Operating System—would not suit end-users.

We worked hard and spent a significant amount of time improving the product in several iterations to ensure that two things happened: one, that it ran on a UNIX OS and was a multi-processing OS. We did this by working with International Computers Limited (ICL) of UK. ICL did the software porting and we enhanced it substantially thereafter. Second, we convinced the British Company PAFEC Ltd to port their design product DOGS—Drawing Office Graphics System—onto the PERQ system. DOGS leveraged the latest developments in graphics and had a simple, straightforward user interface. The DOGS software was for 2D and 3D design, manufacturing, engineering analysis and geographical information systems (GIS). So, we put the PERQ hardware, Unix OS and

DOGS design software together, and OMC's first product, Omega 58000, was born. And with it, OMC introduced CAD/CAM/CAE systems in India.

We launched the Omega 58000 at CSI Convention at Hotel Taj Banjara in Hyderabad in 1983. Our demos attracted impressive crowds. For the first time, people witnessed the power of graphics, computerized industrial drawings and what CAD/CAM/CAE could do for the industry. Our target customer group consisted of defence laboratories and government organizations.

Our first installation took place at BHEL, Bhopal. One of my support engineers installed the machine at BHEL and took the return train to Hyderabad. Even before he reached, we received a phone call that the system was down. Another engineer was dispatched thereafter to fix the computer. We worked hard in the initial days to improve product reliability, stability and customer satisfaction. I insisted on product reliability, as I believed it was critical to OMC's success.

It turned out to be a comprehensive CAD system for the Indian market. I should acknowledge Pradeep Reddy, Vice President of Engineering, and Malla Reddy, General Manager of Engineering, for making Omega 58000 a comprehensive product. When times were tough, we always said, 'We don't want to fail. We'll do everything to make sure the system performs consistently.' And we did just that. Technology talent was at its best. Given the company profile with an amazing founding team including Dr Raj Reddy, and the brand of Tata, attracting the best talent from the IITs was easy. But for the talented team, we would have faced more serious issues with the product. We had no precedent and introducing a new product—especially a technology product—in an unfamiliar market posed several risks and challenges.

While it is fairly difficult to time a new technology into a market accurately, we were conscious that we would have challenges selling our product if we were ahead of time. At the same time, we did not want to miss the bus.

We therefore ensured that our product was robust and reliable, aware that an unreliable product would increase our support costs and create a poor reputation for the new entrant. Next, we chalked out a plan for product positioning, pricing, regions to sell and customer segmentation to target the right clients. Product pricing was tricky in a price-sensitive emerging market. Being the first also meant that OMC had to take on the burden of market development by itself. The company spent a sizeable marketing budget on creating awareness, writing whitepapers on potential benefits and participating in industry shows.

While the new product involved higher customer acquisition costs, it also necessitated that we invest a disproportionate amount of time and effort in educating customers throughout the sales cycle. In-person sales meetings, de-jargoning technical aspects and persuasive communication on how the product would enhance their current business practices helped.

At the same time, we realized that a new product in a virgin market had certain advantages. Customers learnt to trust us as the 'industry's first', offering OMC a competitive edge. The company sustained the first-mover advantage through a multi-pronged strategy. Many pioneers fail to identify the building blocks of sustained advantage such as eliminating customer dissatisfaction by solving their problems. The successful implementation of OMC's strategy reflected the cumulative learnings I had absorbed from Shriram, MICO and HCL. It also shaped me as a CEO.

My experience as a frontline salesman and sales manager at HCL stood me in good stead and helped me push sales and manage sales personnel at OMC. Initially, I took direct responsibility for sales and marketing since it was critical to the company's success. Past experiences are certainly good data points to build the future. I tried replicating the HCL 8C/2 campaign to promote the *Draftsman* system at OMC and was equally successful.

Introducing CAD/CAM workstations was a bold move for OMC and sales were slow to come by initially. Nevertheless, our market segmentation and development acted as critical differentiators in stimulating growth and building a successful brand.

OMC became a rising star and one of the top ten computer manufacturing companies within five years of its inception. Its turnover, which stood at Rs 3.10 crore in 1984, shot up to Rs 15 crore by June 1988. Recognizing the benefits of design automation, many companies followed our lead. The momentum picked up and the Indian market for CAD/CAM/CAE touched Rs 30 crore in 1988, with OMC cornering 50 per cent of the market share.

Policy Reforms: Stairway to Industry Growth

In 1984, the Union Government under Prime Minister Rajiv Gandhi liberalized policies governing computer manufacturing in the country. This facilitated a liberal import of fully assembled motherboards (sub-systems) with processors at reduced import duties. Ironically, trade unions dubbed 1984 as the 'Anti-Computerization Year', though the opposition to computers at this point was much weaker than it had been in the late 1960s. The policy opened up imports but retained some elements of protectionism and achieved the desired results in the hardware sector. Within a year of the introduction of the policy, computer production grew by 100 per cent in unit terms and 65 per cent in monetary terms, while prices fell by 50 per cent.[6]

The success of the computerized ticket reservation system in the Indian Railways changed the attitude of the general population and politicians towards computers. Consequently, the popularity of personal computers grew exponentially. In 1984, we introduced a PC with MS-DOS, a plotter, 2D drafting software (DraftPack 2D) and a graphics library—and called it Draftsman 2D. DraftPack 2D was another novel product from OMC. It was one of the earliest examples of indigenous CAD software in a market dominated by the likes of AutoCAD for 2D drafting work. It supplemented our sales effort with Omega 58000. The awareness of CAD/CAM and its adoption increased steadily in India, and companies like OMC successfully launched new products in line with market requirements and customer acceptance.

Initial hiccups notwithstanding, the product did very well in the market. DraftPack, however, was a low-end product. We then diversified and bought a 3D modelling product from the US, customized it to perform finite element analysis for CAD and launched the higher-end version with 3D modelling capabilities. We called it DraftSmith 3D.

Introducing a low-end CAD product, especially a complete solution, and following it up with product diversification proved to be a fantastic go-to-market strategy. Mindset barriers of customers came down, market accessibility and affordability improved and, as a result, the market size expanded. We had different price points for additional functionality, all catering to the same segment—Computer Aided Design & Drafting (CADD). The more we reached out to the market, the more the inquiries flowed.

Raj played an active role in building the business in the initial years. He encouraged me to dream big. A man of excellent technology vision, his concepts were way ahead of time and, honestly, some were not implementable in the times we lived in. But he was very persuasive, and would repeatedly cajole us in a gentle fashion to try, and we would work—over and over again.

In 1987, I lost my father. Raj was in Bangalore (now Bengaluru) at the time. He called me up to offer his condolences. I spoke to him briefly, hung up the phone, and thought to myself, 'It was nice of him to give me a call.'

Four hours later, he appeared at my house in Hyderabad. He said, 'Mohan, I want to be with you in this difficult time.' It was a moving gesture on his part which touched me deeply. He was empathetic, affectionate and gave us a lot of freedom to operate. Caring for employees is one of the leadership lessons I learnt from Raj. I was quite close to him and did not consider leaving OMC for the first eight years I was there. I continue to have a good relationship with him to this day. He provided me with a great opportunity and I will always be indebted to him.

One of the key reasons for OMC's success was its people. The company had the financial support of the Tatas, technology from

Carnegie Mellon and Raj Reddy's mentorship. These attributes went a long way in attracting the best talent. As the start-up CEO, I contributed by selling the dream of opening a new industry in India. Building CAD software, repurposing an OS for design workstations, working on leading-edge hardware gave the associates enormous work satisfaction.

The output, the team's success and consequently that of the organization became contingent on the kind of relationships that people built. While trust formed the basis of all relationships, respect, self-awareness, inclusion and open communication created a nurturing environment for greater collaboration and cooperation. Attrition was low, reflecting well on the work culture.

Finance was a challenge right from the start. I wish OMC had been better funded in the initial days; it would have avoided the continuous stress on the leadership. In the 1980s, financial institutions charged 18 per cent on long-term borrowings and 20 per cent on short-term working capital borrowings. Lead times for imports were long (the average time for clearing customs was around 10–12 weeks) and many components needed import licences. All this meant we had fairly large working capital needs. In addition, most of the sales were made to the government or government-funded institutions, which delayed payments. For around Rs 18.40 crore of annualized revenue for FY 1992, short-term borrowings were around 200 days covering inventory, work-in-progress and bills outstanding. The interest burden on the company on short-term and long-term borrowings was about 14 per cent of the sales income. This came as a salutary lesson for me that owners should ensure a company is funded well. Constant pressure for funds prevented the management from focusing on sales and growth and made fundraising from banks a tad more challenging.

Screw-Driver Assembly

The liberalization of computers and software import enunciated in the 1986 government policy acted as an impetus to the software export industry.[7] It, however, maintained restrictions on the import of computers (especially those not used to produce software exports) to give a leg up to domestic computer manufacturing. Without a deeper understanding of the nuances of electronics manufacturing and the lack of assembly-line capability and automation, Indian companies became adept at what was derisively described as 'screw-driver manufacturing'.

Manufacturing computers was manual, efficiencies were low, and it became a complex process. Manufacturers started relying heavily on companies in Taiwan, Singapore and Hong Kong to source low-cost motherboards, floppy disk drives, monitors, power supplies, connectors and cables, and even the outer shell. They assembled imported parts and put their own labels and manuals. Manufacturers did the systems engineering and developed appropriate software.

The emphasis on self-reliance and building computers with locally made components was completely buried and computer manufacturing typically became computer assembly with imported parts. In some instances, it was more expensive to import parts rather than a fully assembled computer. However, the availability of locally manufactured computers from many vendors allowed consumers a choice, and competition drove down prices. Nevertheless, OMC did reasonably well. We had 300 to 400 employees, and a turnover of Rs 15 crore by 1988.

In the second half of the 1980s, Silicon Graphics Inc., rebranded as SGI, rose to prominence in the US. Stanford professor James H Clark, who specialized in 3D graphics workstations, co-founded it. I had the honour of hosting him once. Over dinner, Prof. Clark talked about his goal of taking graphics to the next level by replacing Motorola 68000 (a 16/32-bit CISC microprocessor) with an RISC processor, capable of high-performance computing.

We were impressed with Prof. Clark's vision and signed a million-dollar agreement with SGI in 1987 for the technology transfer of their IRIS (Integrated Raster Imaging System) CAD-CAM workstation. IRIS was a powerful personal workstation and had a separate graphics engine (GPU) along with a CPU. It was a step change in terms of the CAD applications it could offer. IRIS could help a design engineer in essential applications such as modelling, finite element analysis and computerized numerical control. An attractive proposition for the manufacturing industry, it turned out to be a huge success; the industry welcomed it and our sales went up. Design engineers could attempt serious design work on a computer and get substantial results for the first time. SGI was pleased with our partnership as a huge market like India had opened up for them.

However, by 1990, SGI found a few more partners in India, who were in direct competition with OMC. SGI expected that it would be able to address the large Indian market better if it had multiple partners. Close on the heels of this development, the Indian government liberalized the policy and gave a go-ahead for computer imports. This flung the doors open to multinationals who could now sell computers directly in the Indian market.

SGI entered the Indian market in direct competition to OMC, selling an advanced version of IRIS—the IRIS Indigo workstation— to break out of the graphics niche and compete more directly with Sun Microsystems and HP with the latest and advanced graphic systems. OMC came under stress. The competition started building as companies started importing the machines and no longer manufactured them in the country.

Import liberalization brought several thousands of PCs into the country, expanding computer usage. This gave rise to small-scale software firms that catered to the software needs of new computer owners. However, on the flip side, technological and design capabilities built during the 1970s and early 1980s eroded. Manufacturing computers in the country was viable only when volumes were high. However, software services had turned into a high-return business proposition buoyed by several government incentives. The Policy on Computer Software Export, Software Development and Training announced in 1986 began to show promising results, with Indian companies capturing the international software market. The definition of 'software export' was broadened to include exports via satellite data links and 'consultancy delivered at the location of foreign clients abroad by Indian software professionals.'[8] This opened the door to the uniquely Indian phenomenon called 'body shopping'. It was time for computer companies to pivot.

My entrepreneurial instincts resurfaced as I saw this as an excellent business opportunity. I had been at OMC for nine years and was getting restive once again. I wanted to break out on my own. I needed to challenge myself. The ambition to become an entrepreneur had been burning inside me right from the day I had stepped out of college. But two triggers fuelled my entrepreneurial impulses again—the first was the fact that I'd turned forty that year (1990). I said, 'If I don't do it now, I'll never do it in this lifetime. This is my last chance. If I miss this window, I'm finished as a wannabe entrepreneur.' I think it is true. Even in hindsight, it was my last chance.

After all, becoming an entrepreneur in mid-life was not a bad idea. In fact, it turned out to be my true calling. I now had the necessary experience in sales, marketing, finance and operations to bring to the table of any business. Experience aside, my aptitude to continuously reinvent myself and my passion to build something new would find a great avenue if I launched my own firm.

The second trigger that pushed me to leave OMC was that its promoters began toying with the idea of selling the company. They had identified a few large corporates and showcased the company. The buyers wanted leadership continuity and made my staying on in the company a condition post-acquisition. One of the directors who was leading the sale transaction had all but committed that I would stay with the firm, post-sale. I dug in my heels when I heard of the clause. It was completely unacceptable. There was no way I was going to work for the new management.

I had a private chat with the said director and informed him that I was not willing to work for the new management under any circumstances. 'The day you sell the company will be my last day here,' I told him.

'You are stalling the sale with your actions and you are being unfair to other shareholders,' he charged. An extremely unpleasant conversation ensued between us. Upset, I headed straight to my friend Rajan Babu Kasetty, whose office was a couple of kilometres from OMC's, composed my resignation letter on his typewriter, and sent it to Raj and Tobi. I thanked them for the opportunity, informed them that I was quitting whilst simultaneously making it clear that my decision was non-negotiable. The director in question had apparently already communicated my intent to the two of them, so my resignation did not come as much of a surprise to either. Given my past conversations articulating my aspirations to become an entrepreneur, when I met them, they expressed their disappointment but quickly reconciled to the fact that I would be leaving and decided to name Pradeep Reddy as my successor.

I was given a year to gradually hand over the reins of OMC to Pradeep. He had joined OMC at around the same time as I had and was serving as its executive director. He oversaw R&D, production and maintenance. Once Pradeep was identified as my successor, I stopped overseeing the operations. Instead, I started focusing on software exports for the company as this division needed attention.

I had a 3 per cent stake in the company when I left OMC. Tobi bought it with Voltas' funds and helped me raise Rs 20 lakh as seed money for my new company.

Running OMC Computers was a blessing in so many ways. I gained the rich experience of running a complex business for ten years. One might say I had technology support from Raj, the best management experience from Voltas and government support from APEDC. We faced tremendous challenges in product development, component imports and clearing customs. But the lessons I learnt about the nuts and bolts of running a business—product development and positioning, negotiating for new technology, handling people, finances, banking and government relationships—were invaluable. It was a rollercoaster ride every day, managing customers and their complaints, repairing the machines, fighting throughout.

OMC gave my business instincts a free run to build the organization from the ground up. By bringing CAD/CAM, a new technology, into the country, OMC opened the door for technology-

led manufacturing across industry sectors. It created a new generation
of engineers in the country with capabilities in design engineering,
which in turn laid the foundation for the ER&D services industry
to flourish in the country. When I look back, my journey at OMC
fills me with the satisfaction of not just selling a product but also
an idea—of introducing a concept, a dream and an industry to this
country. It was a fitting forerunner to my eventual journey as an
entrepreneur.

3

Birth of a Dream

'Do you think it's the right thing to do at this point of time?' Suchi had asked a few weeks before when I told her that I wanted to quit OMC and start out on my own. I could see that the very idea was making her nervous. To her it must have seemed like being asked to jump off an aeroplane without a parachute. Her biggest fear was for the children.

'Our kids are young—they're still in school. Krishna is fifteen, Vaishnavi's just ten . . . How will we protect their future? How will we manage their needs?'

Her questions were valid, as were her fears, but I had already anticipated them. Call it my weakness or my strength, but I like to examine every situation from all possible angles, well ahead of time. Family support was critical to the gargantuan leap I was contemplating. I knew I had to take care of their future before heeding my inner voice. Family came first.

By the time Suchi voiced her concerns, I had figured out a solution. Suchi had an apartment in Secunderabad. 'Let's sell it and invest the proceeds in a commercial property that gets us enough rent to take care of our needs.'

Suchi was game. She sold her flat and bought a piece of commercial property in Chennai. Part of our savings were added to meet the purchase and once the deed was done, we put it on lease to the largest Indian software company then and now—TCS. She was doubly comfortable with her monthly check.

It went a long way in settling her fears. 'I think it'll fetch us enough rental income to keep the family finances in the black,' I told her with satisfaction. 'I promise I won't touch it. Our social status will be undisturbed and we'll still be able to live in the style that we're used to. We have our own home, our kids will continue in the same school, and we'll still have our car and driver. I'm sure we'll outlive this property in ten years, by which time we'll together decide what we want to do with it.'

Suchi had consented but she knew that once I took the plunge, significant sacrifices awaited her down the pike. She realized that once I set up shop, I would become totally immersed in trying to make a go of it, which meant she would have to run the house, take care of the kids and deal with the angst of their adolescent years all by herself. But now that she was convinced that the family's finances were secure, Suchi was prepared to stand by me every step of the way, through thick and thin.

I started serving the year-long cooling-off period at OMC, but my entrepreneurial plans were still weighed down by several silent moments of doubt and hesitation. My career was thriving. As founding CEO, I had built, scaled and nurtured OMC Computers. The company was growing steadily, it paid me well and provided for all the creature comforts, permitting me to keep my family in a certain degree of luxury. I had developed extensive connections across the industry, with several of them vying to hire me at senior leadership positions in much larger companies.

Was I doing the right thing? Should I have allowed myself to stay on as a senior executive, instead of taking this leap of faith to follow my dreams? Was I doing the right thing by attempting to rescript my future? Was it tantamount to sacrificing a promising executive career? What about my family? Was I sacrificing my wife and kids at the altar of my dreams? These questions gnawed at me for several months.

Suchi's questions, too, needed careful consideration. What if I let her down? But by this time, I had bitten the bullet and there was no way to head except forward.

Opportunity, India

As chance would have it, fortune smiled and the business environment in the country became increasingly conducive. Once software came under Open General Licence (OGL) in 1986, imported software packages and tools flooded the Indian market. With this, awareness vis-a-vis software, software usage and, consequently, software skills grew dramatically. Onshore and onsite software development and body shopping emerged as the preferred business model.

Businesses started exploring opportunities to develop software expertise indigenously and export software services. Domestic companies set up links with American customers and their larger computer systems and started working out of India. Soon, offshore development started gaining acceptance with customers and brought tremendous traction to Indian software companies. American companies, too, came to India and set up software development facilities, taking advantage of the existing high-level technical skills and affordable labour costs.[1] Early birds such as TCS, Wipro, Patni Computers and Infosys were growing steadily by the late 1980s. NASSCOM, established in 1988, gave the nascent industry a voice and platform for collective representation. Indian software exports rose from an insignificant number in 1978 to $128 million in 1990.

Independent India underwent one of the worst foreign exchange crises in its history in 1991. Brought about by years of macroeconomic imbalances that eventually weakened the economy, it was precipitated by the Gulf War of 1990. Political uncertainties, double-digit inflation and the dip in confidence of external creditors pushed the country close to defaulting on its external debt.

In July 1991, the newly elected minority government at the Centre announced a slew of policy measures intended to not just stabilize the economy but also restructure it. It turned the crisis into an opportunity. India devalued the rupee and subsequently let the market determine its exchange rate; import licensing with some exceptions were abolished; convertibility (with some exceptions) of the rupee on the current account were introduced; excise duties on several commodities were reduced; limited direct tax reforms were initiated; entry requirements on FDI were eased and private investment in some industries hitherto reserved for public-sector investment were given the green signal.[2]

These and the follow-on policies changed the course of the nation and its economy. The 'licence-permit raj' came to a welcome end and the era of 'liberalization' kicked in, leading to far-reaching consequences for the industry. Economic growth, which had hovered around 3.8 per cent from 1950 to 1990, accelerated to 7 per cent within two years of liberalization.[3]

Under the new policy regime, the government offered several incentives and floated schemes to promote software services exports. The Software Technology Parks of India (STPI) was one of them. This scheme is often credited with the rise of the Indian software industry in the post-liberalization period. STPI, set up as an autonomous society under the Department of Electronics (now Ministry of Electronics and Information Technology), acted as a single window to provide a wide range of services to software exporters, especially small and medium enterprises (SMEs) and start-ups.

Start-ups under the STPI scheme could claim 100 per cent tax exemption on income from software exports for ten years. This helped them to plough back their earnings into the company for further growth. They were exempted from customs duty on hardware and software imported into India as long as they were used for software exports. This saved significant capex for SMEs and start-ups and brought down the cost of computing, making Indian IT services cost competitive vis-à-vis neighbouring countries. As a result, computing and business costs came down and India became a competitive IT destination globally.

The government simplified procedures for multinational companies to set up branches in India as 100 per cent equity companies.[4]

Added to this, a technically savvy influential Indian diaspora in the US opened up opportunities for Indian software companies. The low-entry barriers and asset-light model of software services attracted several technology entrepreneurs to launch businesses.

STPs created excellent infrastructure and ambience for software export companies where there had been none before. It allowed such flexibility that people could plug and play rather than own/ lease premises. The government leased properties from private/ local government players and sub-leased them to small businesses. A three-floor, 1,80,000 square feet space in HUDA Maitrivanam became the first software technology park of Hyderabad.

The offshore business model, technology advancements, availability of low-cost skilled human resources and regulatory relaxations all contributed to the creation of a highly conducive macro-environment that fanned the entrepreneurial aspirations of thousands of educated youths in the country, including mine. To me it seemed like a great opportunity to recruit engineering talent in India and train it to deliver world-class services to global companies.

Zeroing in on Digitization

The birth of an enterprise is a deliberate act. Before setting up my new enterprise, it was imperative that I identified the right opportunity and made the right choice. Decision-making was complex as I had to view all my options from every conceivable perspective— be it technology, human resource capability, scale, market access, solutioning, funding and regulatory.

I travelled extensively to the US in the West and Singapore and Taiwan in South-East Asia during the cooling-off period at OMC. While I brought in good business for OMC selling DraftPack 2D, OMC's 2D drafting software, these trips also opened my eyes to the tremendous potential to sell software services in the American market. These insights corroborated the rationale behind the ongoing flurry of activity and policy initiatives in India that were aimed at boosting software exports. Asking me to focus on exports, in a sense, turned out to be OMC's parting gift to me. I could develop a deep understanding of the software services export markets.

I toyed with several business ideas and finally concluded that while I had the requisite experience in both hardware and software, in the prevailing climate, the larger business opportunity lay in software services.

I decided to ride the tide. Wasting no time, I incorporated Infotech Enterprises in August 1991 to provide 'software services exports'. My wife Suchi became its authorized signatory. I did not invest much thought in the name of the company—as long as it represented my intent, I was content with the name. It was undoubtedly an oversight on my part. I should have weighed the pros and cons of adopting such a generic name with more care.

Once the company was formed, I started wrestling with its purpose. What could I do in software? What could I do that was unique? How could I be distinctly different from the prevailing players in the market? Where could I find a niche market in software in current times that had the potential to become big in the future? If I put my hand into a market segment that was already too big, it would be easy for the incumbents to crush my venture. If it was too small, I would never be able to build anything significant. Where could I start small and create something big, of enduring value? More importantly, where did my experience and passion lie? There were no easy answers.

For about ten years, I had sold CAD software instead of commercial products at OMC Computers. I had inhaled and exhaled CAD, CAM, CAE day in and day out, contributing to the foundation of India's computer-based design engineering industry. 'Should I enter the CAD software services now and leverage my experience?' I wondered.

I believed the potential for CAD software services was enormous but I had no concrete evidence to support my belief with any certainty. I still had my moments of doubt. But in hindsight, they were essential because they helped me to figure out that there were several aspects of the venture that I had not yet dealt with.

I met a few companies in New York to get a barometer reading on the existing and potential design, computing and analysis services to gauge whether there was a real market for it. People waxed eloquent on how the western world was embarking on computer-based drafting in a big way, which had been done manually until then. While companies had started undertaking new drafting work on computers using CAD software, extensive archives of drawings on paper and mylar yet needed to be digitized.

In any manufacturing entity, parts and part families are typically used for several years. Product engineers had to make sure the manually created drawings and the information in them were also incorporated into their systems. I queried if older drawings could be scanned and stored in digital form. I soon realized that when drawings were scanned, they got stored as raster images (the equivalent of a photograph) and could neither be manipulated or edited and nor could engineering analysis be carried out on them. So, the task for companies was to get their old drawings into the computers in an intelligent format (also known as the vector format).

Several companies tried vectorizing raster images using software and basic artificial intelligence algorithms, with little success. A joke that went around in those days was that 'a computer converts 95 per cent of the drawings and leaves behind five per cent and it takes 95 per cent of the time to fix the remaining 5 per cent'. Companies spent millions of dollars in the 1980s to evolve algorithms to recognize patterns and automate the paper-to-digital process. Given the limited computing power and insufficient data, the nascent machine learning algorithms were not efficient enough to justify the investments.

That is when I learnt about a technique called heads-up digitization. It first involved scanning an image into a computer as a raster image. The digitizer then traced/overlaid the points, lines, splines, circles, polygons, annotations and text on the raster using digitizing software. The digitizers thereafter converted them into intelligent vector data and populated the database schema with each feature of the drawing in different layers. It was a fairly laborious process but it was the only way to get accurate replicas of paper drawings and, more importantly, build intelligence into them.

The backlog of drawings that needed to be digitized had high volumes, and it had become quite expensive for American companies to do these projects locally. However, thanks to the affordable cost, technical workforce and scale of operations, they became highly cost-effective when they were shipped to India. The availability of high-speed communication links at STPIs, and the promotion of software exports by the government helped the 'offshore' take-off in a big way. I then stumbled on a few small Indian companies that recently began offering engineering design services, such as scanning and digitizing engineering drawings and paper maps and preliminary CAD work. This reinforced my hypothesis that digitization services were a compelling business proposition.

I researched further and, by October 1991, it became quite clear to me that CAD services had great potential. Digitization offered several advantages. It eliminated the vast storage spaces that paper drawings required. The intelligent digital drawings could be modified, reused, shared with ease and printed at the click of a mouse. On the flip side, I concluded that the return on investment for companies to digitize their industrial drawings was limited as in-house users for the drawings were small and the reuse of old drawings was infrequent.

In comparison, digitizing paper maps, which required similar technology, seemed to present a more compelling case for business. For instance, telecom, electric, gas and water utility companies in the US started digitizing their asset (underground and above the surface) maps. These digital maps enabled them to create digital databases of their assets using a GIS (Geographic Information System), which dramatically improved the utility's ability to manage their assets.

This, in turn, improved operational efficiency, increased service reliability, strengthened safety and regulatory compliance and reduced operating costs. Moreover, the frequency of use of these digital maps was relatively high. Each map had many end users. This prompted companies to invest in digitization. Clearly, it was a low-hanging fruit, ripe for the plucking, for a start-up.

On one of my US trips, I chanced upon a tall, hefty Englishman with dark hair and grey eyes. He was the regional sales manager from Scanning America in New York. Established in 1990, Scanning America was providing document conversion services to private and public entities. Though young, the company had distinguished itself in the market through its commitment to quality, security and customer service and had quickly earned a reputation as a leader among document imaging companies.

One of the benefits of working in OMC was the free access I had to the Tata Sons office on Fifth Avenue, New York City's most expensive and famous business street. I used to operate out of it during my US visits and it inadvertently created the impression among visitors that I was a big gun. I met the said gentleman in the plush environs of the Tata office and took to him immediately, trying hard to absorb everything he was telling me about scanning, digitization and outsourcing services business. He explained how outsourcing would lower the costs for western clients, ensure quality and the early completion of projects. I got a good feel of the business from him; it reinforced my belief in digitization as a potential business idea.

Scanning America was on the lookout for investors at that time; it planned to open a subsidiary in the UK to foray into the European market. He had somehow formed the impression that I was interested in investing in his company. I disabused him of the notion and told him I would not be investing. 'But I am thinking of doing something on my own,' I added.

'Well,' he said, thinking it over. 'I could offer you a consultancy to launch your digitization business in India.'

It was an attractive idea and I told him that it appealed to me.

'We should go to the Birmingham show together and get a pulse of the market,' he suggested.

'Great idea,' I said and signed him on as a consultant.

Later, we met in London and kipped at the Kensington Holiday Inn. I picked up the tab and we went on to attend the event in Birmingham.

Once I returned to India, we worked together for a couple of months. I boned up on the processes and technologies involved in digitization. I paid him the first two instalments, but thereafter the deal petered out as there was no further information forthcoming from him.

By this time, I refined my business idea of map digitization services and chose it as my area of immediate focus. I chalked out the business plan and yet doubts kept assailing me. 'Would the business work? Would it be profitable and survive with time?' I kept asking myself.

There were so many imponderables that there was just no getting away from the questions that kept humming in my head. I finally realized that the plan would remain in flux and there would be no reliable answers until I stopped dithering and actually took the plunge. This meant I had to make dynamic business plans by constantly watching out for opportunities to shape and strengthen the enterprise. If I waited to understand all the risks and figure out solutions, I would not be able to move forward. I had to be selectively blind, keep my calm and smarten up enough to deal with situations and challenges as they arose. And I did possess the nerve and verve to persist with my idea.

As my plans evolved, I discussed them threadbare with my immediate family and friends through that year. They reassured, reinforced and encouraged me to see them through to the end. I did not, however, consult any colleagues or seniors. Nor did I have a mentor to turn to for guidance. I believed that my experiences and learnings in founding and building OMC Computers had provided me with sufficient insight into all the nuts and bolts of how start-ups functioned and I was well-equipped to not miss the wood for the trees.

Hindsight tells me that I should have solicited the wisdom of senior industry colleagues to get more objectivity. They would not only have served as a voice of reason, but also of encouragement. They would have coached me on strategy and execution while opening the door to the prospect of accelerating business. However, engineering services was the least-trodden path in the Indian IT services industry back in 1991 and there were few people I could turn to for the relevant knowledge and experience—or pertinent expertise, for that matter.

Getting Started

Once OMC relieved me, I set about recruiting two GIS engineers and launched the operations of Infotech Enterprises from the precincts of my modest home. My third hire, Sunil Kumar Makkena, was from Suri Computers which was already offering digitization services. It took me a while to convince Sunil about my vision for Infotech. Once he was convinced, he persuaded a few more people from Suri Computers to join us. Sunil has worked with me closely for several years and is still associated with the company in a senior leadership position. I could not muster up the courage to start out at STP-Hyderabad and avail of its facilities. Instead, overcome by an instinct for parsimony prompted by shallow pockets, I converted the dining area of our house into an office space and started working on CAD-CAM workstations. We did several proofs of concept (POC) projects and within a week of Sunil's joining, the quality of our deliverables showed remarkable improvement.

Our first customers were General Motors' Electromotive Division, LaGrange, Chicago and Gabriel Shock Absorbers, Chicago, IL. They were impressed with our sales pitch offering them low-cost digitization services with short lead times and assured quality. We kept our promise, and our clients were happy with the deliverables. This initial success infused us with some confidence. But unwilling to rest on our laurels, I kept at it. I used to learn, explore new tools and techniques and simultaneously train and challenge my colleagues. Conscious of my team's strengths and weaknesses, I gave them directions and suggestions, demanding specific solutions; at the same time, I supported them until they achieved the desired results.

They were interesting times, those early years, as I juggled tasks, functioning as the frontline salesman, HR manager, operations manager, and admin manager, all rolled into one. My only back-end support was Suchi. As there were no restaurants or eateries near our house in Jubilee Hills, Hyderabad in early 1992, tea, breakfast, lunch and dinner were dished out from our home kitchen for all our associates. This was the norm for the first six months. Starting up was a lot like a family affair. Suchi was an extraordinary spouse and partner. As we started shipping out the material, quality issues multiplied. Suchi and I sat late into the night finishing quality checks so that we could get corrections done the next day.

Suchi actively monitored the company accounts. She was authorized to sign cheques and made sure salaries were paid on time in my absence. She kept a close watch on expenses and had a fantastic memory. A ready reckoner, she could quote instantly and exactly, up to the last decimal point, how much we had spent on any item and what our exact salary bill was in any of the preceding months.

The law mandated that a company should have three directors on its board. I asked my old friend, former colleague and perennial confidante, Rajan Babu Kasetty, to join as non-executive director on the Infotech board. I made the offer over a meal at my house at 347, Jubilee Hills. Simple, straightforward and intelligent, he was an obvious choice. He was talented and a quick learner. What was more, our friendship spanned twenty years and he was someone I trusted completely. Rajan and I had a lot in common. He was an electrical engineer with a passion for design and engineering. We had started our careers at Shriram Refrigeration as management trainees on the same day. We met on the red bus at the Shriram gate while heading home from work and had struck up a friendship that firmed up over the years. He was immensely helpful. Rajan, too, had harboured entrepreneurial aspirations. In fact, he had tried his hand at starting a company much before me. Unfortunately, he had suffered some setbacks. He understood the business well and would play a highly supportive role in the building of Infotech. Whenever I had a bad day, it was Rajan who I would always turn to. I would call him, confide in him, discuss and debate issues with him. I came to regard him as extended family.

Life moved on, more or less on an even keel, with the usual minor hiccups. One day, however, we were struck by a mini-disaster. Krishna was sitting at the dining table when its legs suddenly gave way. Luckily, some swift thinking and even quicker reflexes exhibited by our engineers saved the day. They not only managed to hold on to the tabletop, but also rescued the workstations and data from an ignominious end. It had been a foolish lapse. We had known that table was meant for dining and not digitizing maps, but we had not given the matter much thought. Wiser after the fact, we strengthened the dining table, added more worktables around it, acquired two more systems and resumed operations. As the volume of work increased, we realized we needed more space and resources. We opted for Maitrivanam and STPI-Hyderabad as the default alternative to set up our new facility.

The minimum leasable area at STPI-Hyderabad was 2200 square feet. I approached its director, J.A. Chowdary, for a smaller space. Chowdary, a government officer, was quite supportive of the industry and displayed enormous flexibility. He agreed to partition the area. Just as I was on the point of accepting the offer, I smelt the coffee and realized there was more business coming our way. I flung thrift to the winds and mustered up the courage to dispense with the partition and leased out the entire the 2,200 square feet of space. Once our tenancy was inked, I returned to my primary focus—business, and left the task of tackling the interiors to Suchi. She was the one who spruced up the space, procured the furniture and turned it into a functional office.

We were about six people at the time. We got two cabins built, one for me and one for Sunil to share with a couple of floor supervisors. We had five desks made—for five people to work per shift—and had a centre table for the floor supervisors. We left the rest of the space open.

I was prudent in my spending, right from the start. I did not take a salary for the first year and took a nominal salary for three years after that. CAD workstations were expensive, software costs were steep and the business would be viable only if we run the operations in shifts. We started working in two shifts initially, then optimized to three. The financial model was such that asset utilization went up substantially when we operated two shifts and the gross margins hovered at around 70 per cent.

Being a new business, Infotech involved a host of spending decisions such as salaries, technology, marketing, office space and administrative expenses. I had to make trade-offs while allocating the available finances as I believed spending should be in proportion to billing and revenue. This required continuous discipline in optimizing costs and minimizing risks while delivering business value and maximizing profitability.

I hired a receptionist-cum-admin staff with two years' experience and trained him in writing, communication and documentation. My associates wondered why I was spending time training this newbie when I could have easily hired an experienced person with good admin skills. But I maintained that we need to use our resources wisely and expand only when it was required. I made my colleagues understand that my financial prudence would benefit the company and everyone else in the long run.

We added twenty-five workstations, plotters and scanners over time and, as we grew, I ensured that resources started flowing in so that the associates did not lack anything. We arranged for things as the need arose. As business grew, we expanded the premises. By March 1995, we had over 100 people working in two shifts. We leased extra space to accommodate the increasing headcount, eventually occupying 25,000 square feet between the fifth and sixth floors of Maitrivanam. My family and I were delighted. We had started on the right note. I was relieved that I had chosen the right service offering and go-to-market strategy. I had lofty ambitions and felt that Infotech was cruising in the right direction.

In his book *Outliers*, Malcolm Gladwell argues that there is no such thing as a self-made man, and super-achievers are successful because of their circumstances, families and appetite for hard work. In retrospect, if it were not for my family's support, the conducive business conditions in the country in 1991, my persistence and hard work, and my openness to quickly learn and adapt on the go, Infotech would have remained an unfulfilled dream.

4

Growing Pains

'Okay, I've got the business off the ground. What's the next logical thing to do?' I was having a quiet moment to myself and, as usual, that's when the noise in my head began.

I could almost hear Lewis Carroll whispering, 'My dear, here we must run as fast as we can, just to stay in place. And if you wish to go anywhere you must run twice as fast as that.'

Carroll was a mathematician before he took up writing and mathematics was my favourite subject, both in school and college—when I did not have my nose between the pages of some interesting book. This fascination with numbers made me adept at playing with them. My training as an engineer had sharpened my logical and analytical skills, investing me with the art of analysing any situation from multiple perspectives. It made me question the status quo and empowered me with the ability to identify problems, simplify complex situations, find solutions and continuously improve them through an iterative process.

When I started writing computer programs and ran use-cases, I quickly arrived at the outcome range with mental calculations alone. This is probably a lot truer with finance. I crunch numbers for fun and often, when my colleagues run calculators in a meeting, I juggle around with the figures in my head and race to the final digits, albeit not to the last decimal.

These core skills came in use whenever I viewed my start-up with a magnifying glass and started looking for the next mountain to scale—and there were several.

Scaling Delivery

People often equate entrepreneurship with the starting up of a company. It's not wrong, but neither is it right, because the picture is incomplete. Once an entrepreneur kick-starts operations, he needs to turn his attention to bring scale and growth to the organization. But growth does not simply take care of itself and scaling-up is an even bigger test. It requires an incredible amount of energy, great dedication and strategic planning.

An example: our initial service offering—digitizing paper maps and drawings—had started gaining traction. It was the year 1993, and Infotech was still in its formative years, when we received a call from Ushwin Desousa, Senior Manager at Hindustan Lever Limited (now Hindustan Unilever Limited—HUL). Introducing himself, Desousa went on to discuss the matter at hand. He said, 'India has more than 6 lakh villages and HUL has customers in each one of them. Most of them are the "hard to reach" variety. Demographic profiling and mapping would be a formidable tool for us to address the business potential more efficiently. Instead of the conventional distribution system, we're looking for a way to get rural dealers to reach predetermined points on state and national highways on a weekly basis to collect our products because our trucks travel there on predetermined routes. We believe this will be the most efficient way for our product outreach to penetrate rural India.'

He paused for breath and I made a few encouraging sounds. 'Well,' he enquired. 'Do you have the technical capability and capacity to develop such a system for us?'

'Wow,' I thought, taking care to mask my rising excitement. To me an inquiry from HUL in itself was a godsend—and that too with such a concrete opportunity—so I was in seventh heaven. Never one to dilly-dally when an opportunity came my way, I asked for some more information, taking care to let him know that although we had not dabbled in a project like this so far, I would be able to figure out if we could handle it, if he let me know precisely what it entailed.

He waxed eloquent on the proposed project and I heard him out attentively. In the course of our conversation, I realized that the project involved both software and data and had tremendous business potential. 'Let me think it over,' I told him at the end of our talk.

I reviewed the conversation I'd had with Desousa in my mind. It was quite a forward-looking project for the times, necessitating extensive use of mapping and database technologies. The software component was small and I was sure we could handle it.

I contemplated taking up the challenge. While there were numerous risks, the customer touchpoint was very supportive. It was a fairly large business opportunity for an early-stage start-up and we could always resell the data if we got it right.

After making an assessment, we made our proposal to the customer. We priced it in a way that it would just about cover our costs, our logic being that if the project was successful, we could subsequently sell the country's map data and make a profit. We were poised to learn the hard way that, on such hollow assumptions, coffers generally lie unfilled.

We faced several challenges in the execution and most, if not all, were centred on maps. In the pre-digital era, procuring maps— of similar scale, currency, and of restricted areas—was a nightmare. There was no map data of India or census data digitally available in the early 1990s. The maps in paper format were outdated and the 1991 census data was yet to be released. Source distortions due to scaling and ageing of paper maps was another stumbling block. Integrating data from census maps of districts and villages that were not to scale and fitting these district maps into state-level maps was yet another Sisyphean task.

We used several mapping techniques and finally managed to create a single map database of the country in a GIS tool and linked the attribute data from census and HUL's historical sales data. We delivered a solution that could optimize the routes to get the best coverage of the most populated villages to maximize HUL's reach. Using the data and the tool, HUL could capitalize its sales and optimize the distribution points.

Despite all the impediments, the overpowering impulse to please our customer—propelled by that Japanese belief *okyakusama wa kamisama desu* (the customer is God) drove us to work day and night to not merely customize and deliver the project, but to deliver it to HUL's satisfaction. That was also when I twigged Robert Burn's precept about well-laid plans of mice and men—we could not sell the data we had tailored to HUL's needs to any other customer! While we did not lose money, in our eagerness to bring scale to the operations, we had bitten off more than we could chew. Sager after the fact, I realized that we had taken on a large project without the appropriate domain expertise to drive and scale it.

Digitization those days involved manual processes and was consequently prone to human errors. Besides, customers demanded 99.5 per cent accuracy on digital databases. While they were aware of the challenges involved in achieving such high levels of accuracy, their applications were meaningless if the data was inaccurate. The addressable market was large, and we recognized that the scalability of our business was contingent on sustaining the quality of our work. The high manual component in the process meant individual skills, attitude and commitment to the project were critical factors in determining output quality.

These were the early days of digitization services market, and we found very few experienced engineers/technicians who were cut out for the job. The small band of experienced associates we had worked with dedication to uphold our promise to provide prescribed quality. But when we scaled to larger projects and started recruiting scores of engineers to meet our burgeoning need for techies, our consistency vis-a-vis quality went for a toss. This was when the realization dawned on me—we could not rely on individual competence alone— the variation in skill was too wide!

To combat the problem, we started putting processes in place.

We inventoried the drawings, defined the process, created checklists for every task we performed in digitizing a paper drawing and carried out multiple quality checks before shipping. We mapped the journey of the drawings from their entry into our facility to their exit. We trained people to adhere to the laid-out procedure. This enabled us to become compliant with ISO 9002 standards (in 1994). We adopted industrial engineering and data entry techniques and invented the maker-checker concept.

Things changed dramatically after that. We won new business and scaling up, as a result, became easy. We started hitting new milestones every year, each one unique. Office space expanded with every new order. There was never a dull moment and the energy that flowed was positive and brimmed with a sense of purpose.

After we became an ISO 9002 certified company, people said projects delivered by Infotech were flawless. But we still faltered on a few deliveries. I kept telling my associates, 'It's not just about writing the process, it's also about making sure people read and follow them flawlessly.' We put in a significant amount of effort into training people. Yet, we continued to face quality issues.

Scaling up was the ultimate test for Infotech's start-up team. The increased flow of projects and customers stretched us. Our conventions, roles, rules, skills, systems and practices fell short in adequately serving the influx of demand, creating friction and frustration.

So, we laid down procedures to share information and enable teams to function efficiently. As teams evolved into sizeable units, we handed them the necessary authority to perform while simultaneously holding them accountable for outcomes. They were provided with all the requisite processes, tools, training and technology to complete their tasks. Tools to automate some steps and monitor errors at every stage were developed. We emphasized planning and forecasting and created feedback mechanisms to iterate and improvise continuously. These actions brought stability to the operations and professionalized the enterprise. As we did not have a cogent framework to transition to scale and maturity, we evolved through experimentation.

During this phase, I learnt that as founder CEO, I needed to work 'on' the company as opposed to working 'in' it. It was vital that I focused on key activities that would move the start-up strategically forward or else progress, if any, would be slow. I saw myself increasingly transforming into a facilitator and skilful delegator whilst moving away from being a hands-on doer and micro-manager. I started nurturing people who could take up responsibility and ownership as future leaders, instilling the right behaviours and values in them.

Several opportunities appeared. Collins Bartholomew, the world's oldest commercial mapping company, which had been in the business of producing maps for around 200 years, came knocking at our door. Established at Edinburgh, in the United Kingdom in 1826, it was the largest publisher and supplier of atlases globally. The firm had a challenging project for us: it wanted us to digitize world maps.

By then, we had leased out an additional 10,000 square feet in Maitrivanam (apart from the initial 2200 square feet we rented) and had about 250 people working for us. Bartholomew wanted us to finish the work in five short months, which meant we needed to hire and train another 120 people, to ensure that the project was completed within the stipulated time. I sought ideas from the team. How were we going to accomplish this rapid ramp-up?

Unwilling to lose Bartholomew, we worked out a solution within the existing infrastructure and facilities. We started night shifts— and ran them for three to four months to meet our commitments. Associates who were good at work extended excellent support to new hires. We ensured associate safety at night and paid them an additional allowance. We procured Esri software licences and kicked off the project.

We digitized the first set of maps and sent them to Bartholomew. Pat came an urgent message—'we need to talk'. As the communication arrived late at night and our customer was located in Edinburgh, I waited till it was early morning in Scotland before calling up.

I had a highly upset client on my hands. 'What have you done?' asked an irate voice. 'We can't see the maps on our screens, and those that we can are not useful at all.'

Over the course of the conversation the voice at the other end pointed out that the maps needed a projection system. 'We specified this earlier,' said the representative from Bartholomew, sounding slightly calmer now. He emphasized the essential requirement of using a projection system to accurately depict various features on a map.

Caught on the wrong foot, I apologized profusely. It appeared that our engineers, for some reason, had ignored the specification given by the customer. Realizing that we had tripped up, I spent the next few minutes soothing my customer's ruffled feathers and promised to fix the problem at the earliest.

We got to work immediately, now that the realization had hit us that maps required a 'projection system' to serve as a reference. We reworked the maps as per Bartholomew's specifications and won their confidence.

A crisis had been averted, but working with Bartholomew had opened our eyes to the fact that Infotech was not a geospatial company. It was merely a digitization company that took paper drawings from utility firms and produced intelligent data using Automated Mapping and Facilities Management (AM/FM). Wiser after the fact, I figured out that if we wanted to climb up the customer value chain, we had to add domain capabilities. I also realized that our lack of domain expertise was the primary reason we had not been able to improve and resell the data we had created for HUL. We quickly recruited geospatial specialists who, in turn, trained our staff. It was our first big move to get well and truly into geospatial data creation and systematically build our geographic information systems (GIS)/geospatial technology expertise.

We did manage to deliver the Bartholomew project successfully and it turned out to be one of our first benchmark projects. To prevent our assets and new associates from falling idle, lest their utilization declined, we ensured the continuity of projects. The lessons learnt from Bartholomew, such as planning, rapid ramp-up, infrastructure, training, subject-matter expertise and cross-skilling, became our best practices. And this was cascaded across the organization to guide and inspire the creation of more such successful projects. With each new project, we bettered ourselves. We learned the hard way but we became experts at it.

Within a short period of time, 'digitization at scale' became our core competence. Infotech had a diversified portfolio of CAD and geospatial services—5–10 per cent of the volume was CAD, and the rest geospatial business. This service offering gave us enormous business traction and our volumes swelled. We maintained quality at large volumes, made sure we delivered consistently, on time and at an affordable price. We walked the talk and customers began to notice us. This model was so successful that business grew at a CAGR of 65 per cent between 1996 and 1999 (Rs 4.90 crore revenue in 1996 to Rs 22.10 crore by 1999). The company serviced all the projects offshore, but secured them against global competition. At one point, Infotech had the largest data conversion centres globally. By the turn of the century, it was Asia's largest geospatial/GIS service provider.

Another big project we landed was with Fugro, a Dutch multinational company and the world's leading geodata specialist. It wanted us to digitize a utility company's assets and come up with the integrated database. It was a large AM/FM project and had all the makings of a huge challenge. I was a bit apprehensive since we were required to build new skills within a short time. But my team was confident and we picked up the gauntlet. Fugro was anxious about deadlines and its representatives visited us at regular intervals to check if we were on track. They were pleasantly surprised with our progress. After we had completed the project, Jos Anneveld, Director of Fugro, visited us and announced an incentive for all the associates on the assignment. It was the first time that associates at Infotech received an incentive directly from a customer.

Infotech managed its project flow efficiently and seamlessly transitioned resources from one project to another. There was never a situation where the company was short of skilled associates or had excess resources on the bench. While we invested heavily in hiring and training people, we were careful about attrition and project continuity. In this field, when it rains, it pours. Yet, we managed our operations in a watertight manner and handled the demands and sensitivities of different geographies well. Our system and process orientation played a vital role in ensuring the scaling of operations.

We ramped up our geospatial technology capabilities by putting together a team that understood the engineering involved in creating the AM/FM maps for telecom and power distribution utilities. Data becomes meaningful only through software and, as a logical extension, we had the opportunity to extend our offerings to software services. Infotech built its capabilities to offer enterprise-level end-to-end solutions. This strategy allowed us to get closer to our customers and understand their needs better. It helped us ascend the geospatial value chain and increase the value-addition per associate.

If I have to attribute Infotech's growth and sustenance in the initial years to one factor, it was the result of successfully exploiting the 'PPT' framework. PPT in popular parlance is the file extension for PowerPoint, but for us it stands for **P**eople, **P**rocess, **T**ools, technology and training with the **C**ustomer being central to all the activity. We institutionalized the PPT framework and the practice is still in force at the company.

We turned the biggest challenges for the operations—quality, affordable cost and on-time delivery—into the guiding strategy for success. The company did everything possible to deliver quality consistently, and provide value-added services, but it was never the cheapest in the market. In fact, our quality promise became our competitive advantage. Several competitors tried the cost route to beat us, without much success. We scaled our operations to such an extent that at one point Infotech simultaneously ran 30 geospatial projects—small and big—with around 6,000 associates in different geographies.

Partnering to Scale

An enterprise, in its scaling-up phase, faces numerous challenges that are often of an order of magnitude more difficult than just starting the venture. Infotech's growth ambitions meant we had to develop a powerful sales and marketing engine in-house. But I was painfully aware that it was often an expensive and slower option for business expansion, especially in export-oriented enterprises. Setting up a sales front overseas and bringing it up to scale with our service offerings was daunting for an entrepreneur like me who did not have adequate means to invest.

I thought it prudent to look outside the enterprise. A potential route I contemplated was to enter into partnerships and nurture them. I felt that Infotech, despite its limited financial ability, could create and deliver business value faster with alliances and craft a wider peripheral bandwidth. I decided to take the partnership path. However, identifying and nurturing non-competitive, complementary partners was not going to be plain sailing.

I scouted for partners willing to identify business prospects, bid on contracts, close projects, define the process to us, interface with clients and promise customer satisfaction. In turn, Infotech guaranteed appropriate production processes, delivery of the product/service as per customer specifications, project management, quality and customer satisfaction.

It was a tough task trying to convince large distributors/ marketing companies to partner with us in the early years of business as Infotech had neither the track record nor the brand identity to flaunt. I discovered that it was easier to persuade acquaintances, friends and relatives to enter into partnerships.

My earliest target was Karlu Rambhala, a school friend who had become an American citizen and lived in Washington, DC. Karlu and I had gone to high school together in the early 1960s in a small town called Kakinada. We had been like two peas in a pod both in and out of class for the three years we were there. Our friendship survived school and we both graduated as engineers. Karlu became a marine engineer while I opted for mechanical engineering. Later, he followed me to the University of Michigan.

After he had finished his masters, Karlu stayed on in the US. During the period under discussion, he was working for a marine engineering consulting company and had a wealth of experience in CAD/CAM systems. Karlu was sharp and bright and I was envious of the mop of hair he had on his head. We would meet up occasionally during my trips to the States and I thought he would be a great partner as he was familiar with the American market and, even more importantly, he had the CAD/CAM domain knowledge.

I made several trips to Washington, DC, to convince Karlu while he squired me around to the best stores in town to give me a 'debonair touch'. He had a great sense of fashion and a sharp eye for style and would prod me to pick the best suits at Nordstrom. Not content, he would then frogmarch me to a store in Tyson's Corner Center in McLean, VA and gently nudge me to pick up a few insanely expensive suits. He was a great believer in quality over quantity. I allowed him to spur me into sartorial elegance, becoming considerably lighter in the pocket as a result of his efforts. I, in turn, kept at him to switch to business. At the first instance, he laughed at me; on the next occasion, he paid attention to my exhortation; and, by the sixth attempt, he was on board. My persuasive efforts had worked! Now that he himself was convinced, Karlu got to work on his senior colleague Pat Callahan and persuaded him to jump ship to 'join the business' as a partner. It was a great way to kick-start our business overseas.

We then prevailed upon K.B. Reddy, a close relative of mine, to join us as an independent sales consultant. KB is an amazing salesman (he had never sold CAD, though), the kind who can sell igloos to Eskimos. He can strike up a conversation with anyone and is a great magnet for potential customers. Karlu and I thought he would be excellent at softening up customers before we engaged them in serious technology discussions. KB turned out to be an asset and was key to our sales success in the initial years.

Karlu founded Infotech Enterprises, Inc. (which did not have the same ownership as Infotech Enterprises Pvt. Ltd—the Indian entity). He became the CEO, Pat the COO, and KB, an independent sales consultant. The understanding between us was that they would take care of sales, customer interface (both pre-sale and post-sale) and quality control in the US, and we would deliver services from India.

We envisaged working with multiple partners from each country to ensure we had a good pipeline of prospects and a continuous order flow. In the company's long-term interest, I needed to guard against exposure to a single market, limited customer base and a single partner. It was important to de-risk the business and reduce customer and geography dependencies.

A few months before I left OMC, I met Jean Milan in Brussels. We became good friends. At the time, Jean was CapGemini's Belgian operations director and had good business connections in the local market. I decided to strike a similar partnership with him in Europe. I coaxed Jean to become an entrepreneur. He incorporated InfoCAD Enterprises BV. As in the US, this too was an independent company. Jean was great at sales but did not know anything about CAD/CAM. We agreed that he would manage sales and customer connect in Europe and we would deliver services from India.

We replicated the partnership model and forayed into the Australian market as well in 1994. Here, we tied up with CANData, and even landed a few good projects through the company. I handed over the Australian business to Ranga Mohan Rao, VP of sales, while I focused on the Western markets.

Our partners bid for contracts. Before each bid, we would give them our cost estimate and the timeline involved for its execution in India. While our partners awarded us fixed price contracts based on the quotations we submitted, their final bid to the end-users typically included their marketing and sales overheads, customer interfacing expenses and the cost of regular customer interaction. The model took off well.

We created detailed contracts, defined metrics to assess value, and established formal systems and structures, as we were aware that effective interfacing was essential for a successful partnership. Karlu and Pat were fanatical about quality to the extent that I felt they were nitpicking. They would throw an entire batch back at us if they spotted a single fault in one drawing. That said, their obsession was probably a blessing in disguise, as it hammered home the importance of quality to the point we turned into nitpickers ourselves!

Alliances are complex affairs, often demanding a high degree of interdependence, an ability to navigate and actively leverage significant differences between the strengths and operating styles of partners. The alignment of partners' profiles, long-term vision, passion, work ethic, trust and communication are critical for a mutually beneficial partnership. Two to three years into the relationship, I acknowledged a mismatch. I had a long-term vision and wanted to grow rapidly, while my American affiliate had other ideas. They were making good progress with federal contracts where we had no role to play as these were to be executed onshore and, in some instances, needed security clearances. When we realized our business objectives were divergent, we decided to go our separate ways. In 1996, we severed ties with Infotech Enterprises Inc.

In Europe, Jean was content. He was chary of risks and plodded on as a one man-army for five years. He was a gentleman in a world that rewarded sharks and was happy making do in the Benelux market. Volumes were small, but Jean was satisfied. It was a lifestyle business for him.

The Australian business did well and CANData was always prompt in its payments. But a few years on, the firm ran into trouble due to differences between the partners. This was the time when we lost Ranga Mohan to cancer and witnessed a significant slowdown in our Australian revenues.

Clearly, we needed like-minded partners who were driven by similar ambitions, values and drive to succeed. Where would I find them?

Partnership Trouble

We searched the market for possible partners and found one in Smartscan, a GIS services provider in Boulder, Colorado. Mickey Fain, the founder and CEO, was a brilliant mind and a pleasure to work with. I lobbied with the firm to become its outsourcing partner. Once the deal was inked, Mickey and his team helped us to enhance our processes and upgrade our quality standards. We started deploying tools instead of throwing bodies at complex problems. We built up a great relationship with Smartscan and successfully delivered the King County conversion project. Close on its heels, Mickey won the proof of concept (POC) for San Diego County. The POC was complex, and the customer quite demanding. We sent four Infotech engineers to San Diego to help Mickey. He poured in a lot of effort and investment but couldn't get the dues for the final phase of the project. Smartscan eventually declared bankruptcy in 1998.

We started over. The search for large and financially stable GIS service providers keen on leveraging services from India to stay competitive in the American market began all over again. We identified the top ten GIS service providers in the US and decided to devote 90 per cent of our time exploring partnerships with them. The top firms in the sector were small in size, typically turning $20–25 million in annual revenue. I negotiated a successful collaboration with one of the top players in the GIS services market—MSE Corp in Indianapolis, Indiana. K.B. Reddy played an important role in identifying the partner; he also built an amazing rapport with the senior leadership. Randy Sage, the then COO, saw merit in outsourcing. We worked hard to convince the leadership, especially Sol Miller, who was founder and chairman, and signed a technical services agreement with the company.

Soon, the digitization supplier market in the US witnessed consolidation. Analytical Surveys Inc (ASI), a Nasdaq-listed company with similar revenues, acquired MSE. ASI was aggressive and acquired the top four GIS services companies in about eighteen months to consolidate itself as the largest GIS services company at that

time. We started working closely with ASI, thanks to the influence
of the MSE leadership team. Based on Infotech's performance and
leadership, ASI entered into a long-term agreement with Infotech.
We signed a deal to provide data conversion services using ASI's
proprietary mapping software, at a cost that was considerably lower
than that of ASI. The contract envisaged minimum services of $33
million (Rs 142 crore) over five years with the sale of the ASI-
owned, India-based Cartographic Sciences to Infotech thrown in to
sweeten the deal.

This strategy cut ASI's costs and extended its global reach.
Sid Corder, then president of ASI, explained the Infotech alliance
in a 23 June 1999 press release. 'Increased worldwide demand for
GIS services has prompted our efforts to increase the company's
global capacity,' he said, adding, 'We have taken several key steps
to grow our domestic capacity in recent years, and those efforts
will continue.'[1] The Infotech partnership proved so beneficial that
ASI moved more of its data conversion work to us. ASI finished
up 1999 with a revenue of $113 million. It won business from the
American market consistently, gave us work continuously and paid
us promptly. Infotech was on a roll.

And then the partnership hit a roadblock. Its shareholders
alleged that the company had overstated its income and earnings
and had issued materially false and misleading financial statements,
violating generally accepted accounting principles (GAAP).

On 27 January 2000, ASI announced that it would have to
make additional adjustments to its previously declared revenue
and earnings for the fiscal 1999 as a result of misstating the cost of
completion projections for certain contracts. This wiped out millions
of dollars in profits and the firm was in deep financial trouble. These
developments were perturbing, as ASI was our biggest customer and
its outstanding payments to us ran into several millions.

The Securities and Exchange Commission (SEC) filed charges of
fraud against three former ASI executives (they reached a settlement
later). It was a rainy day in August at the turn of the millennium;
the monsoon was in full pelt and I was at my nephew's pre-wedding

ceremony. For two-and-a-half hours, I sat in my car at the wedding venue, amidst all the celebrations, arguing my case with Hamid Akhavan, vice president of ASI, to release our payments. It may have been my powers of persuasion or just sheer good luck; whatever it was, ASI paid most of its outstanding dues and the relationship ended amicably.

Then, as luck would have it, the opportunity to acquire ASI reared its head. The idea was exciting, but I decided to adopt a cautious approach, as I always did. It was a cross-border transaction between two publicly listed entities governed by two different regulators (SEC in the US and SEBI in India), and ASI was beleaguered by legal challenges. We employed the services of a team of Hong Kong-based attorneys who specialized in cross-border transactions.

I flew to San Antonio, Texas (where ASI had its new headquarters) with the legal team and our CFO. We stayed at the Hilton Palacio del Rio, a beautiful twenty-one-storey hacienda-style hotel famous for its original artwork and distinctive royal Spanish theme. Our first day ended with a call from our attorney, late in the evening, requesting a breakfast meeting the next day at a picturesque riverfront coffee shop.

Over breakfast, our attorneys steadily and clearly enumerated the risks in the acquisition. Some ASI executives were already under litigation with SEC and the company was also bang in the middle of a class action suit. 'You never know how many more might crop up in future and all liabilities will rest then with Infotech. The risks can't be ring-fenced easily and the potential damages are difficult to estimate,' they cautioned. 'It'll be difficult for an Indian company to handle US lawsuits. In fact, we strongly recommend that you avoid this transaction, at all costs.'

More than sufficiently forewarned, we yielded to their judgement specially as the risks were far too many for a company of Infotech's size at the time. I decided to pass on the opportunity.

By this time, Infotech's business was making steady strides, but most of our growth was courtesy our affiliates. Some of our strategic partners were market leaders in their countries of operations.

Infotech ranked among the top five GIS/geospatial companies in the Asia-Pacific region and had customers in all five continents. We had several projects under our belt but enjoyed credit for none of them, as everything we had done over the years had been routed through our business allies. Our North American enterprise was not scaling to its potential, thanks in the main to our partnerships. The opportunity before us was enormous but we couldn't capitalize on it as we were far too remote from our customers—and the layer of separation, I recognized, was a direct consequence of our partnerships.

'This isn't working,' I told myself. 'We need footprints—lots of local footprints to serve our customers effectively and scale up the business.' But this would require dexterous balancing to ensure that we were not perceived as a threat by our existing partners.

In July 1999, we established a legal entity called Infotech Software Solutions, Inc. (ISSI) in Riverside, California in the US. Rajan Kasetty, who until then had been a director on the board of Infotech India, moved to the States to oversee operations. It was our first wholly owned subsidiary. To our partners, it had been launched primarily to address the commercial software market.

Our decision might have appeared to be reactive, but its time had come. Instead of chalking out plans based on assumptions, I find it prudent to make continuous adjustments using a build-measure-learn feedback loop. This steering process helps me gauge when to continue along a chosen path and when to take a sharp turn.

As we heralded our presence in the US, we discovered there were already six companies in existence going by the name of Infotech Enterprises in various states in the country, in addition to the one that had been established by Karlu. But we persisted with the title and decided to make an impact with our brand. ISSI sold commercial software, with ASI as our GIS services partner. The move disturbed Karlu to the extent that he later changed his company's name to Avineon.

All start-ups have a true north and so did Infotech. Ours was to become a thriving, global and sustainable business. To this end, I did everything strategically to steer Infotech towards this goal.

Partnering for Technology

Digitization services was an interesting business. It had a large addressable market, was manually intensive, had low realization per person, good margins and could be quickly scaled with the right processes. All the same, I recognized fairly early that as time went by, competition would catch up and the market share would shrink. We needed to move up the value chain as quickly as we could. As digitization became commoditized, our service offerings would be of more value to our customers provided we extended software services to our mix, in addition to data.

We identified the top two GIS software providers—Esri and Smallworld. Esri was strong in the traditional GIS/geospatial market. With its ArcInfo family of products, Esri flourished in government markets across the world. We tried to convince the firm that we could partner it to provide GIS/geospatial services for its customers.

Esri did not give us work but it allowed us to qualify as an Esri-recognized vendor to provide digitization services. It then handed us some parcel maps to digitize. It was a fifty-hour job and Esri had a rigorous evaluation process. My team set to work.

I tried to inspire them. 'This is an important opportunity, guys. If we qualify as an Esri vendor, we'll be in big business.' I used to work out of a small cabin at that time, which gave me a bird's-eye view of how my team laboured over the job. The significance of the task was apparent to them and they slogged till they almost dropped.

Noting their stress, I called Sunil to my cabin. 'I know you guys are working hard. Stop getting hassled. Even if we fail, it doesn't matter. I have complete confidence in all of you and that's not going to change. Even if there's no work for the next three to four years, the company can stand it. Just do your best and stop feeling so pressured. The world will not end.' The tension eased and they lumbered on. I kept a hawk's eye on their progress until the job was done. Then we relaxed.

We received the results of our labour in a week. The Esri quality group had found our work 99.99 per cent compliant. Esri recognized us as one of its qualified vendors, which meant we were now an authorized Esri service partner. The letter from Esri brought a dramatic shift to our business. It was a defining moment for Infotech. I cannot recall using another document as extensively to win contracts. Without the Esri brand, it would have been hard to convince customers of our ability to produce quality work. Jack Dangermond, Esri's founder, is a visionary in developing GIS software. The credit for architecting the growth of the global geospatial industry is his. His work ethic and ability to remember people and recall conversations is stupendous. He continues to be a friend and still leads the company.

We also worked closely with Smallworld which was based out of Cambridge in the UK. Infotech developed a long-term strategic partnership with Smallworld to distribute their GIS solutions and consulting services. We produced several customized applications on their platform. Our relationship evolved to a stage where we supported part of their product development from India. The partnership worked well. Wherever possible, they pushed our software and digitization services as an add-on to their platform. It was a small company when we first met, but later emerged as a world leader in GIS technology solutions for the telecommunications and utilities markets. GE Power Systems acquired the company in the year 2000, and the brand continues to this day as GE Smallworld.

Over the years, we also built relationships with CadKey and Bentley, both notable CAD software companies in the industry. We used Bentley's Microstation extensively at Infotech. We were platform-agnostic and maintained relationships with all CAD companies—formal and informal. At one point, we became the largest AutoCAD users in India. Partnerships formed the foundation on which we built Infotech and alliances with software vendors enabled us to respond intelligently to customer needs and move up the value chain.

5

Expanding Offerings

Krishna had just finished his class ten examinations. He still had two years of Intermediate (as it is known in this part of the world) to go through before he would be ready to tackle his undergrad studies. He wanted to become an engineer and had set his sights on the Indian Institute of Technology (IIT)—the Mecca for all engineering aspirants in the country.

Admissions into the IITs was by no means a piece of cake—not with lakhs of students appearing for the entrance test annually to compete for seats that ran into four digits for all six IITs in the country. Faced with these daunting statistics, we opted for the usual route to the IITs in these parts—coaching classes!

Enter Chukka Ramaiah, more famously known as 'IIT Ramaiah', who was and is adulated by all wannabe engineers and their anxious families as the best ticket into an IIT. I chanced upon Ramaiah through a friend and apprised him of Krishna's ambitions. 'Send your son to me,' he said graciously. 'I'll make sure he gets into an IIT.'

Elated, I fixed Krishna's admission into his coaching classes and went home triumphant. But not for long. We were aghast when we discovered that his classes started at 3.30 a.m.! Even worse, they were run from a location that was 15 km from our home. Shoulders sagging, we tried for some optimism. How bad could it be? Very bad, as it turned out. Infotech was still a neonate; I had to travel to keep the company afloat and Suchi had to be up at 2 a.m. to make sure Krishna reached his coaching classes on time, with tiffin, etc.—whilst juggling between company affairs and household chores during the day.

Fed up finally with the gruelling schedule, we approached Ramaiah, hoping to lobby for a more reasonable shift. 'We'd like to move Krishna to a class that runs in the evening,' I said.

Suchi, who had by then inveigled her way into Ramaiah's affections by taking over as his unofficial medical consultant (she had taken to supplying all his medicines) complained that it was getting very difficult to send Krishna to his classes.

Ramaiah was unimpressed. 'Early morning classes are the best. Mind is fresh after the rest.'

'I can't cope,' wailed my wife. 'Neither can Krishna. He's tired throughout the day and finds it hard to stay awake during his regular classes. I have too much on my plate and this place is too far away. You must shift him to a later class.'

He unbent a little, noting her very real distress, came up with a suggestion. 'Don't be so stressed, amma. Move your house. I've seen an apartment just next to the school. You move in. Problem solved!'

As far as suggestions went, it was impractical and we were clearly at an impasse. Ramaiah held very definitive opinions on the receptivity of the human brain in the wee hours of the morning and wasn't going to have a hand in downgrading Krishna's mental faculties by shifting his timings! We gave up the battle, did not move house and our lives continued at the same breakneck pace until Krishna finally threw up his hands and said, 'Enough is enough!' It had been a harrowing time for him. His board exams were round the corner and the coaching classes were just too hectic. Krishna didn't get into IIT, though he did sail through the state engineering exams with a respectable rank.

A fresh debate broke out within the family. Were private engineering colleges worth considering? Our opinion was a unanimous

'No!' So, what were our options? We could send him to America. But it was May already—would there be sufficient time? Could we afford it? It would definitely cause a huge dip in our finances. In the end, Suchi and I, true to our forebears, decided nothing was more important than Krishna's education. We were prepared to bite the bullet.

I got in touch with the head of admissions at Purdue University through a second-level contact. She said, 'If you have the application, fill it up and send it to me. I'll make sure you get an I-20 in the next forty-eight hours.'

And she did. It was the year 1994. Krishna headed to Purdue, while I went back to ideating Infotech's expansion.

The most important asset of a new company, I figured, is its fresh thinking. Business history is replete with examples of how small groups of people bound together by a common purpose have changed the world for the better. Many start-ups are fortunate enough to find a niche market for a service or product with a large addressable market. Infotech was part of this privileged set.

As we grew and stabilized, I watched our digitization service offering churning out profits. A fresh thought struck me. Should we plan our growth by riding the wave as long as we could? I quickly discarded the notion. It was a flawed approach and tended to ignore the reality that the digitization wave would plateau at some point and probably trammel our ambition to build a sustainable global business in the long term.

I then wondered how we could scale and make the business predictable and profitable in the long run. How could we broaden our range and expand our market share? What new products and services could we build to develop the market? How could we mitigate future risks? What could we do to protect the company from competition and volatility in the marketspace? These questions catalysed us to explore the market further.

When we were an Rs 1–2 crore company, scaling the business was top priority and we scrambled for it, recognizing that it could give us a lot more bandwidth to invest in the core business. Besides, as a start-up, Infotech had the right size, appetite and agility to quickly build new service lines from the ground up—beginning from zero to one.

We started expanding our core CAD and GIS/geospatial business into software products and application development services. It was an adjacency to our existing offerings; we could leverage our knowledge and expertise; it seemed a natural progression to move up the customer value chain.

At the same time, I acknowledged that we should continue our focus on digitization and our financial and human resources should not be used to diversify at the cost of the existing offering. If we spread ourselves too thin, it could bring the entire business down.

Infotech forayed into software product development with a drawing management solution called MODES (Management of Drawings and Engineering Systems). From the mid-'80s to the early '90s, engineering departments the world over had transformed their paper drawings and designs into digital form. The digitalization happened quite rapidly thanks to the simplicity and efficiency of the CAD applications. However, there was a dire need for an efficient way to index and search this large repository of vector drawings and scanned images (raster) through software. Moreover, the traditional method involving multiple iterations between the designer and reviewer was proving to be a choking point. More importantly, a 'digital' tool was required to communicate the design intent or changes while working in teams. We developed MODES to specifically address these needs.

Infotech sold MODES in Europe through a partner under the brand name EuroArchiv. We were not as lucky in the US as we could not find a distributor for the product there. We chose a partnership model which permitted us to receive royalties for our product and allowed us to continue investing in it. However, we soon realized that the model was faulty as it yielded limited or late customer feedback and insufficient intelligence on market requirement, a factor which was critical to sustained product development.

We then developed our mapping products on a concept we called 'Viewing Equation'. The platform had the functionality to have maps created by one user, modified by three users and viewed by any number of users. We struggled for three years (1994–96) and eventually launched our first product MapView in 1997.

While marketing MapView, we met Rainer Ziegler, CEO of CARDy Karten-Informationssysteme GmbH. Ziegler was marketing Cardy Karten, a digital map product from his company. We showed MapView to him. Our team worked day and night to present a demo at his office in Moenchengladbach, a suburb of Dusseldorf, Germany. The end result was heartening—Ziegler's jaw dropped when he saw the speed at which our maps were running!

'I'm really impressed with this level of product sophistication from India,' he exclaimed in a thick German accent.

Ziegler quickly firmed up his plan to travel to India for more detailed discussions. We finalized the product specifications and signed the contract to customize and enhance MapView to his needs. We delivered the product with another demo at his office a few months later; he was absolutely delighted when he saw the 'closer to printed maps' kind of display.

'*Zis ees wonderful!*' he said, in rapture. He threw a party for us at an Indian restaurant in Dusseldorf and treated us to his favourite chicken tikka and dal fry to demonstrate his utter delight. It was a gesture that reflected a strong customer commitment.

Although the development effort was technically successful (with a fully functional product and state-of-the-art technology) and we had proved our competence without a hitch, the product was late to market. Our challenge was that we did not know how to shape our development into a 'commercial product'. Ziegler sold the product IP subsequently to Vodafone for fleet management applications.

We continued developing MapView and built several applications around its core technology. We did not have a customer, so our team began by experimenting and developing product PoCs. They created all the functional blocks for GPS and designed a vehicle navigation system as proof of concept and called it GeoLogic. We pitched the idea to the state road transport corporation. We were ahead of the times. We were pushing for a buy-in from a potential customer in the pre-Google Maps era and although our technology excited officialdom, it did not spur it into action; our POC failed to take off commercially.

Fast forward to 2003. We ran into Giuseppe Carnevali, CEO of Navionics, an Italian manufacturer of electronic navigation charts, who was on a trip to Hyderabad to get ocean maps digitized. Navionics had a marine navigation solution for pleasure boaters. The solution ran on Navionics' own device—a personal digital assistant (PDA), pretty much like today's smartphone but with far lesser computing power and storage space. The software and map data would sit on a small 'SD card-like' storage. So, the use case that Navionics saw in GeoLogic was to just give another card to its captive users as an add-on application. He would plug it in and navigate on the road and eventually offer it as a full-fledged car navigation system. Giuseppe Carnevali used to call this multi-modal transportation system. A huge business actually!

Navionics also knew that this new solution would be accepted only if it was better than that of the existing leading provider in the industry, TomTom. Our product was benchmarked against TomTom. The good news was that we delivered a much smaller disk and memory footprint, were faster in computing routes, provided better quality navigation instructions and timing but lagged behind on schedule and user interface (UI) features, making it less appealing as a consumer product which was what it was meant to be! The UI was a huge gap that we just did not see! But Navionics wanted a ready-to-ship consumer product. It took over the development of the product.

Despite the business setback, my association with Navionics was not without its lighter moments. I travelled to the Navionics headquarters in Viareggio, Tuscany, Italy, a lovely town with easy access to beaches and monuments. The closest airport to the town was Pisa International Airport, and on one of my trips, I went by Giuseppe's recommendation and stayed at the Grand Hotel Dumo, which was a stone's throw away from the Leaning Tower of Pisa. The highlight of that trip was a lunch I had at a popular beach with the company's COO, Pedros, at the famous Bango Ristorante Florida. We sat in a hut-like structure of the restaurant, feasting on the 360-degree view of the sea and the surroundings and chatted desultorily over cocktails and shrimps with tartar sauce. I noticed that we were the only people on the beach who were respectably clad—a sudden shortage of cloth appeared to have afflicted the rest of the beach! For me, what was even more surprising was the fact that the beach was jampacked, despite the fact that it was a working day. I had dinner that night with Carnevali at the hotel I was staying in; it was to become the starting point of a long and wonderful friendship between us. Business is not all about specifications, POs, delivery and invoices. It is also about building long-lasting relationships which weather business challenges.

We kept lagging in product development and quickly realized that product development was a highly competitive space, needing higher-order skills, substantial R&D investments, different business models and more.

This was during the initial days of digital navigation. There weren't many models to emulate and nor were there enough off-the-shelf technology tools. We struggled—mainly because our approach was aligned towards services and so were our functional skills. We had moved without trying to discover the archetype that was best suited for a successful software company. We muddled along using the traditional trial-and-error method, stayed open to experiments, learned on the job, failed and finally course-corrected. We were one of the pioneers in the industry and developed several variants. DigitalPages—a kiosk-based digital Yellow Pages—was one. A digital kiosk did a quarter-century ago what smartphones do today with mobile internet. DigitalPages was an interactive consumer information system integrating GIS, multimedia and database technologies. These were early days for digital yellow pages. Airport authorities evinced interest, but we could not turn it into a profitable business model.

Developing bespoke software products became our unique proposition. The Council of Scientific and Industrial Research

(CSIR), Government of India recognized our R&D unit. This helped our brand. It allowed us to write off our R&D expenses and get some tax credits.

Infotech steadily built its geospatial product portfolio in product-as-a-service model, without losing sight of engineering. The company simultaneously had a product software services play going on. AutoCAD became the dominant supplier for computer-aided drafting (CAD) systems. CADKEY, Microstation (from Bentley), CADAM, Pro-E were distant competitors to AutoCAD. Organizations often used multiple copies of these software. Although their functionality was similar, they were not interoperable. Even though IGES was a recognized standard, there were no comprehensive tools to provide a consistent output. We developed a tool to read different file formats and effortlessly switch between CAD files created in different software. After a while, AutoCAD made its file formats so complex that it became difficult to evolve our tool to keep up with the changes and we finally abandoned the product.

We provided product development services to CADKEY and Smallworld. CADKEY was amongst the first CAD software with 3D capabilities built for personal computers. Infotech assisted CADKEY in developing its CAD software products suite. Over the next few years, our work with the firm became a reference to leverage ourselves powerfully into the CAD software market. We built add-on software products on top of the Bentley Microstation platform.

In the 1970s and 1980s, the early years of using computers for design and engineering applications, large corporates such as Boeing, Pratt & Whitney, Westinghouse or GE developed CAD software in-house. This required deep investments and these companies used their homegrown products for design, engineering and analysis. To us, it was a business opportunity to port the software on a different hardware as new faster and cheaper products became available. We maintained the code written for mainframes on the native platforms. Our software services business continued to grow year after year. We scaled this business well.

The expertise in CAD/GIS software product development was very helpful in strengthening our software services portfolio. We supported customers who wanted bespoke development of an application or wanted to migrate their existing products from the ever-changing operating systems—Mainframe to VAX to UNIX to Windows etc. This continues to be a strong practice at the company.

Breaking into Pure-Play IT Services

Infotech grew reasonably well in the first five years, achieving revenues of Rs 7.10 crore ($2 million) in FY1997 with a headcount of about 175. But we were not growing on par with other IT industry peers.

Doubts crowded my mind. Could CAD and GIS/geospatial become sustainable businesses in the long run? Our competition was declaring fantastic results quarter after quarter and yet Infotech was merely growing at a modest rate. What more could I do to expand the company's footprint? I was flustered by the fact that CAD and GIS/geospatial still had not shot ahead of the curve. It was growing at a much slower pace as compared to IT services.

Our mixed success in product development did not deter us from exploring other avenues. Several openings came our way. But I was cautious. We had to make smart choices. We could not afford to fail. I studied the evolving business environment and decided to test the waters in software development services with an eye on the Y2K remediation opportunity. Looking for the next big break which can bring about growth is typical of every entrepreneur and I was no different.

I explored the market for a potential acquisition, preferring that to building the business ground up, which would take longer. We found SRG (Systems Research Group) Ltd, a Hyderabad-based commercial software development company, as a desirable target for acquisition.

SRG was co-founded by Radha Krishna, a serial entrepreneur whom I had known since my days at HCL. An excellent systems architect and people's manager, in his previous venture RADIG Cybernetics, Radha had partnered with HCL for software development. We shared a great rapport and I admired his business acumen and leadership skills. Once we had zeroed in on SRG, it did not take me much time to convince Radha and his partners to merge their company with ours. SRG was in the throes of a financial crunch, and joining hands with a growing company like Infotech which had strong business prospects and robust financials was a relief for the firm.

SRG became Infotech's new division and gave us a quick entry into the commercial software market. The division swiftly grew into a full-fledged IBM AS400 solutions provider and Infotech became a 'Partner in Development' and 'Solution Development Partner' for IBM. We commissioned SRG to develop an ERP product—EWIS (Enterprise Wide Information System)—a flexible, customizable solution for small and medium companies covering all functional areas of an enterprise such as marketing and sales, finance and accounts, manufacturing operations, personnel and administration. It had the functionality of a mainframe ERP with the convenience of a desktop application.

The product did well initially but later ran into inevitable snags such as upgradation in functionality, user interface and speed. After a while, we decided to call a halt to the development and sales of EWIS. However, we continued to support existing customers, developing bespoke commercial applications for industries such as logistics and forex dealers.

In 1999 we recruited Rajeev Lal, an old friend and colleague from my days at MICO, to run and expand the business. Rajeev had extensive experience in software development both in and outside India. He brought more rigour to the processes in the software development group. We quickly managed to get the SEI CMMi Level 5 certification.

We made a serious attempt to onboard international customers in the year 2000. During a weekly review call, Martin Trostel, who headed our German operations, said, 'Mohan, we've received a request for a proposal from Metro, the fourth-largest retailer in the world in terms of revenues.'

'It seems like a great opportunity but a difficult one to win.' I was excited but cautious. 'What are our chances of winning the bid? Should we even bother bidding at all?' I queried.

'It'll be a tough fight,' Martin admitted. 'We have to offer something unique to grab their attention and win the contract. Lowballing the price could be a good strategy,' he said, unfurling a stratagem we could adopt.

'Martin,' I said thinking hard. 'If we lowball the price once, we'll never be able to regain our price point.' I turned over his suggestion in my mind and then conceded. 'But you have a valid point. It could win the deal for us.' I agreed to back his line of attack.

To our surprise, we won the Metro contract and managed to deliver the IT services successfully. The account scaled as much as $3 million in annual revenues with reasonable margins.

On the other side of the Atlantic, our office location in Riverside, a hundred miles east of Los Angeles, California, limited our accessibility and attracted few potential customers in the US. Rajan, therefore, pursued every possible avenue irrespective of its potential.

Infotech had a few onsite opportunities but the resources we sent from India, while skilled, had little exposure to the Western world. Rajan struggled to make them adapt to the working culture in the west and ensure that they became productive within the first few weeks of their arrival. Our company had half a dozen overseas and several domestic SME customers and the division generated good revenues. We had about 150-200 developers in software services but wrestled to scale further. We found it difficult to position ourselves as a strong commercial software services contender, especially with a large CAD/GIS software and services business.

Balancing Act: Digitization vs Software

Digitization and software services businesses are like chalk and cheese, despite the perceived similarities in their business and operating models. Digitization involved repetitive and regimented manual processes that converted paper-based data into intelligent digital format for customers. It required lower-order skills. Software, especially software product development, was based on creative and intellectual processes requiring aptitudes of a much higher-order. Software product businesses needed high upfront investments and had long lead times for revenue flows.

It also entailed higher risks in achieving product success in the market. Even its management styles were unique. A digitization business needed managers to act as people's champions, requiring them to train, mould and constantly monitor associates' efficiencies while in software development, managers were not required to micromanage. Both these businesses are exclusive of each other. The resources, too, are not fungible. I do not recollect one instance where I moved a resource from one division to another. Digitization/geospatial became a profitable division quite quickly, generating positive cash flows even though it required enormous effort on our part to get our act right to ensure quality, on-time delivery and affordability.

Software processes are very diverse from digitization. The quality benchmarks are different. A fairly large amount of effort went into building quality into our software groups. Certifications like ISO 9001:2000 (in 2001) and CMMi Level 5 (in 2002) brought a reasonably large process standardization and discipline, enhancing customer satisfaction. We needed high-calibre software professionals to compete against the big domestic software service providers. Salary levels were different, as were the need hierarchies. Consequently, we saw two cultures evolving parallelly within the company. Putting both of them under one roof was one of the most challenging tasks I tackled at the company.

Furthermore, the software services business required a completely different leadership. I must confess I did not have the bandwidth to focus on it after Infotech found success in engineering services in the year 2000. As a result, it lacked strategic thinking, affecting the corporate entity's positioning. I believe we also did not have the right go-to-market strategy. The traditional model for software development services was to place engineers at customer sites onshore. As the relationship progressed and these engineers gained enough knowledge of a customer's business processes, software development was moved offshore. That was how most of the big players grew in the market. But our go-to-market strategy was largely driven by the offshore model and, as a result, we were constrained by a weak sales engine.

Moreover, while we could build good differentiators in the engineering and geospatial business, we could not do the same in the pure-play IT business. Among other strategies, we tried using it as an extension of our engineering business, without much success. A combination of all these factors made me question where we stood as an organization and in which segments we should build our reputation.

When people talk about strategy, it is typically about an organization's plans and how it intends to achieve them. But to me, what a company does not want to do and the reasons behind it are equally important. When something is not working, it is good to cut one's losses and move on. The commercial software business had taken us to a point where we had to take a call. We carved it out into a subsidiary in 2010 and finally divested it in 2014.

In the initial years, the company diversified its business portfolio with multiple ideas, products and services. But during our growth journey, we had to prioritize a select few offerings based on market potential and our ability to ramp up the business and build capabilities to manage those choices.

I do not regret my decision, but a few questions still linger. Could we have done better with the software business? Was it a prudent decision to get into it in the first place when our minds and hearts were in the engineering software and services business? The final call was sticking to our core competence: providing software development and engineering and digitization services in the broad functional areas of CAD and geospatial.

My experience has taught me that companies tend to reap diversification rewards when they are synergistic and have a cohesive operating model tying independent business units together. The role of the corporate is to bring value-adding strategies for individual business units. It is only then that a diversified company's value will be greater than the sum of its parts. It is essential to align the corporate's role and activities with the needs and opportunities of its portfolio businesses. Once you set the portfolio and parenting strategies, disciplined capital allocation will help translate the strategy into action. This experience brought with it several learnings that stood us in good stead in the future.

6

Bold Overseas Acquisitions

Infotech went public in April 1997, giving us the financial muscle to take a few bold steps. After battling business limitations with the partnership model, we started exploring the acquisition route to gain a geographic footprint and get closer to the customer. Once we had set up office in the US, Europe was our next logical growth market, and the UK the obvious beachhead. Several eyebrows went up as we started looking to acquire companies internationally. In those days, it was unusual for an Indian company of our size to buy companies in the West, and especially in the UK.

When Transition Partners Ltd, a boutique American investment banking firm, got in touch with me with an exciting proposal, I dove deep into it. The company on offer was the UK-based Dataview Solutions. Dataview was into business geographics and its primary area of focus was geodemographic analysis. It was a small outfit, working out of a single office with an employee strength of around twenty-five professionals. Its business profile attracted me as it was engaged in designing, developing, marketing, licensing and supporting software products, application development tools and data products in the European geospatial market. It had customers in banking, telecom and retail. Geoff Kendall, who had founded Dataview in London in 1992 and the other major shareholder, John

Kendall, were looking for an exit option as Geoff planned to move back to his native Australia.

We studied Dataview's investment memorandum, projects and customers and tried to understand the business through multiple conversations with the senior management team. I studied their numbers and found that the firm was profitable, growing and debt-free. It had a reputed customer base, a well-laid out management structure and ticked most of the significant boxes for me. After several discussions over the phone, I said, 'I can come and see you next week in London.' The reaction on the other side, I was to find out later, was, 'Wow, this guy is going to come all the way to London to see us.'

I met the team in London in early 1999 and held a series of discussions with them—all of them promising. It was time to take a decision. Would it be an aye or a nay? I gave serious thought to the offer on the table. Dataview's expertise and its work with customers such as British Telecom, NatWest and Orange was impressive. With Infotech's strengths and scale and Dataview's clientele, I believed our synergies could pull off a lot more. We foresaw an explosion of capabilities and scale when we cross-sold our data and software services to existing customers.

Another major plus was Dataview's vastly capable leadership team. I was personally impressed with its general manager, John Renard. John bought into the transaction and agreed to stay on. He holds a senior leadership position at the company today. I viewed him as a great addition to the management. Geoff, who had been involved in the actual running of the business, sweetened the deal even further, by agreeing to remain in the company for another two years.

John later told me that when the sale process started, Dataview expected that either another UK company or a US company looking for a European bridgehead would buy it. Infotech was late to the process and Dataview already had two other offers. However, it quickly became clear that I had really taken the time to understand the business and my willingness to come and visit the firm at such short notice tipped the scales in our favour. Infotech became the company's preferred bidder. But there were still a few hiccups lurking round the corner.

At the fag end of the deal, Geoff Kendall and family suddenly went silent, giving me a lot of anxious moments. Gene and Terry, the peerless duo from Transition Partners, stepped in and calmed me down, explaining the phenomenon as the 'lost dog syndrome'. 'You'll occasionally find dogs running astray and competing with cars on roads. They catch up with the vehicle but end up losing breath. At this point, the dog is lost,' they told me. 'The Kendalls,' they explained, 'have got what they wanted and they're probably feeling a bit lost at the moment. Give them time, they'll be back.' And they were—much to my relief.

We concluded the acquisition and made the announcement in August 1999. It was a small takeover but an important one. For a company of Infotech's size (Rs 22.10 crore/$5.26 million revenue in FY1999), acquiring an overseas company like Dataview for Rs 7.60 crore/$1.8 million in cash and another Rs 7.60 crore /$1.8 million in stock to be earned in two years was a bold move for an Indian IT firm.

It was a challenging cross-border transaction what with Transition being based in Boulder, Colorado, Dataview in London and Infotech in Hyderabad. However, with a shared focus that hinged on a successful outcome, the transaction was completed in a relatively short time.

A small aside: the takeover almost did not happen because both sets of lawyers forgot to include the cost of the international funds transfer into their final calculations—a tiny amount compared to the purchase price—but a potential problem, nevertheless. Fortunately, it was a time when people still carried cash and we were able to cough up the necessary money and put it on the table. The transaction took place as planned.

The acquisition helped us to insulate ourselves from the negative impact of the US economic slowdown when the dot-com bubble burst at the turn of the millennium. Our revenues stood at Rs 160 crore ($33.32 million) in FY2003, reflecting the steady European revenue growth post the Dataview acquisition, offsetting the US slowdown of 2002. The acquisition also impacted our engineering services business positively.

Initially, Dataview was apprehensive about working with a much larger group (Infotech had 850 people) but everyone, barring one mid-level manager, stayed back. We used the words 'acquisition' and 'merger' interchangeably in internal communications to soften their anxiety. Our effort to integrate the operations and cultures of both outfits paid off; employees at Dataview set aside their disquiet and settled down. They started to understand the projects and type of work that best suited Infotech and focused on the opportunity that was blossoming. Culturally we were quite different, yet our values were very similar. This acted as a unifier and helped us to concentrate on the bigger picture and work towards our common goals. There were the inevitable mistakes in the early days, but perseverance and a willingness to learn from each other helped us overcome the obvious challenges of culture and lack of proximity. A passion for, and expertise in, all things geospatial definitely helped.

A couple of years earlier, I had met Martin Trostel at Hannover Messe in Germany. This was around the time I was exploring the German market in search of a good distributor for MODES, our CAD product. Martin had a CAD product and distribution company, Advanced Graphics Software (AGS).

My first interaction with Martin set the tone for our future relationship. Martin was a man of few words, with a sympathetic ear and a deep understanding of the European CAD/CAM market. I quickly perceived that AGS was the right fit for selling MODES.

Martin liked MODES but was astute enough to say that he would only engage with Infotech in an exclusive contract with royalty-based transactions and no firm commitments. Martin had a clear vision of how he would position the product. He wanted to re-brand it as EuroArchiv to leverage the equity of his existing brand. I thought the deal was worthwhile under the given circumstances and agreed to the retail price and royalty he proposed. We celebrated the signing of the agreement with a dinner at Indisches Restaurant

Kashmir in Leonberg, which became a regular haunt as our relationship flourished over the years.

Martin and I developed a strong relationship, driven by values. AGS was a small business, but Martin ran a tight ship, insisting on both profitability and cash flows. He wrote product reviews in German magazines to generate sales leads which yielded reasonable business month on month. Martin paid our royalty very promptly. By the fifteenth of every month, payments would arrive without even a day's delay for revenues generated in the previous month. He used to attach a spreadsheet of the day-wise sales. He was very strong on transparency and ethics.

After a year of working with Martin, it occurred to me that acquiring AGS would be a great value add for Infotech. The company would get a foothold in Germany and ready access to the Western European market. Moreover, we would gain a brand that was already established in the German CAD/CAM product market space.

I broached the topic with him. 'Martin, AGS is closely aligned to Infotech's core capabilities—our CAD products. If we work together, the potential synergies and opportunities will help us cut costs and grow the business across the European market. You should consider Infotech acquiring AGS.'

Thoroughly taken aback, Martin rejected my offer instantly. 'No thank you, Mohan. I like my independence and prefer to run my own business.'

I tried to soften the proposition, feeling that I had made the offer out of the blue without preparing him for the move. 'Think about it, Martin, don't view my proposition as an intent to buy out AGS and subsume it into Infotech. It would be a merger—a coming together of two independent entities that would continue to work with their sovereignty intact. I assure you I'll give you enough independence to operate the European business.'

Martin stuck to his guns and politely refused my offer yet again.

I did not give up. In the course of my business trips to the US and back, I made it a point to stop over in Frankfurt and spend time with Martin while I waited for my connecting flights. Our conversations never extended beyond a couple of hours but I made sure we developed a deeper rapport. The mutual trust and respect we shared blossomed even more over time and Martin began to thaw. Within a year, he had started seeing the merit in combining forces with me. Infotech acquired AGS in October 2000. Infotech Enterprises GmbH, MollenbaschstraBe, Leonberg, a small town in the German federal state of Baden-Württemberg and 16 km west of Stuttgart, became the beachhead for our forays into continental Europe.

I started travelling to Leonberg frequently, and that was when I had my first run in with Martin—not over work but food! Meals never loomed large in Martin's scheme of things and he would invariably forget all about lunch, but for me three meals a day were critical to my daily routine and I refused to entertain the notion of skipping them. Like many other things, I slowly convinced Martin to at least eat a sandwich at the Cafe Eleni, in the Leo-Center Shopping Mall which we had started frequenting, thanks to me. However, let it not be said that Martin was a poor host. He always insisted on taking me out for dinner at the Kashmir. It was rather paradoxical that I was eating Indian food in Germany! The food was reasonable and I developed a fondness for the place because this was where Martin and I had many a conversation on how we would go about building our European business.

I promised Martin independent functioning as long as he aligned his goals and strategies with those of Infotech. AGS was an important acquisition because we realized that having a company in the UK did not necessarily mean we had access to the markets in continental Europe, especially Germany. It was a good example of how a partnership could evolve into an acquisition.

With the ASI relationship running into deep trouble, our GIS/geospatial business faced serious challenges in late 2001. But our efforts with other customers—multimillion-dollar projects from the Dutch multinational, Fugro, KPN Telecom, Triathlon—the Canadian geomatics company, CANData, the Australian company, and our European acquisitions (Dataview and AGS) ensured our business remained resilient. The two acquisitions in Europe formed a new Europe, Africa and Middle East division within Infotech Enterprises Europe and strengthened our regional presence.

After losing the ASI business, we started scouting around for an acquisition in the US to establish a strong local footprint in the world's most prominent geospatial market. We gave a buy-side mandate to Transition Partners Ltd. Once again, the task fell on Gene Copeland and Terry Schreier, the same investment bankers who had represented Dataview's sell-side mandate. Gene was the 'good cop' and Terry the 'bad cop'—or at least those were the roles they played but as a team they were perfect! And very impressive. They identified VARGIS LLC as a potential target. VARGIS was a pioneer in commercializing digital earth imagery and was into geospatial mapping products and services. It was also a prime contractor of the multi-year US state and regional imagery programmes. Greg Tilley was its co-founder and president.

In January 2004, we acquired VARGIS and retained its current management team, operating it as an independent entity under Infotech. Greg was a perfect addition to our US leadership team. He understood the geospatial sector well, especially the photogrammetry market. The acquisition gave us a well-established platform to address the geospatial needs of government, utility, telecom and transportation clients in the US. The acquisition positioned us for aggressive growth in the North American GIS/geospatial markets.

We created three strategic business units (SBUs) within Infotech Software Solutions Inc to better manage the diversity and reach of our US business—GIS/geospatial services, operating from Sterling, Virginia, engineering services from East Hartford, Connecticut and software services from Riverside, California.

In all three acquisitions (Dataview, AGS and VARGIS), the CEOs stayed with us. Handling these new leaders was no picnic. They had been full or partial owners of the target companies and their egos were understandably sensitive. Each of them hailed from a different culture and had a unique background. We had to handle all three with kid gloves to avoid upsetting them while making sure we brought out the best in them after the acquisition.

There were also a few instances where we came across some hesitation in selling to an Indian-owned company or working for Indian leadership. But once these initial wrinkles were ironed out, our acquisitions by and large brought excellent customer connect and enjoyed a great relationship with associates.

To get the best out of the acquisition, we always made a thorough evaluation of the leadership. We gave them appropriate positions along with the comfort of working with a larger company. Whilst giving stability and security to their roles, we simultaneously provided opportunities for growth. For instance, Martin Trostel worked as the CEO of our fully-owned subsidiary in Germany and provided leadership for engineering services in Europe. He worked with us for more than fifteen years after the acquisition and retired on a happy note. We told all of them that we would run the business through them in a light-handed M&A style. Considering the fact that cross-border acquisitions were notoriously tough to pull off in those days, I would say Infotech's early investments were quite a success.

In hindsight, though, these three acquisitions taught us several lessons. We certainly expanded our global footprint through the acquired local talent, including their CEOs. We won customer confidence as the local leadership gave more customer comfort. However, we erred in terms of product-fit.

Dataview Solutions was a geospatial company and I thought, 'This is the right company to buy.' But it was only after we acquired it that we realized the challenges before us. Infotech was into 'professional geospatial' business, proficient in digitizing assets, infrastructure, facility management and parcel mapping. Dataview was into 'business geospatial', providing geodemographics and business intelligence solutions that were further down the geospatial market continuum. Although we worked with similar customers in the telecom and utility sectors, Infotech served the operational and technical aspects of customer business, while Dataview addressed the sales and marketing side. The buyers in these organizations were different—VP of operations for asset mapping and VP of marketing and sales for business geospatial solutions. Project volumes were larger and sales cycles were longer in the professional geospatial segment.

The Dataview acquisition also threw up abundant troubles on the operational side, especially around sales. A sales professional of Dataview, used to handling a ticket size of the order of $10K, was overwhelmed at having to close deals of $100K magnitude monthly, which were the norm for sales personnel at Infotech. We did not realize business geospatial had much smaller deal values and would not scale to those in the professional geospatial market. Their salary structure and sales incentives were also different. So, we had to rejig our sales structure and get a different set of sales professionals and allow those who could not adapt to leave.

We faced similar challenges with AGS, a low-cost CAD product reseller. It had marquee customers such as Bosch, Siemens, Alstom, etc., but the buyers of these CAD products were different from Infotech's clientele. While the VP of engineering made decisions for CAD services outsourcing, design engineers decided on the low-end drawing archival packages. We miscalculated buyer synergies before the acquisition. While deciding to buy AGS, I prioritized customer connect rather than the product value proposition. We took the EuroArchiv product business and sold it for a while. But it did not work out for very long.

We also made a similar mistake with VARGIS, which was more of a photogrammetry company and worked mainly with county and state governments. The sales cultures were different. We quickly moved salespeople from India to supplement and crank up the sales engine.

'Learning' is the tritest excuse touted in management books when execution fails. It gives comfort to the doer and listener. It offers solace to organizations—large and small—which depend entirely on entrepreneurial innovation to survive. But one cannot take it to a customer, shareholder or private equity investor. It does not pay the bills, nor does it build reputations or brands. Learning is an expensive investment for an entrepreneur. Yet, it was the most vital ingredient in transforming Infotech into a sustainable company.

The one question I ask after a day's work is: What is the lesson? How can I sow the 'learning' of today to harvest the 'growth' of tomorrow? What elements of strategy, product development, quality, sales, marketing functions can I improve to realize the company's vision?

This relentless root cause analysis and follow-on action has yielded favourable results over the years. After all, entrepreneurship is about dynamic decision-making and learning; it's not about being risk-averse.

Infotech's early acquisitions highlighted the need for a thorough screening mechanism to support a transaction, including due diligence in scrutinizing its technical and business aspects. They also taught us that buying companies should be treated as a business process. Acquisition mistakes are common and I made my fair share of them. Fortunately, they were calculated risks that eventually paid off. We learnt from our slip-ups and took corrective measures. On an aggregate, if we weigh the positives and negatives, the scale tilts overwhelmingly towards the former. These acquisitions allowed us to meet our strategic goal which was to expand Infotech's geographical footprint, to facilitate its rapid growth in subsequent years. As we continued to work on strategic relationships and pursue acquisition prospects, we became wiser with our choices.

7

Driving Growth:
Aerospace Engineering

Was Einstein's philosophy of science correct when he said that 'the creative principle resides in Mathematics'?[1] Perhaps. But can creative impulses alone act as propellers to give wings to dreams and pilot them towards success? Champions, as Muhammad Ali once said, aren't made in gyms. They're made from something they have deep inside them—a desire, a dream, a vision.[2] I had been dreaming of building a global engineering services company in India for a long time, and once the desire took hold of me it would not fade—my vision became a living, breathing entity taking on a parallel life of its own. But then reality stepped in and my grand plans hit a roadblock even before they took off.

In the early 1990s, large multinationals looked askance at engineering outsourcing. They zealously guarded their products as though they were crown jewels, and were extremely sceptical about outsourcing their core competence. They were particularly apprehensive about IP and associated protection laws in countries like India. As a result, we took a detour and found a potential adjacency with a large addressable market in digitization. We started digitizing maps and engineering drawings, moved up the

GIS/geospatial value-chain, created good revenue streams and were recognized globally as a credible service provider.

But I never took my eyes off my first love: the engineering services business. This was the premise that drove Infotech's IPO in March 1997. I kept my promise to our shareholders and re-launched the engineering services division in 1997–98 with much greater focus and rigour.

We started out with a small team, working on opportunities that came our way in dribs and drabs with specialized design engineering services such as 3D models of mechanical components, finite element modelling and analysis and building NC machining codes.

Our first customer was the Ford Motor Company. Thanks to a lead by an industry colleague, we clinched the deal and executed the finite element modelling and analysis of an engine block. Infotech continued to work for Ford, and yet for three consecutive years, our annual billing was no more than $100,000. We tried several tactics to scale the account without success. Ford preferred to outsource to local service providers with automotive expertise, which Infotech lacked. Moreover, its outsourcing strategy was tactical and projects were awarded on the twin basis of its need and workload.

To step up, we recruited Rajendra Velagapudi from Bharat Earth Movers Limited (BEML). He brought knowledge of the engineering product life cycle to our table and set up formats, templates and risk management plans for engineering services. Within a few months, we had streamlined our processes and obtained ISO 9000 certification for our engineering services. The process experience of our geospatial division came in handy when we laid out the processes for engineering.

Enter: Pratt & Whitney

One sunny afternoon in February 2000, Manohar Rao, an old friend from my Shriram days, called up. The call came while we were up to our necks preparing for the NASSCOM India Leadership Forum

(NILF, now renamed NTLF) in Mumbai which was scheduled for the next day.

'Pratt & Whitney (P&W) are here in Hyderabad tonight. They're hosting a dinner at Hotel Grand Kakatiya. I've worked with them for the past two years and I think you should meet them.'

My ears perked up. Pratt and Whitney (P&W), the American aerospace company (a division of United Technologies Corp, now merged with Raytheon Technologies), was and is one of the largest manufacturers of aircraft engines in the world. I don't typically miss a networking opportunity but in this case, my principles stood in the way.

I declined politely. 'Manohar Rao *garu*, to be honest, I don't know much about Pratt & Whitney. Besides, I don't like gate-crashing a dinner without an invitation. It's against my personal rules.'

'That's not a problem! I know Pratt & Whitney's country manager. I'll get a fax invite sent to you,' Manohar insisted.

He kept his word and I received the invite. Unlike a few entrepreneurs, who consign networking to the bottom of their priority list, I recognize its benefits. I leverage my connections and never miss an opportunity to meet new people. Nor do I arrive late for meetings. Punctuality is a trait I have always prized and I do not think it adds to one's stature to keep people cooling their heels. I was at Hotel Grand Kakatiya at 7.30 p.m. Little did I realize at the time that this routine networking event was about to change Infotech's destiny.

I cast my gaze around the dimly lit room. Manohar was hobnobbing with a small group of people comprising representatives from Satyam Computers and a few smaller companies; they were all engrossed in muffled conversations and appeared oblivious to the world at large. There was no sign of Pratt & Whitney executives anywhere. The clock ticked away and 7.30 p.m. turned to 8.30 p.m., but there was still no sight of the Pratt & Whitney team. Just as I was beginning to get restless, the eighteen-member delegation from Pratt & Whitney walked in. The team, on a *Bharat darshan* at the time, to familiarize itself with India, was on a sharp lookout for partners; its flight to Hyderabad had been delayed.

The first task of a salesman at a networking event is to recognize the decision-maker. I had precious little time, but I quickly identified the decision-makers in the team—Ed Crow, vice president of engineering and Jyothi Purshottaman, CFO.

I chatted up Ed Crow over a glass of wine.

'What are you drinking?' he asked.

'Wine,' I replied.

'What kind of wine is it?' Ed questioned.

'It's an Indian wine made entirely out of grapes grown in India,' I answered and then proceeded to treat him to a detailed story about Golconda Ruby Red, the first wine ever made in India. The brand was available only in select markets in south India. It possessed a unique flavour.

My story piqued his interest and Ed ordered a glass of Golconda Ruby Red. Ed liked it and enjoyed his introduction to an authentic Indian wine despite its 'cough syrup'-like taste. He appeared to enjoy our conversation and eventually asked, 'Mohan, what are you doing tomorrow?'

'I'm off to Mumbai for a NASSCOM event,' I responded promptly.

'How about the team visit your office tomorrow? We would like to spend an hour with you to know what you do better,' Ed suggested.

I was surprised. I'm not given to changing my plans at the drop of a hat. But in this instance, I instinctively replied, 'Sure, Ed! Let's meet at my office tomorrow morning.'

Infotech had inaugurated its Madhapur (Hyderabad) headquarters just twenty days prior to this conversation. We had about a thousand associates working on the first two floors, but the rest of the building was just a shell. We were consolidating people from other offices at various locations in the city. Our in-house cafeteria and other facilities were yet to come up.

Ed and his team visited Infotech the next morning, and we ended up spending two-and-a-half hours together. In addition to my corporate pitch, our team showcased Infotech's nascent engineering capabilities. Honestly speaking, we had only served Ford Motor Company till then and were eager to expand. We took the Pratt & Whitney team around our floors and demonstrated our process compliance, quality and timeline adherence. We also explained how we measured the productivity of each associate on an ongoing basis and the process that was extant to improve the same. Our efforts to please customers and customer testimonials caught their attention.

This introductory meeting with Pratt and Whitney turned out to be quite productive. By the time it ended, we had an invitation. 'When are you coming to East Hartford?' Ed inquired, before getting into the car that was waiting for him.

'Whenever you want me to,' I responded with a firm handshake.

Within a fortnight, I was in East Hartford, Connecticut, at the Pratt & Whitney's global headquarters, meeting Ed and his team for a second time. By the first week of April, Pratt & Whitney's team was back in Hyderabad to take the conversation forward.

We finalized a five-year strategic partnership with Pratt & Whitney, US. The engagement involved delivering a range of software services, solutions and engineering services for product development and maintenance. We agreed to create a centre of excellence for the company to provide mission-critical services intrinsic to its business. Infotech's Pratt & Whitney project became the most significant engagement by an Indian company in outsourced engineering services at the turn of the century.

Within two months of issuing the purchase order (PO), Pratt & Whitney started negotiating for a stake in the company. I ensured the terms of investment included a volume commitment to engage at least 500 engineers undertaking Pratt & Whitney work. We offered a 15 per cent equity stake in the company with an option to further enhance it to 18.4 per cent by 2003 with equitable terms to both parties. Charles (Chuck) W. Ayer, the financial controller with Pratt & Whitney, represented the company on the Infotech board. Chuck contributed significantly in evolving our association into a long-term strategic relationship.

Pratt & Whitney knew we did not have domain capabilities in aerospace, much less aircraft engines—one of the most sophisticated equipment ever designed and built by humans. But it was aware of Infotech's strength to rapidly scale projects. The company recognized our abilities to measure outcomes, analyse results and fix deviations. Even more importantly, it recognized that the Infotech leadership could be trusted and was invested in making the relationship successful. The upshot: 'Don't worry,' we were told. 'We'll teach you all there is to know about aircraft engines.'

Pratt was highly successful in moving some of its manufacturing work to China and its strategy was to move its design and engineering work to India. Infotech was the first foreign firm to which Pratt & Whitney began outsourcing its engineering services. It was a new concept for the company and it was keen to make it succeed. The move proved to be a win-win strategy and contributed to the success of both companies.

It was a new experience for Infotech's engineering services division to work with customers in aircraft engine design. Since this was a complex and safety-critical activity, we knew it would take us time to make a business impact for the customer. But we were more than willing to embark upon this long and arduous journey.

For the first two months, Infotech recruited twenty-five people each week. We organized walk-ins in Bangalore (now Bengaluru), Chennai, Pune and Mumbai. Once the right candidates were identified, offer letters were issued on the spot and they were onboarded at the earliest. A majority of these early associates continue to work with the company in various business units even today.

Pratt & Whitney took three of our associates, Rajendra among them, to its East Hartford headquarters. They were put through rigorous training and were made to interact with various module centre teams. Our team went through an orientation on Pratt & Whitney's systems and processes, the tasks it intended to outsource, the challenges in outsourcing that both parties foresaw and the additional facilities/support that it would need from Hyderabad. In addition, the teams agreed to the processes that would strengthen collaboration and cybersecurity, especially firewalls, as the customer IP was precious.

It was a world that had not yet learned the joys of high-speed Internet or videoconferencing and the work involved was extremely sensitive. Pratt & Whitney desired fail-safe connectivity between its offices in North America and the Infotech India offices. It agreed to pay for it. For the first time we encountered a customer who needed 100 per cent redundancy and therefore facilitated the installation of optical fibre connectivity, one via the Atlantic and the other, trans-Pacific. They were also used for audio calls with just an extension number from the client premises. This ensured 100 per cent uptime, and considerably improved our engagement and collaboration with the customer. The act in itself was significant as it reflected how invested Pratt & Whitney was in the relationship. At our end, it meant a great opportunity and also a big responsibility to contribute to its long-term success.

In the first year of our engagement, about 100 experts from Pratt & Whitney visited Hyderabad. A similar number of associates were deputed from Infotech to East Hartford for training. The teams were eventually grouped into various module centres—compressor, combustor, turbine, externals and mechanical systems, to name a few.

As our teams began to work with their counterparts at Pratt & Whitney, we faced a fresh hitch—the thick English accents and poor communication skills of our associates! Our customer found it difficult to understand them and vice versa. Our associates would frequently infuse regional accents to hilarious effect. One incident in particular stands out. We were in the middle of a conference call when a Pratt & Whitney representative announced that he would be coming to Hyderabad the following week.

One of our engineers was so excited by this announcement that he said, 'You are comingaaa?'

There was a prolonged silence as the person on the other end struggled to decipher what he meant. He finally got it and confirmed that he was indeed.

We met this obstacle head on and put our engineers on a structured month-long training in 'accent neutralization' and threw in a formal writing course for good measure to enhance their written skills.

We created e-learning modules for new associates. By the time they completed their three-month orientation and training, they had gained a fair understanding of the work and processes they would execute and were confident of facing the customer.

Ramping up the Account

For the first six months, Pratt & Whitney outsourced low-end work such as product definition and class-2 engineering changes. It allowed us to understand the engineering change management (ECM) process and the reasons for modifying the designs. This knowledge came in handy when we worked on new component designs later.

Apart from change implementation, we handled aftermarket engineering services. Infotech developed detailed repair manuals to disassemble engines, prepare parts cleaning processes, inspect parts, and rebuild/reassemble. These, too, helped our teams understand why and how a certain component failed and the mode and frequency of failure; we would then loop the input back to our teams which were working on new component designs.

Most of the initial work pertained to engineering software and mechanical design and engineering. Pratt & Whitney then involved us in a software development project for verification and validation. We developed products and platforms—one of them was a portal for engine maintenance. We expanded this by slowly engaging in software development for avionics. We developed a tool to move its existing software programmes from UNIX to Microsoft Windows platforms. Some of the products we developed in 2001/2002 are still being used by Pratt & Whitney and maintained by our teams.

We made numerous mistakes in the first few months, but each of them turned out to be an opportunity for learning. Pratt

& Whitney was as eager to make the partnership successful as we were. Instead of fault-finding, it handheld us and kept the team morale high.

Pratt & Whitney stationed a senior engineering outsourcing manager in Hyderabad to bridge the gap between teams. He played a vital role in making sure both sides worked closely and deepened the rapport. On behalf of Infotech, Rajendra handled the relationship quite responsibly and sized up to all the challenges, initially in delivery and later in scaling the account. As our engagement grew in volume, I brought back Ashok Kumar (who had gone through a brief stint in overseeing geospatial services delivery, previously) to Infotech to head the delivery of engineering services. Ashok had a flair for aerospace engineering and a wealth of knowledge about engineering outsourcing which helped us to gain customer confidence.

Expanding the scope of engagement and business with an existing customer is as important as acquiring new ones. After six months, Pratt & Whitney came up with a fresh proposal. 'Here are two components. They're cracking and failing in service before their designed service life. Can you analyse why and suggest a fix?'

We grabbed the opportunity with both hands. We set up an integrated product team (IPT) with capabilities in design, stress analysis, thermal analysis, materials, repair process and manufacturing and launched two pilots. Pratt & Whitney promised to shadow us but allowed us a free hand to work on the pilots.

Customer expectations were high. We knew this was the opportunity of a lifetime. Failure was not an option, and success was not guaranteed. But it was definitely worth a try. So, we worked our hearts out to develop a solution the customer teams had not thought through. We had no legacy to live up to and were therefore free to think out of the box. Our teams, young and spirited, analysed and understood the root cause of the failure of the components and came up with a series of suggestions to improve the design. We had analytically validated, simulated and convinced ourselves that we were on the right track before offering a solution that worked within the constrained environment of the engine.

It took close to eighteen months to work on these pilots, and the solution led to two patents. They were so successful that Pratt & Whitney regards them as a benchmark in tackling field problems. Our team was nominated for the Pratt & Whitney leadership awards—the highest award in the company. Though we did not win the prize, for a company with just three–four years of aerospace experience, it was a moment of great pride to be nominated to this coveted honour. The pilots had won us customer confidence. Pratt & Whitney was now certain that Infotech was ready to shoulder larger responsibilities with less supervision.

This moment marked the next phase of our relationship. We expanded from providing discreet services to solutions. IPT became our second-level engagement with the firm. Infotech began to take ownership of engine parts in the field and started improving the design through corrective action. The tenor of our problem statements changed. Assertions like, 'This part belongs to us. We'll take care of any failure that may happen to it on the field. We'll also manage any design changes on the part in its service life,' became frequent phrases that we started trotting out to the client.

The Pratt & Whitney account scaled well beyond our expectations. It was a fine culmination of customer demand and our ability to deliver quality services on time, every time. In a way, fortune too favoured our efforts. Within two years, Pratt & Whitney accounted for about 50 per cent of Infotech's revenue.

We slowly started taking ownership of not just parts but individual part families—stators, cases, rotors, mechanical components, externals, brackets and tubes. We fixed hundreds of problems for the customer and, while doing so, we learnt a lot more about engine design and manufacturing.

As the account turned larger and more complex, we felt the need to manage full customer experience—from the front-end sales process to ongoing service and support. Transparent processes, consistent and open communication, clearly defined ownership and well-laid out protocols for coordination with multiple stakeholders were put in place across geographies, functions and teams to enhance it.

Infotech wholeheartedly embraced Pratt & Whitney's business operating system—Achieving Competitive Excellence (ACE)—in 2002 and relentlessly forged ahead to improve standardization in our teams. Our ACE journey helped us craft well-defined account management practices and tools to monitor customer service, customer value and customer growth.

Gradually, we communicated a credible quantified value proposition (QVP) for the services, a key differentiator in price negotiation. Before negotiations, our cross-functional sales team analysed industry cost curves, gathered market intelligence and modelled scenarios to understand and quantify the best alternatives for the customer and put forward the optimal pricing deal. Infotech won several awards for innovation and productivity year after year; they were worthy testimonies of our value creation. These exertions helped us turn Pratt & Whitney, our largest customer, into Infotech's growth engine.

Taking Charge: Engine Subsystems

Over time, Infotech worked on several engine programmes including the state-of-the-art GP7000 and supported the customer in redesigning a few existing components while Pratt & Whitney handled most of the new components. We then offered support in designing new parts. Initially, we landed small projects in the new engine programme.

As our engagement intensified, it necessitated a daily interaction with our customer to better understand their needs and get hold of its inputs so that they could be translated to the team back in Hyderabad. The aim was to bridge the gaps and provide exceptional service. To this end, we stationed customer engagement and account managers in East Hartford. Excellent service may retain the customer for a while, but that alone will not ensure account growth. We realized that the key to fast-track business growth lay in creating customer value. Our engagement and account managers were consequently encouraged to develop an owner's mindset and think and act like passionate entrepreneurs while working with Pratt & Whitney and identify its unarticulated needs.

Our teams continuously tracked the health and viability of the account, gaining deep insight into customer requirements while determining and directing us to the areas that needed improvement. Our willingness to operate in uncharted seas helped us develop the muscle to think new, innovate, incubate ideas and create novel and commercially viable services. Even though adjacencies and whitespaces were beyond the scope and framework of existing projects, we proactively monitored opportunities that were monetizable and pitched them at an opportune moment. After all, acquiring a new customer is five to ten times more expensive than retaining and scaling an existing one. I have observed that customer retention has a significant and positive bearing on a company's profits. These efforts, which were centred on products, processes and business model innovations, enabled us to upsell, leading to portfolio expansion.

The working vibe between the teams was positive and friendly. They had freedom and guidance throughout. At the same time, we held our teams accountable for their actions while making sure organizational support, not just from me but from every department, was available to them when projects threw up challenges. Team spirit was high, and there was an air of informality without any undercurrents. Everyone was on the same wavelength and aimed to please the customer. One may call it company culture—a culture that was triggered by individual curiosity, nurtured by organizational aspirations, coupled with a personal desire and drive to succeed.

In around 2008, Pratt & Whitney launched a new engine programme called GTF—Geared Turbo Fan programme (since renamed Next Generation Product Family or NGPF engine programme). This state-of-the-art engine promised to deliver a 16 per cent increase in fuel efficiency, 50 per cent reduction in noise and 50 per cent reduction in carbon emissions over existing engines. This was music to the ears of the aviation industry and expectations were high. New engine programmes typically involve investments worth billions, and companies such as Pratt & Whitney embark on new programmes, perhaps, once in twenty years.

We proactively identified twenty new features that could be part of the engine, features we were confident of developing independently and pitched our ideas to Dave Carter, vice president, Pratt & Whitney, during one of his trips to Hyderabad. Our pitch surprised Dave, but he encouraged us to present it to the team in East Hartford.

We took our pitch to their chief engineers and zeroed in on a few component ideas. Sensing our fervency and confidence, Pratt & Whitney entrusted us with part of the new project. We proved our capabilities by executing these tasks flawlessly. Infotech gradually found its way into the new programme and started engaging in new part development, transforming ourselves into a value-added partner instead of a supplier. By 2010/2011, we ramped up our engagement to a level that the company was executing a substantial amount of the engineering work on the NGPF engine. We ended up supporting it with 350 additional engineers and enabled it to file a number of patents and create new intellectual property. To this day, our work has helped Pratt & Whitney file more than fifty patents.

The NGPF programme progressed at breakneck speed on the one side. On the other, Pratt & Whitney intended to repurpose the flight-proven turbofan engine into an industrial gas turbine, which could be a cost-effective solution for utility providers. They inquired if we would like to redesign, validate and manufacture the hardware of certain parts at a significantly lower cost without compromising functionality and safety. The company was ready to make Infotech an exclusive supplier of the components for a period of ten years, but on a risk-share model.

We weighed the pros and cons of the business case. Up to this point, Infotech had executed customer POs but it had never invested in a customer programme or taken complete ownership. Could we do it? We decided to set this as our new target. Taking the risk, Infotech invested a quarter of a million dollars upfront and grabbed the project. We were required to significantly re-engineer some modules/components to bring down the cost and put about a hundred engineers on the job. In essence, what was expected of us was to provide systems engineering and systems integration to the extent we would more or less function as deputy to Pratt & Whitney's chief engineer.

Pratt & Whitney handheld us in the course of the project and we produced the engine parts; they tested successfully in Florida and eight sets of hardware were delivered. Infotech recovered its investment and had a great learning experience. It continues to be an ongoing project.

As our engagement and value-add grew, over-reliance on a single vendor (Infotech) became a concern for the customer. Even though the senior management was confident of the relationship, others worked overtime to de-risk the dependency. A large company like Pratt & Whitney had strong reasons to consider de-risking. Even for us, over-dependence on a single customer was a risky proposition. We could not prevent competition. But we increased our value-add to a level that even though we lost some work to the competition, it was only limited to those projects where the margins were low or we had an inherent weakness in skills.

Pratt & Whitney successfully fired the first NGPF engine in 2013. By 2015, the amount of engineering work on NGPF slowed down substantially. We started worrying about keeping our band of well-trained engineers engaged and occupied with interesting projects. After some brainstorming, we recognized that though NGPF delivered the promised functional efficiencies, the cost of the engine was exorbitant. We proposed compelling cost-optimizing solutions to the customer and signed a long-term partnership, again in risk-revenue sharing mode. The project entailed that we invest and execute class I and II engineering changes and receive part of the savings accrued to Pratt & Whitney upon engine shipment. This was a great business case that brought forth our teams' entrepreneurial spirit and leveraged the client's trust in us while kicking up the value momentum a notch higher.

I managed the Pratt & Whitney account during the first ten years of the association and was rather possessive about it. I tended it carefully, letting it mature into a long-term strategic partnership between two multinational institutions.

Part of the credit goes to the Pratt & Whitney US leadership. Their commitment to the long-term partnership is an endorsement of our business competence. They taught us the nuances of managing large customers and their expectations. In the true spirit of partnership, Pratt & Whitney focused on making Infotech a shared success story and we leveraged that confidence, expanded the account strategically and nurtured it to remarkable levels of growth and maturity.

Capturing UTC Business

United Technologies Corporation (UTC, now part of Raytheon Technologies), the corporate body that owned Pratt & Whitney, had many divisions and subsidiaries. Pratt & Whiney Canada was a Pratt & Whitney US division but with a different identity and leadership. Their product offerings, too, were dissimilar.

For Infotech, it was logical to take the initial success with Pratt & Whitney US to Pratt & Whitney Canada. But they were on the verge of creating a captive in Bangalore (now Bengaluru) and had just issued job offers to twenty engineers. It was difficult to coax them to change their strategy. I was determined to give it a try anyway and flew to Montreal to persuade the Pratt & Whitney Canada leadership to throw in their lot with us.

I had a simple proposition: Infotech was better equipped to manage outsourcing engagements. We were cost-effective and could ensure that Pratt & Whitney Canada did not run into problems with sub-scale operations. Pratt & Whitney Canada was culturally different from its US outfit. I had to pull all the tricks in the sales playbook to convince its leadership that Infotech's value proposition was sound.

Their leadership finally relented and accepted my proposal—albeit with conditions. The provisos were as follows: we were to honour the job offers that had already been extended; the engagement was to be located in Bangalore (now Bengaluru); it was to be secluded from

Pratt & Whitney US and Pratt & Whitney Canada would manage the projects. We went through some initial hiccups, but over time we managed to smooth out all the rough edges in terms of quality and on-time delivery. We continue to have a great relationship with the firm.

We then trained our gaze on Hamilton Sunstrand (which became UTC Aerospace Systems and, subsequently, Collins Aerospace), as it was also in the aerospace business. There was a free exchange of people, information and processes between Pratt & Whitney US and Hamilton Sunstrand, making things a bit easier for us. However, engaging and coordinating with Hamilton Sunstrand's geographically dispersed teams was like a labour of Hercules.

While our Pratt & Whitney engagement was heavy on mechanical engineering by virtue of content and was centred on one product family, i.e., aircraft engines, our Hamilton Sunstrand engagement focused on electronics and embedded software. Their product portfolio is diverse, catering to several dozens of aircraft systems such as propellers, auxiliary power units (APU), actuation systems, air management systems, electric systems, nacelle, lighting systems, etc.

As Infotech scaled its engagement with Hamilton Sunstrand, it rapidly moved from providing engineering services to build-to-specification (B2S) engagements on a few critical sub-systems. We bagged a contract to design, build and qualify the Bus Power Control Unit (BPCU) and Overvoltage Protection Unit (OPU) for the company. The BPCU is used to control the distribution of electrical power between various distribution busses on the aircraft. The OPU compares the sampled voltage to a reference voltage, both critical electrical systems in an aeroplane. We successfully delivered the hardware, catapulting from pure engineering services to design-to-build solutions.

Success in one UTC subsidiary encouraged us to approach others as well. We built engagements with their aerospace subsidiary Sikorsky and to a lesser extent, with non-aerospace entities such as Otis and Carrier (now independent corporate bodies). We swiftly realized that the 'one size fits all' strategy was unsound. Though these firms were part of a large conglomerate, their businesses, cultures, processes, technologies and business models were varied. While we carried the best lessons forward from our anchor customer, we needed to invest time, energy and effort to understand each subsidiary and adjust our propositions to suit them individually. Despite tremendous efforts to tailor our pitch and actions for individual fit, our relationship with them never blossomed.

Sikorsky was difficult and frustrating. Every customer meeting went well, giving us the hope that a contract would follow. In hot pursuit to strike a deal with the firm, at the time, I would frequently drive with Sampath, our account manager, from Hartford to Stratford where Sikorsky was headquartered. It was about 80 kilometres away and we used to take about an hour to reach our destination. We normally devoted the driving time to intense discussions on strategy for the impending meetings. On one such trip, I broke off in mid-sentence, noticing that Sampath had turned pale.

'What's wrong?' I asked, wondering why he was looking so squeamish.

'S-sir,' he stammered. 'The brakes have failed.'

It was my turn to pale. The volume of traffic suddenly began to look ominous. 'We're done for,' I thought, sending up a silent prayer to all the Gods I could think of.

With great presence of mind, Sampath quickly drove the car onto the shoulder of the road straight into the lush green grass adjoining the highway. After a few minutes the car came to a slow stop and I heaved a huge sigh of relief. It had been one of the scariest moments of my life.

We didn't spend too much time congratulating ourselves on our lucky escape. We had a bigger problem on our hands. We needed a car pronto if we were to reach on time for the meeting. We called a cab and asked the driver to step on it; he did and we made it to the meeting by the skin of our teeth. Customer commitment was always a priority at Infotech. The first thing I did once we were back at our office was to sanction a loan for Sampath to buy a new car.

Despite the prolonged chase, the Sikorsky account never took off. It may have been because the US government's export control laws prohibit the export of sensitive technologies, thereby making the company chary of outsourcing defence-related work.

Otis design work, on the other hand, had a large local content, as it designed elevators based on exact building sizes. This constraint did not lend itself to outsourcing at a scale that would make it a viable proposition for us. Carrier was operating in the consumer durables space of air-conditioners and its product life cycles were short. Our limited knowledge of air-conditioning and elevator technologies also placed us at a disadvantage.

In a few instances, referencing our success with other subsidiaries was a drawback. Apart from understanding the product and processes of a potential customer, we needed to understand the people and culture in each account. Sometimes, professional rivalries within the multinationals put us in an unfavourable spot.

These aggravations notwithstanding, working with large multinationals such as UTC offered several pluses. Infotech did things right and scaled the account satisfactorily at incremental sales and marketing costs. We used the first success as a launchpad to provide services to other divisions and subsidiaries while simultaneously building product, process and people knowledge. From a $600,000 customer account in FY2001, Pratt & Whitney and other UTC subsidiaries have been closing in on $100-plus million since FY2015 and have 1500-plus engineers, which was the largest team supporting Pratt & Whitney and Collins Aerospace.

Beyond UTC

Often, by strategically aligning with one customer, a company runs into challenges with its competitors. After building a strong relationship with Pratt & Whitney, we found it difficult to get any substantial work from GE or Rolls Royce, Pratt & Whitney's biggest aircraft engine design and manufacturing competitors. We failed to breach their ramparts; despite myriad attempts to invite them to our facilities, countless assurances to protect their IP, facilitate their centres at different locations, have separate leaderships and build Chinese walls, they were unmoved.

This did not stop us from hunting and farming other players in the aerospace industry. We began working with Boeing in 2004 on a small XML conversion project and soon got involved in the design and stress analysis of the complete aircraft wing. We then had the opportunity to support the Dreamliner programme for mid-body integration for stress analysis and wing leading edges design support. These programmes provided us with ample experience in Boeing tools and core design process standards, helping us win projects of greater scale and scope. We had 400+ engineers on Boeing projects at one point, delivering 24X7 support in engineering for the first time.

Our engagement with Boeing brought us several accolades over the years, including Pride@Boeing, Boeing Performance Supplier Award and the prestigious Boeing Supplier of the Year awards. Of the pack of 4000-plus Boeing suppliers spanning thirteen categories, we stood out year after year, reflecting our intense commitment to the customer. No other customer showered us with as many awards. The award ceremony was a black-tie event—and we had a crisis on our hands. None of us had tuxedo-type suits! We were relieved when we discovered that they could be rented for a fee. The tuxedos arrived a couple of hours before the event and had to be handed back the next morning. Following the dress code was our way of adhering to customer instructions to please them to the utmost. Once it became apparent that we would be receiving awards on a fairly regular basis, I evaluated the cost benefits of getting a tuxedo stitched instead of renting them every year. I must confess that being rigged out in style to receive awards at these grand affairs that closely resembled the Oscars was gratifying in the extreme.

However, this relationship was and continues to be tactical, unlike our strategic engagement with Pratt & Whitney. We are, nevertheless, striving hard to turn it into a strategic relationship to attain more customer stickiness and ensure a continuous flow to de-risk the business. It's a journey with no destination.

At some point, while working with Pratt & Whitney and Boeing, it dawned on me that our aerospace business was concentrated in North America and a good geographic spread was crucial if we wanted to de-risk it. To this end, we entered into a partnership with GKN Aerospace, UK. GKN, a Tier-1 supplier to Airbus, is involved in engineering design and manufacture of aerostructures. We engaged in a pilot project and built on its success, diligently pursuing the customer until we won a full-scale project to design and analyse fixed trailing edge composite panels. We swiftly ramped up the requisite skills, facilitated immediate deployment and had multiple engagements with the firm over the years.

Our aerospace capabilities got a step change when we embarked on our journey with Airbus to develop cabin and cargo solutions through software verification and validation. Infotech invested heavily in scaling, upskilling people and setting up systems. Over the years, we worked on several Airbus programmes. But we repeatedly encountered difficulties in our bid to make it to the Airbus Engineering Strategic Supplier (E2S) list. Despite our capabilities and best efforts, we could not make it to this biennial list. Airbus used the list to evaluate companies and decide whether they had the requisite skills, capabilities and familiarity with its functioning. Although we had the required competence to execute high-end aerostructural designs, we lacked the knowledge of Airbus' design standards. It was a classic case of which came first—the chicken or the egg. We could only become familiar with Airbus standards if we worked on its products but we never got the opportunity to work with the firm directly. We were asked to work with Airbus engineering service providers to familiarize ourselves with Airbus standards, but this too was a dead end as there was always a conflict of interest between the service providers. The company Cyient then forayed into aerospace electronics with Airbus Germany.

We partnered with Vought Aircraft Industries, US (later acquired by Triumph Group) and started supporting the aerostructural component design and development activities. Our commitment and competency prompted Vought to expand its engagement to seven other sites. After Triumph acquired it in 2010, we began working with Triumph Aerostructures (TGI business unit) and were recognized as a preferred engineering supplier.

In 2012, Triumph Aerostructures won Bombardier Aerospace (BA) 7500 programme for wing development, and Infotech became the preferred engineering supplier to support the BA programme.

As we continue to expand our aerospace business, my mind wanders back to our humble beginnings. Serendipity gave Infotech an entry into this extremely challenging technology and safety-critical industry. We had no domain knowledge back in 2000. Yet, we didn't play by luck to grow the account, we focused on mutual returns. Our curiosity to learn, spirit to persist and unceasing endeavour to succeed propelled us to channel our energies into building versatile capabilities and expertise in the industry. Our determination to be distinct drove us to be bold and venture into spaces that others found difficult to enter. This nerve, verve and commitment hurtled the company into an accelerated growth orbit.

8

Riding High with New Verticals

G. K. Chesterton's words whirred in my head. In Chapter 2 of his book *Orthodoxy* he has written: 'The poet only desires exaltation and expansion, a world to stretch himself in. The poet only asks to get his head into the heavens. It is the logician who seeks to get the heavens into his head. And it is his head that splits.'[1] He was so right! Here I was flying high, riding on my success with Pratt & Whitney and yet I was perpetually on pins and needles over the company's future. Success does not naturally beget success and I was not prepared to rest on my laurels. I was constantly haunted by the thought that there was a very fine line between surface and substance, and I felt that I needed to bridge the continuum between present and future successes through constant reinvention so that we kept up with the everchanging demands of the market.

Our success with Pratt & Whitney was making me uneasy because several stakeholders and I had lately started questioning our excessive customer dependency on the firm. A solo customer and single vertical left the company vulnerable and open to risk. 'The only way to reduce our dependence on Pratt & Whitney,' I once quipped to my team, jokingly, 'is if we stopped getting additional business from them.' I had made the remark on a light note, but my misgivings were very real. I quietly resolved to keep one foot firmly rooted in our current success while concurrently shifting gears to seek success in other segments.

My mind made up, I set about segregating the non-Pratt & Whitney business, christened it as 'manufacturing' and got Executive Director Sudhir Sethi to head it. Sudhir had joined the company board in the year 2000, as a nominee of Walden International (our investor). Walden subsequently exited India and Sudhir joined Infotech as a full-time executive director, heading the non-UTC business. I continued to handle Pratt & Whitney and the rest of the UTC (now Raytheon Technologies) account.

There were a few small projects coming in and with some fifty people engaged. We created a playbook for multinational companies looking to outsource. We educated prospective customers and directed our efforts to develop the market for outsourced R&D services in product development, maintenance and manufacturing, showcasing our Pratt & Whitney work to win their confidence.

In 2003, I became a member of the NASSCOM Executive Council and it provided me with the perfect platform to get vocal about the unique requirements and challenges of engineering services versus pure-play IT or BPM services. This proactive engagement led to the creation of the engineering services council (ER&D Forum) at NASSCOM which became responsible for launching several initiatives for the sector over the years.

NASSCOM's lobbying coincided with the huge global demand for IT services and helped to bring about favourable policies to stimulate the rapid growth of the domestic industry. Its efforts to grow the pie as a priority—exports worth $50 billion by 2008 (a target set in 1999)—helped ignite a spirit of cooperation at a broader level, even as intense competition continued between individual companies.[2]

The organization also played a crucial role in opening up new markets. It actively campaigned and promoted the Indian IT industry's capabilities and represented its interests internationally, elevating its brand image. This helped to build up the trust of developed nations in the Indian IT outsourcing story and attracted several multinationals to the country.

Bombardier Transportation (BT) came to India in 2003 at around the same time that I had joined NASSCOM. It was searching for outsourcing partners. Representatives from Bombardier Transportation visited and evaluated several vendors—Infotech was one of them. I received the team at the Hyderabad airport on a Sunday.

Charbel Bachaalani, a senior director, was leading the India engineering/offshoring initiative for Bombardier Transportation. Charbel's leadership was multifaceted—his expertise spanned technical, commercial and programme management. He was highly committed, could judge all situations from every relevant viewpoint and arrive at business solutions in the firm's best interests. Charbel was a very tough negotiator and kept us on our toes.

The evaluation was in the initial stages and the Bombardier Transportation team was worried about Hyderabad as a location. They had heard that it was prone to periodic bouts of communal tensions and that the northern part of the then combined state of Andhra Pradesh was a hotbed of left-wing extremism. Figuring that any attempt on my part to allay their fears would not be as useful, I quickly arranged for them to meet with the late K. Vidyadhar Rao, who was minister for large-scale industries in the erstwhile Andhra Pradesh government. It was a very calibrated move.

Vidyadhar Rao swiftly eased the team's concerns. 'You should pose this question to the *darwan* (guard) of your hotel. He'll tell you how friendship is flourishing among various communities in Hyderabad today. Violence is a thing of the past. The city has not witnessed a single incident of violence in the past three–four years. Your worries are misplaced. Left-wing extremism runs along a corridor extending from Nepal to Sri Lanka. A small strip passes through this state, but the government has successfully blocked it.'

He closed his argument with a sweetener for the Bombardier Transportation team. The city of Hyderabad was not only safe—its government was pro-industry!

Rao's lecture seemed to do the trick, because discussions progressed thereafter, both in India and at Bombardier Transportation's office in Montreal, Canada.

During one of our trips to Montreal, a senior colleague and I stayed at The Queen Elizabeth Hotel. It was a well-known hotel in downtown Montreal and extremely high-priced. I normally avoided pricey hotels but Bombardier Transportation talked me into staying there as it was peak winter and snowing heavily. Their headquarters was located in the same block as the hotel and the buildings were interconnected. This meant we did not need to hit the road and brave the vagaries of the weather. Our meetings wound up fairly late in the evening, after which my colleague and I went up to the concierge to inquire where we could find a nearby restaurant for dinner.

He looked us up and down once and swiftly had our measure. What he saw at a glance were two Indians wrapped in layer upon layer of warm clothing to ward off the weather. Unsuccessfully trying to hide a grin, he pulled out a paper map and pin-pointed a restaurant called Le Taj. 'Le Taj is at walking distance. You'll reach the place comfortably in ten minutes flat,' he informed us.

Being inured to the chill, he did not take the snow into account and since we were suffering from acute hunger pangs, we were prepared to suffer the frost. The thought of an Indian restaurant was an added attraction. We plodded through the streets meticulously following the concierge's instructions. We kept looking for Le Taj and just couldn't find it, until we realized that its front entrance was buried in snow! Our resolve to find the restaurant is a reflection of the typical salesman's attitude to 'never give up'.

We anticipated winning Bombardier Transportation's aerospace business, basing our confidence on the credibility we had built with Pratt & Whitney. But we were in for a rude awakening. Bombardier Transportation offered us a contract for its rail transportation division on a build-operate-transfer (BOT) basis for three years, instead. We had never undertaken a BOT transaction before and I was reluctant to bear the overhead of recruiting people, training them and subsequently keeping them occupied with projects before eventually transferring them to their India centre when the contract ended.

Bombardier Transportation insisted the project had to be on a BOT basis. As negotiations gained speed, we sensed that the contract was drifting away from us. Call it luck or destiny, we accidentally heard about the BOT proposal offered by a competitor.

My mind started pinwheeling as usual. 'What's the worst-case scenario?' I deliberated. 'I can lose the contract today, or I can give it up three years later. Who knows how matters will turn out in three years? Things might change, they might even become more favourable if we work our heads off. I should pick up the contract now and worry about everything else later. If we manage to win customer confidence, we can always renegotiate the contract at the end of three years.'

Now that all the cobwebs in my head had been swept clean, I decided to take the plunge and we made an attractive offer. We bagged the business. I remember the day distinctly. It was at 5 p.m. on a clear September evening in 2003 when Bombardier Transportation verbally told us that we were in. Jubilant, I took them to the Hotel Grand Kakatiya to celebrate.

In the course of the festivities that evening, a couple of members from Bombardier Transportation took me aside and handed me a lemon. 'Mohan, we've included an additional clause into the contract. We want you to know about it.'

'What is it?' I inquired softly, even as my heart sank. I had a grave foreboding that I was not going to like what I was about to hear.

They then proceeded to describe the essence of the clause. In a nutshell, they insisted the contract would be valid only if a particular senior executive remained on the team and the company's rolls.

'If the executive leaves the company, we will terminate the agreement,' they cautioned.

This surprised me and I sensed that something was amiss. I tend to get forceful and decisive when the situation demands and clearly this was an occasion that necessitated a strong pushback.

'If this clause is present in the contract, I will not sign it,' I told the team firmly without becoming overtly aggressive.

That night I tried my best to persuade the team against including the clause. My contention was: How can an institution such as Bombardier Transportation make a contract with another institution such as Infotech and yet say its validity is contingent only on one individual's presence? As the founder, I had put my life on the block to nurture the company. Infotech's identity and interests were paramount to me, and no single individual would or could take precedence over the organization.

The team could not escalate matters and take it to its senior management as I had already met Laurent Beaudoin, the chairman, during my previous visit to Montreal and he had a good impression of Infotech and its leadership. We signed the contract the following morning without the clause. Trust is essential for me in any relationship and one of my senior colleagues lost it during the transaction.

Sceptical after the incident, I appointed my son, Krishna Bodanapu, as account manager for the Bombardier Transportation engagement. I wanted someone I could rely on to be part of the relationship. After pursuing electrical engineering at Purdue University, Krishna had started his career at Altera Corp and Infotech Europe before moving to Infotech India. He became central to the account while I remained at its periphery.

Krishna visited Darby, UK, the first site of our engagement with Bombardier Transportation. He won them over and bagged the project. The relationship began on a modest scale with a team of six members working on technical publications, making changes and corrections to documents in response to the red line mark-ups. Krishna provided the oversight as the team executed the first project and delivered it to the satisfaction of the customer.

The unique facet of the Bombardier Transportation account is its complexity. Unlike global industries such as aerospace and defence, which design in one country and manufacture in another, rail transportation is local by nature. It is a dynamic and highly competitive industry. Rail transport manufacturers typically design, build and sell in the same country for a specific project. For this reason, the BT team was spread across twenty-six locations. This presented the first degree of complexity.

The second degree of complexity was posed by the twenty-six locations that were in as many different countries. The sites had different languages, cultures and even design standards. Our ambition to build a global engagement for a localized industry meant we had to model the engagement in a way that it would make sense to all the teams concerned. We had no precedent in the industry. But we had the intellectual and technical freedom to define our actions.

We underestimated the complex nature of the account initially and did not do a particularly good job. But once we understood how Bombardier Transportation's European offices worked and how they differed in functioning from their US operations, we learnt to manage the nuances involved and started delivering excellent work, quickly spreading our engagement to all their sites. This was an inflection point that helped us grow the account.

At around this point, we felt it was essential to map the value stream we were delivering to the customer. Carving out the areas of our competence, we standardized them across sites and service offerings. We took the common denominators across various locations, cross-pollinated the best practices, established an excellence centre and named it Bombardier Transportation Engineering Centre India (BTECI). BTECI became a microcosm of Bombardier Transportation in one location. It facilitated Bombardier Transportation's standardization programme and helped it to extract the value of being a global company. This was another point of inflection in the engagement.

BTECI started gaining the attention of all Bombardier Transportation sites and divisions, including mainline, metro, locomotives, light rail vehicles (LRV), bogies, propulsion and controls, and rail control systems (signalling systems). The divisions were quite spread out, with some of them having multiple sites all over the world. We gradually started working with all their engineering divisions.

Quite early on, Prabhakar Atla began supporting Krishna in managing the account and was eventually responsible for the sales and relationship management. Prabhakar had joined Infotech as a marketing manager but veered into and excelled in business development and sales. Over the years, Prabhakar rose to shoulder the responsibilities of multiple business units, including rail transportation. He currently serves the company as President and Global Head – Aerospace, Rail & Communications business unit.

We built up the team in mechanical engineering, technical publications, software development, embedded electronics, software testing and signalling and got involved in several rail, metro rail and high-speed rail projects across the world.

Our ability to build domain expertise and deliver projects successfully encouraged the customer to regard Infotech as a product development partner and awarded two projects to us. We successfully developed the products, produced prototypes, tested them and had them qualified and certified. Today, these products are still running in several trains worldwide, the Delhi Metro being one of them. Pleased with our success, Bombardier Transportation then offered us a chance to try our hand at software development and testing of the Train Control Management System (TCMS). We set up an elaborate lab with forty test tracks spread over 3000 square feet for TCMS testing for various projects across the world.

BTECI executed 125,000 hours of work for the Delhi Metro. The proximity of Infotech's Hyderabad location served as an advantage for this project. In another significant project, BTECI executed 350,000 hours of work for Crossrail, London. The project marked many firsts for the excellence centre. It was an interesting experience in resource building. We managed to build unique resources that combined knowledge, skills, organizational values and systems/processes.

We tried to place the customer at the centre of our activity to understand problems from their lens, so that we could deliver appropriate solutions. And we did this over and over quite well. But at the same time, we were often caught up in a value paradox. Should we focus on delivering superior, affordable, differentiated value to customers, or should we provide shareholders with immediate, increased dividends and earnings? Should we focus on earning customer delight and customer loyalty or focus on delivering short-term profits and buybacks?

We realized that the answer lay in pursuing none of these exclusively. We had to win by striking a balance between creating customer value and profitability or shareholder value, as they were intrinsically linked. We could not cost-manage our way to enduring profitable growth. There was a stage when we agreed to everything in the contract in our nervousness to win the deal. But this approach often brought us grief. 'Buying' business may work for a short time but is not sustainable in the long run. When we learnt to ensure quality growth of the top-line, it paved the way to an enduring bottom line.

We had developed quality systems for engineering services that had proved successful in our work with Pratt & Whitney and assumed we only had to replicate them for Bombardier Transportation. As it turned out, mere replication was not enough. We had to contend with numerous quality issues, problems of idle time billing (which Infotech had to absorb) and poor-quality resources. By the end of three years, Krishna ironed out all the wrinkles and had the BOT contract renewed for another three. At the end of the seventh year, we had the BOT clause removed. It was another inflection point in our journey with Bombardier Transportation.

Under the BOT clause, we functioned as an extension of Bombardier Transportation. It nurtured and grew us with an anticipation that the team would integrate with the parent at some point. Once we spun off as an independent entity, we gained intellectual, spiritual and technical freedom to scale ourselves up and contribute as a partner, and in some cases even challenge it in spirit.

The testimony to Infotech gaining that spirit of freedom can be found in the 'cost on track' project. We assessed all its products and platforms and advised the company to take the cost out by optimizing the design. We also presented many ideas, filtered them, executed a few and got paid based on the outcome.

As our largest non-aerospace account, Bombardier Transportation clocked over $50 million in revenue in FY2020 from a modest $150,000 in the first year of our association. Today, it is the largest global rail transportation engagement by volume and value creation by any engineering or IT services provider (not just offshoring) in the world.

When I assess the reasons for scaling the account revenue significantly, three aspects stand out. One was the absolute clarity we had about engineering services, the competencies we needed to build and the contours of the partnership we had to nurture.

Next was our ability to execute meticulously. Our focus on execution was not merely limited to delivering project commitments but also in building a governance system for the overall engagement. This was a distributed engagement and at any given point in time, we were working on ten to twenty programmes across the company's twenty-six sites spanning multiple time zones with task sizes that were as small as ten hours up to 1,00,000 hours. We churned out not less than 2000 such individual work packages, each year. To tie everything together, we institutionalized a robust governance mechanism right from project management to programme management, site and executive levels on both sides.

Bombardier Transportation was keen on outsourcing work to BTECI and reducing at least 20 per cent of its engineering headcount. We set up cost KPIs and monitored them diligently, in addition to other parameters such as quality, headcount and utilization. Divisional and site coordinators reviewed the metrics and made sure outsourcing operations were smooth. This structure of governance remained robust and consistent throughout the engagement, especially at the executive level. Krishna would chair all quarterly review meetings.

The third dimension was relationship management. Despite several structural and CXO changes at Bombardier Transportation, Krishna maintained a strong executive connect. He was purpose-driven. Even as he meticulously monitored the quarterly results, he impressed upon teammates that their work was not just for quarterly/annual benefits but for a larger purpose, which was broad, sustainable and value-driven.

At the same time, he was pragmatic. He meant more than he said and did more than he meant. Customers, especially senior executives, sensed this and related to it. More importantly, he led from the front. In any customer conversation or programme, he was happy to roll up his sleeves, step into the conversation and do whatever was needed to fix an issue. This was one reason the CXOs of Bombardier Transportation could connect well with Krishna and trust the company with more outsourced work. Our Bombardier Transportation experience is a good example for entrepreneurs to follow when they are moving from early growth to managing/leading organizational transformation.

Our next customer, quite akin to Bombardier Transportation, was Alstom, its direct competitor and current owner. In the early stages of our discussions, given that we already had an established engagement with BT, it was clear to the Alstom leadership that we had the required domain knowledge and skills to build a global engineering partnership in rail transportation. But the crucial question was our ability to manage data confidentiality, a genuine concern given that engineering capability is a key competitive differentiator for all rail OEMs.

We addressed the issue head on. By this time, we had already built large global engagements in various industries. For example, in aerospace, we were already working with companies that were direct competitors and had already put a robust data confidentiality framework in place. This included a complete physical isolation of all centres, an assurance not to move key engineering resources from one relationship to another without appropriate approvals and a strong engagement governance mechanism to provide leadership oversight on all vital issues. But the trick was to demonstrate that our structures worked. To gain confidence, we offered the Alstom leadership a chance to have direct conversations with our key clients in aerospace. Alstom agreed. Apart from connecting with our clients to assure itself, Alstom also put us through rigorous audits before concluding that our credibility was sound.

Once Alstom was sufficiently convinced, the company provided us with our first major opportunity to support its high-speed rail project in Europe. We then set up our Alstom—Cyient Engineering Centre in Bangalore (now Bengaluru), ensuring that it was 600 km away from BTECI (in Hyderabad).

Establishing credibility and making a start was only the first step. It was also important for us to ensure that we sustained Alstom's trust by ensuring the integrity of our operations year after year. Which we did.

In rail projects, we typically get involved with the client at the bidding stages and, as a result, a lot of sensitive information comes our way. For instance, both Bombardier Transportation and Alstom bid for the Kanpur and Agra metro rail. We were involved in the pre-bid activity of both companies and possessed information relevant to both the companies that could have helped the bid of the other.

But customer confidentiality is a value we hold dear in the company and we naturally did not use the information to benefit one company over the other. This meant that we had to expend our energy to protect customer data, IP and brand image. We ensured that the account teams were committed to confidentiality of plans, strategy and proprietary information when they worked with competing customers. To this end, well-defined and elaborate conflict mitigation tools, security and QA policies, firewalls as well as policies for training and audits, were put in place. The fact that we segregated customer information without any overlap earned us brownie points.

It was a great moment for Infotech when Alstom recognized our efforts by awarding us with the 'Best Supplier of the Year' award in 2014, an avowed testimony to the fact that keeping a promise was as important to us as making it, as it strengthened our credibility.

Credibility is an enterprise's currency and assumes centrality in creating, sustaining and expanding business operations. Our customers were inclined to engage in long-term relationships with us as we were mindful of their market reputation. One would rarely get to see such fiercely competing firms working with one service provider.

Eyeing the Opportunity, Challenging the Status Quo

Invensys Rail, the railway signalling division of Invensys Group of the UK (bought over by Siemens Mobility later), was another transportation customer we landed. Krishna managed this account as well and built a great relationship. One day, he came back from Invensys with an interesting tale.

'I came across something strange,' Krishna told me with a puzzled air. 'I noticed several elderly Indians working at Invensys Rail (in Chippenham, Wiltshire, UK). While I was waiting in the lobby, I saw an elderly gentleman walking down the staircase with difficulty. I wanted to reach out and help him climb down the steps, but held myself back as I thought he might get offended. I wonder why Invensys hires senior citizens.'

I wondered too and said so. We both agreed that his discovery was peculiar enough to merit further investigation.

We dug deeper and found that the elderly gentleman who had caught Krishna's eye was among several contract workers who possessed an IRSE (Institution of Railway Signalling Engineers) licensing certificate—a global certification. Very few people could lay claim to the accreditation, and Invensys only hired certified signalling engineers for its onsite projects. Invensys always cited a shortage of accredited signalling engineers as an excuse for not scaling the project.

I challenged Krishna with a gleam in my eye. 'We need 200 IRSE certified signalling engineers. How long would you take to build that capability in Infotech?'

Krishna was optimistic. 'I'll make sure we have 200 certified signalling engineers on Infotech rolls within the year,' he promised. I smiled, pleased by his confidence.

We were soon to discover that there were many a slip betwixt cup and lip. The hunt for certified engineers swiftly uncovered the dismal fact that it typically took an engineer the documentation of seven years of work to procure the prized certification. We hired signalling engineers, put them through rigorous training, followed up with meticulous day-wise documentation of their work, present and past, to produce the required evidence of their experience so that their certification could be fast-tracked. We catapulted from the initial five signalling engineers we had to 200 signalling engineers with IRSE certification. We managed to groom them within just six months! It was a prominent milestone. We absorbed all of them into the Invensys project, ramped up the account and scaled the business.

For me, this is entrepreneurship. Spotting and prising open a business opportunity that exists right in front of us is often a huge task. First, we had to confront our assumptions. Next, we assessed the issues at hand. Understanding the reasons for a problem opened up the way. Once we found the solution and implemented it, we unlocked the opportunity. We had an eye for counterintuitive solutions which often made us view unsurmountable challenges as crucibles for creativity and business model innovation.

Four-Filter Strategy: Entering New Verticals

By 2005, Infotech's engineering services business gained significant traction, especially in the aerospace and rail transportation sectors. At the same time, we lacked sufficient understanding of the market and the long-term opportunity that lay ahead. That was the case with most players in India.

In 2006, Booz Allen Hamilton (BAH), commissioned by NASSCOM, came out with a report titled 'Globalization of Engineering Services: The Next Frontier for India'. The report predicted that the global spend on engineering services, which was $750 billion in 2004, would cross $1 trillion by 2020. The report stated that India could capture 25–30 per cent—as much as $50 billion in annual revenues of the total $150–225 billion market for outsourced engineering services—by 2020.

The report reinforced my conviction that our future lay in the engineering services business and product design market. But I also recognized that Infotech needed a lot more brand and visibility to tap this potential. We raised $63.3 million from General Atlantic Global Partners, a private equity firm, in 2007 and started exploring new business segments.

My argument was that if companies like Pratt & Whitney and Bombardier Transportation were spending millions on product design, so would companies in other verticals. We applied a four-filter strategy to identify prospective verticals and companies to target and began by first understanding the product design market vertical by vertical—and identified promising sectors. After that we zeroed in on potential sub-verticals; we then shortlisted the top spenders in each sub-vertical. We realized that we could only build long-term strategic partnerships with companies that had a large engineering practice and decided to pursue only the top 50/100 companies in each vertical/sub-vertical.

As a fourth filter, we researched which of these top companies were already working with our competitors. Project complexity is relatively high in engineering services and it is not easy to switch service providers. As a result, in the early days of outsourcing, customers were keen to develop long-standing partnerships. So, we filtered out companies that were working with the competition, distilling our list further and shortening it down to those prospective customers who could give us the best returns for our efforts. Once all four filters had been applied, we ended up with a list of must-have customers for our sales engine to target. We then started scouting for new verticals and customers.

An interesting customer win in 2009 was Westinghouse Electric Company, the US-based Westinghouse Electric Corporation's nuclear power venture. Meena Mutyala was vice president of engineering and CEO of its Indian entity. We made contact with her through a mutual friend. We were in possession of intelligence that we were the last entrant in the deal and that Westinghouse was already in conversation with a few competitors. I pitched Infotech's capabilities vis-à-vis large IT companies to Meena over a dinner, in an attempt to convince her that we could accomplish far more for them with our intense customer focus.

Westinghouse wanted its future partner to possess both domain knowledge and engineering know-how to optimize project outcomes. While Infotech scores were top-notch in engineering expertise, scepticism ran high regarding our limited or practically no insight in the nuclear power sector. To allay Westinghouse's apprehensions, we organized a workshop in Cranberry, Philadelphia and invited representatives from Pratt & Whitney and Bombardier Transportation to share their experiences of how they had built complex practices from ground zero along with Infotech in aerospace and rail transportation, respectively. Our key customers impressed upon Westinghouse the significance of the business model and our experience in handling technology to deliver mission-critical projects. This strengthened Westinghouse's confidence in Infotech's ability to deliver in a new and complex domain.

We parleyed with them for about six months before clinching the deal. Infotech signed up with Westinghouse Electric to set up the Westinghouse India Engineering Centre (WIEC) at our facility in Hyderabad. We spent another year pursuing authorization from the Department of Atomic Energy to exchange nuclear information, without which we could not get into the nuclear power business in India. It was quite a rigorous process involving both US and Indian interests vis-à-vis the exchange of sensitive nuclear information. We had to detail the infrastructure that was being built, explain the technology control plan and put together a framework for the seamless exchange of information before the government believed Infotech had all the credentials to execute this highly-sensitive project.

Meena's husband, Dr Brahmaji, a senior Westinghouse employee who managed the programme, extended his support to our team in the initial years on various functional areas of plant engineering and talent recruitment. We started providing discreet engineering services on the 'turbine/conventional island' and 'balance of plant' sections and progressively built expertise, acquired additional licenses and approvals and started supporting 'nuclear island' (the heart of the nuclear power plant)-related work as well. The engagement started with 20–30 engineers, expanded to about 300 and stabilized at around 200 engineers.

The strategic partnership enabled Westinghouse to strengthen its engineering capability for its global nuclear energy business. Getting into the nuclear power plant business was a breakthrough for Infotech. Expanding beyond engineering services, we started providing support services; these included supply chain and back-office processing, five years ago, from our engineering centre in Prague, in the Czech Republic; it was designed to service specialized nearshore engineering solutions.

Creating a footprint in new verticals was not easy. We knocked at several doors without much luck and plotted different strategies to break into the automotive market with little success. We were probably late to that market. It was already heavily competitive and the entry barriers were too high. By 2008, we had little to show for all the efforts we had put into the automotive sector and decided to suspend our investments in the area.

It was a hard decision, but its time had come. As an entrepreneur, I had to discern when to exit a particular strategy. I used data and logic to assess the situation and weighed my options. When I realized we were wasting time without any positive outcomes, I kept my sentiments and pride aside and proclaimed, 'Let's not stretch ourselves any further. It's pointless to continue investing for little or no returns. It will just end up costing the company an arm and a leg.'

Automotives aside, two verticals we monitored closely were off-highway vehicles and telecom. We tried multiple approaches to win customers in these sectors with no success. We thought through the situation, recognized we could not bring growth through organic means alone and chalked out a strategy to acquire existing suppliers of large customers.

The telecommunications industry had always been a key market for Infotech from a geospatial-services standpoint. We identified

My parents, Nagi Reddy and Ratna Kumari.
They gave highest priority to our education.

Three generations: My maternal grandparents, parents, me and my sister.

Along with my siblings when I was
eleven. We were always a team.

As president of the Mechanical Engineers Association,
College of Engineering, Kakinada, 1971.

Sucharitha, my wife, my pillar of strength.

Our children, Krishna and Vaishnavi, our joy.

Savouring the family moments with children and grandchildren.

At the launch of Booz Allen Hamilton's report 'Globalisation of Engineering Services: The Next Frontier for India' in 2006. The report prompted Cyient/ Infotech to launch engineering services in several industry verticals.

My first NASSCOM Executive Council meet along with IT industry stalwarts in 2003.

Unveiling Cyient logo along with my successor Krishna after the rebranding exercise in 2014.

Moments of pride: Standing out of a pack of 4000-plus Boeing suppliers spanning thirteen categories year after year and receiving the awards in Oscars style.

Spearheading NASSCOM presented momentous opportunities to host Prime Minister Narendra Modi. At the Start-up India event in San Jose, USA, in 2015.

With Prime Minister Manmohan Singh and Louis Chenevert, chairman of UTC. Louis apprised the Indian prime minister on UTC's accomplishments.

NASSCOM Executive Council meets Telangana chief minister K. Chandrashekar Rao on Cyient campus.

Double delight: Receiving Hyderabad Software Enterprises Association (HYSEA) Lifetime Achievement award and Best Exporter of the Year award from Vice-President Venkaiah Naidu, in 2018.

Lifting the Geospatial World Hall of Fame award.

Receiving E&Y Entrepreneur of the Year award (finalist) from Arun Jaitley as Rahul Bajaj and Kashi Mimani look on.

Sharing my joy of receiving Hyderabad Management Association's Lifetime Achievement Award with my wife, Sucharitha, and Telangana IT minister, K.T. Rama Rao.

At the inaugural of T-Hub 1.0 along with Ratan Tata, Telangana governor
E.S.L. Naraimhan and IT minister, K.T. Rama Rao.

When President Ram Nath Kovind graced IIT Hyderabad's 7th Annual
Convocation ceremony as the chief guest, in 2018.

When an opportunity knocked to serve as the honorary consul of the
Federal Republic of Germany for Telangana and Andhra Pradesh, in 2016;
Sharing the frame with German ambassador Martin Ney.

Digitizing tomorrow together: Hosting two heads of state on behalf of NASSCOM—Angela Merkel and Narendra Modi—at the Indo–German Summit, in 2015.

Receiving the Padma Shri from President Pranab Mukherjee in 2017. I wish my father were alive to see me receive this incredible honour.

Former President A.P.J. Abdul Kalam supports frugal innovation for eyecare at Srujana Innovation Centre, a joint initiative of Cyient Foundation and LV Prasad Eye Institute.

Empowering tomorrow together: Our children studying in Cyient-adopted government schools.

Children from Cyient-adopted government schools along with Telangana governor Tamilisai Soundararajan cheer blood donors at a mega blood donation camp organized by Cyient Foundation.

network plans and designs as an excellent growth area and chose the acquisition route because the market was moving rapidly and we did not want to lose time developing these capabilities organically.

After evaluating various options, we found a good fit in Wellsco, a focused engineering services provider to the US telecom industry. Headquartered in Paragould, Arkansas, it counted some of the US's largest telecom companies as long-term customers. The acquisition went well, and Infotech gained access to the deep domain skills and experience of the Wellsco team. Their strong, long-term customer relationships and US delivery capabilities served us well. We moved up the value chain from a digitization service provider to a leading network engineering services provider. We won AT&T as a customer and set up a global network engineering centre. It became a point of reference in the telecom industry, helping us win customers like Windstream and Verizon.

Working from the same strategy playbook, we offered to acquire Daxcon Engineering Inc in 2010 to enter the off-highway and heavy equipment market and gain Caterpillar as a customer. Daxcon was an engineering services company focused on heavy equipment engineering, commercial vehicles and aerospace, based in Peoria, Illinois. Its long-standing relationship with Caterpillar appealed to us. After several rounds of negotiations, Mike Daxenbichler, its CEO, turned down our proposal.

After a long and disappointing day at Daxcon, Krishna, Bhanu Cherukuri and I drove to Peoria airport to fly back to Chicago. Waiting in the lounge area, I reflected over the day's events. Peeved at the idea of turning tail, I decided to try my luck once more and called up Mike. 'I've just been thinking over our meeting and I'd like to know what's holding you back,' I said. 'Is there anything I can do to address your concerns? I can always stay back and we can go through your apprehensions once again,' I offered.

Mike agreed. I dropped my plans to fly to Chicago and took a cab back to the city. Mike and I met up over dinner and had a long conversation. His concerns were mainly about working with an Indian company, losing control of operations and becoming a small cog in a large wheel. I tried to quieten his anxiety and told him how Infotech had absorbed Dataview and AGS and arranged calls with John (Renard) and Martin so that his fears could be put to rest. By the following morning, Mike had agreed to sign the deal.

Daxcon was part of a focused strategy on our part to acquire customers by acquiring their suppliers. The company was a strategic fit. It gave us domain expertise in heavy equipment engineering and commercial vehicles, brought us long-term customer relationships and created US delivery capability. This complemented Infotech's broader delivery capabilities and footprint, allowing us to build a strong presence in the heavy engineering segment quickly. It delivered more than our acquisition thesis.

We secured the Caterpillar account through Daxcon. As luck would have it, Caterpillar decided to route projects through its captive in India. We signed a contract with its India entity, only to realize that getting business from it was going to be a gruelling task as it viewed Daxcon as a competitor. It took some deft balancing on our part to build trust and win some business, but the account scaled back dramatically within a few months as the off-highway market went into a downturn. We were faced with a setback; a year after acquiring Daxcon, it had lost half its revenue!

In every acquisition, we typically define the objectives before the transaction. But often, an acquisition decision per se is neither right nor wrong. It usually becomes clear only in hindsight. The transaction and integration consumed a lot of management (of Daxcon and Infotech) bandwidth. Apart from the additional issue of ensuring returns on investment, despite all our precautions, the team had to brace for new challenges when the market reality changed. Industry dynamic aside, the combined business had to deal with multiple markets, competing customers, complicated product/ services portfolio, people and operational complexity. The synergy and the cultural match we had with the Daxcon team helped us to tide over the obstacles. It was successful because we were intensely focused on the strategic logic and business case, right from its inception, and worked hard on each milestone in the course of our plan to achieve the desired end state, no matter how far it was into the future.

The significant benefit that accrued to us in buying Daxcon was the footprint we gained in the off-highway and heavy equipment areas. We could not have matured our nascent business in this domain nor successfully pursued several Fortune 500 companies in the sector without the domain expertise we acquired through Daxcon.

Diversification through new verticals was the company's game plan in sync with the conventional management wisdom of not putting all the eggs in one basket. While this strategy allowed us to reduce dependence on the aerospace sector and de-risk the business, it also made us bend our backs and face new challenges every day. This facilitated the company's transformation into a versatile and mature engineering services player with an envious portfolio and an admirable track record.

9

Acquisitions to Enter New Markets

'Mohan, have you heard the news?'

We were in the middle of hectic preparations, working out the final agreement with Time To Market (TTM) at San Jose, California. The firm specialized in ASIC (application-specific integrated circuits) design and embedded software solutions for networking, communication, automotives, medical technology, consumer electronics and semiconductor industries. Everything was on course when during a frenetic day of attending to formalities, Bhanu Cherukuri, our VP of Strategy, burst into my room with the above question. He looked disturbed.

'No. What news?' I inquired.

'Lehman Brothers has announced bankruptcy. It has triggered a major turmoil in the financial markets,' he informed me, worry lines writ large across his forehead.

'Oh, I see. Didn't we send the final version of the agreement to Time To Market only last evening?' I queried after garnering some more details on this highly unexpected market development.

'Yes, we did. But we still have a choice,' Bhanu cautioned. 'There's still time to take a step back.' In effect, he was asking me to reconsider and withdraw from the proposal.

'No, Bhanu. we don't have a choice. We've made a commitment and we'll stick to it. We are going to buy Time To Market,' I asserted. We honoured our commitment and braced ourselves for the moment of truth.

How had we ended up here?

To cut a long story short, it all began during our early forays into the engineering services, when we focused only on the mechanical side of product design, even though a product is an integrated system of mechanical, electrical, electronic parts and embedded software. This limited our addressable market. By 2001, we recognized that our strategy was flawed and decided that the time had come to set foot in other areas, especially electronic design services (EDS). By investing in building up our EDS capabilities and a laboratory, we ventured into designing and developing hardware and physical boards; it was a new business line for Infotech.

We started approaching multinational companies to showcase our work. By 2002, we were designing and delivering printed circuit boards (PCBs) to a subsidiary of Danaher, an American conglomerate dealing in professional, medical, industrial and commercial products and services.

Infotech developed multilayered boards with eight to ten layers of complex circuits and multiple functions housed in enclosures and embedded them with software (firmware in digital parlance). We then cross-compiled them to specific microcontrollers and microprocessors and developed validation and verification tools and test jigs. They were designed and built in 'plug and play' mode, to enable the customer to fabricate a new system around them without putting in too much effort.

These PCBs helped the customer retrofit the electronic boards which had become obsolete as their components were either unavailable or the suppliers that produced them no longer existed. In most cases, it did not have proper documentation of the technology or components used in the boards. Infotech redesigned these boards with microcontrollers and components that had an availability of twenty years, supporting them with documentation; we managed to achieve cent per cent functionality of the original boards. The customer found them cost-effective and saved hundreds of thousands of dollars just on the design itself. Pleased, the firm proceeded to introduce us to ten other subsidiaries of Danaher and we quickly scaled the account.

The next big spurt in our EDS and embedded software business came in the course of our work with Bombardier Transportation (BT). About a year into our association with the company, one of its teams visited us from the US looking for help to redesign two control boards that were hovering on the edge of component obsolescence. The customer was in dire need. Repeated attempts at redesigning the said boards were affecting the firm's overall focus.

A particularly desperate customer representative impressed the urgency of the situation on us. 'This is my first visit to India and I'm sure—given the brilliant Indian engineers in our team back in the US—there's every chance that we'll come across someone here who can help us.'

Without much ado and to the customer's immense delight, we provided a low-cost solution to its problems by providing a retrofit instead of redesigning the two boards entirely, at a speed that stunned the firm. Our contribution saved the company hundreds of thousands of dollars and heralded a new phase in our relationship. We were soon providing embedded electronics support to several Bombardier Transportation sites across the US, Canada and Europe.

An immediate outcome of this experience was that Infotech began to explore new territories and ventured into totally unknown domains such as railway signalling. We developed an advanced Level 3 signalling system, a communication gateway, map generation tools and remote platform display tools. At one point, we had about a hundred embedded systems engineers working exclusively for Bombardier Transportation.

As Infotech branched into new verticals and nurtured them, it also built an EDS laboratory to step up its capabilities to support customers such as Invensys in rail signalling, Philips in consumer products and medical devices, and Airbus in avionics.

We expanded our engineering base with several domain experts across product design, prototyping and manufacturing to address new customer requirements on the go. Our specific embedded software development skills led us to the VLSI (very large-scale integration) design base using semiconductors.

Our EDS team functioned as a horizontal, and the verticals leveraged this functionality whenever an opportunity presented itself. For instance, Philips wanted us to develop a remote controller. We combined the functionality of 600 remotes and developed a single device that met the functional requirements of the customer. After a certain point, our EDS function moved into the business verticals adding value to their core engineering capabilities.

The 2006 Booz Allen Hamilton report, *Globalization of Engineering Services: The Next Frontier for India*—as mentioned earlier, had reinforced our conviction regarding the potential of engineering services. It had simultaneously opened our eyes to the electronics design and manufacturing segment, that was much larger than the mechanical engineering services market. The report forecast that hi-tech/telecom (including semiconductors, consumer electronics, telecom, computer systems, and medical devices) were likely to represent the largest slice within electronics design and manufacturing.

I did not react to these predictions for over a year but increasingly felt that Infotech should not miss this opportunity. We had built enviable mechanical engineering services capabilities, had a fair play in EDS and embedded software, and harboured aspirations to move towards system-level product design. This made it imperative for us to augment our capabilities in electronics hardware and make inroads into semiconductor design and engineering.

Business success relies on quick, fact-based decision-making. But these industries were huge and transforming swiftly. Understanding the industry ecosystem could take several years, and we found ourselves on the horns of a dilemma: what is the right decision? To wait until we had gained a good understanding of the market, or to take the plunge without overthinking too much and adapt ourselves along the way?

Organizations always make trade-offs between the velocity and quality of decision-making, but speed does not necessarily have to undercut the merit of a given decision. The active time frame for a decision is very short, so as entrepreneurs, we have to take wise and prompt decisions, hold our ground and expand further. We had wasted valuable time earlier by dithering endlessly and, as a result, lost out in the automotive space. There was no way I was going to repeat the same mistake.

Hi-tech is a large spender and complements our strong mechanical engineering talent while simultaneously adding to our EDS capabilities. So, we took a strategic decision to enter the semiconductor business through the buy route. We started scouting around for relevant companies and finally zeroed in on Time To Market (TTM), a San Jose, California-based semiconductor design services company. It was the year 2008. Just as we inked the deal, Lehman Brothers declared bankruptcy, creating massive shockwaves in markets worldwide. Bhanu, our VP- Strategy, reacting to the general market mayhem did try to talk me out of the deal, but I stuck to my guns and we stayed on course.

Once the formalities of the acquisition were complete, Infotech launched its semiconductor practice. Time To Market's ASIC design strengths complemented our existing prowess in field-programmable gate array (FPGA), board design and embedded software development. As a combined entity we were capable of providing end-to-end design services to the semiconductor, telecom and computing industries.

It did not take us too long to grasp how the economic recession triggered by the fall of Lehman Brothers had affected the semiconductor business. Before the acquisition, Time To Market had given us a long list of its customers, most of which were start-ups. As liquidity became tight in the market, these start-ups went belly up and, within a short spell, Time To Market's customers disappeared one after the other and, even worse, some stopped payments. It took us twelve months to turn around the acquired entity.

Our only takeaways from the acquisition were an understanding of the market and the company's skill base. It appeared that we had more or less acquired a body shop. Besides, the semiconductor industry was highly cyclical with frequent waxing and waning of capital and R&D investment inflows, consolidation and expansion, marked by shifts in global competitor positioning. But we stood our ground, demonstrating our strategic focus in the new market. Infotech geared up to build its capabilities, broaden its customer base and pitch itself as a trusted partner that could provide comprehensive chip and systems design.

We started taking ownership of the complete life cycle of ASIC chips—from prototype to mass production to post-production testing and qualification—providing turnkey solutions. This gave us the ability to think holistically from a systems perspective on how products function with individual parts from several engineering disciplines: mechanical, electrical, electronics and embedded software. It was a unique achievement for an Indian services company and helped us to position Infotech in the global semiconductor arena.

However, we did not report good traction and scale for several reasons. The competition was ahead of us, both in competence (skill) and customer relationships. Semiconductor and our core mechanical engineering services were like apples and oranges from a business standpoint. Business model differences, talent disparities and operating cost variations abounded. Moreover, the semiconductor business needed us to be closer to the customer geographically. It took us a while to get aligned with the realities of the sector. This apart, I must admit that our own ability to execute was not up to the mark.

At every turn, we kept looking for people who could introduce us to prospective customers. We screened company after company and used every sales technique in the book to win clients. At the same time, we scouted around for private-equity players to fund our business growth.

We specifically looked for potential investors who had connections in the market and could open customer doors for us. With this strategy in mind, we chose General Atlantic Partners (GAP). William (Bill) O. Grabe, who subsequently became managing director of GAP, joined our board of directors as a nominee of the firm. Before he joined GAP, Bill had worked with IBM and had extensive corporate connections; these came in handy when he introduced us to some marquee customers in the semiconductor business.

Over time, I came around to the philosophy that if I took a decision based on data instead of gut feel, it might not turn out as expected for two reasons—either the assumption from the data was wrong or our execution was below par. The Time to Market acquisition was a bold and strategic move by Infotech. We could not have anticipated the events that took place eighteen months later, but since the decision per se was correct, I believed there was scope for course correction. Despite the macroeconomic and industry headwinds, we held fort and kept a keen eye on the market as we worked hard to turn the business around.

A step-shift in our semiconductor capabilities came when we acquired AnSem NV. in 2018, a Belgian company specializing in advanced analogue, radio frequency and mixed-signal integrated circuit design. AnSem, a spin-off of the University of Leuven, was supported by *imec*—the research and innovation hub of nanoelectronics and digital technologies. The acquisition expanded our capabilities to offer turnkey, custom, and smart analogue front-end chips and sensors to capture data with this acquisition. We integrated these with home-grown IoT and analytics capabilities, courtesy our 2014 acquisition of Invati Insights. The Ansem acquisition was made at a time when our clients and focus industries had begun to go increasingly digital. AnSem strengthened Cyient's position as a digital solutions provider.

New Horizons: Medical Technology and Healthcare

A customer we actively pursued soon after branching into new verticals was Philips. We met Cees Wesdorp, CTO of Domestic Appliances and Personal Care, Philips in his office at their headquarters in Amsterdam, the Netherlands. It was extremely well designed with a wonderful view of the Amstel River.

Cees has the best mind I have ever encountered on healthcare technologies. He had an extraordinary knowledge of how technology would have a great influence on diagnosis, treatment and prevention. We signed a contract with the company in 2005 and invited Cees and his team for dinner that evening to an Indian restaurant for a meal of tikka masala and naan, which we washed down with a glass of mango lassi each. We continued to talk about the future of medical technologies and how it would help doctors to take care of a lot more patients, especially in developing countries where the doctor-patient ratio was very low.

The conversation was riveting and we were sitting in the basement with a 2-foot-high window view of the street. In between bites and the constant flow of words, I could not help noticing the endless pitter-patter of high-heeled sandals and leather shoes, as people walked by. The food was delicious, the service was quick and the staff super friendly. I felt a sense of benign contentment with the world at large.

We started providing product design engineering services to Philips' personal health electronics merchandise such as razors, shavers, trimmers, female beauty products, and domestic appliances such as coffee/beverage machines and vacuum cleaners. By this time, Philips was an established brand and globally popular for its consumer electronics products. However, it soon embraced a deliberate strategy switch to transform and position itself as a healthcare and medical technology company, eyeing the enormous opportunities unfolding in the twenty-first century. We saw merit in aligning with its strategy and used our work for Philips as a stepping stone to gain a footprint in the medical technology sector in the long term.

In the first few years, I took a personal interest in nurturing the account and matured it from a project-based engagement into a larger centre of excellence (CoE) engagement. Along with our customer, we forayed into precision diagnostics, connected patient-care monitoring, diagnostic imaging and several other solutions. These became the springboard for the medical technology practice within Infotech. We started out as a tactical supplier but grew and became one of Phillips' three preferred partners, contributing to 80 per cent of its engineering work over the years.

In 2005, Philips was exploring the possibility of carving out its business in Klagenfurt, Austria. The unit manufactured personal-care products for women. I went with my team to Klagenfurt, Austria for due diligence. The Philips team presented their 'epilators' technology for hair removal with great flourish and harped endlessly on its superiority over waxing.

We were keen on the acquisition as it would assure us of a steady stream of revenue. But by the time the Philips team arrived in Hyderabad for discussions, some organizational changes had taken place at Philips and we could not arrive at a consensus on key issues such as exclusivity, minimum guarantee, margin and price. We finally dropped the proposed acquisition.

As we worked with Philips, we noticed the medical devices industry was witnessing a paradigm shift, thanks to the increasing consumerization of healthcare. The sector started exploring the outsourcing market aggressively as healthcare costs skyrocketed and competition from low-cost device manufacturers built up. To top it all, the lifespan of medical devices fell sharply due to rapidly changing technology.

Our next significant engagement came when Thermo Fisher Scientific began exploring India as a possible location to set up a captive centre in 2009. The global economy was in recession, and Thermo Fisher was constrained in making huge investments. Eyeing this as a strategic opportunity, Infotech offered to develop a centre in the 'co-location' model. We established a Centre of Excellence that housed associates of both the companies under one roof while Infotech ran the operations.

I envisaged several advantages in having the customer on our premises. One, while winning the customer, we could gain intimate knowledge of its products and business lines, which would help us to deliver top-notch quality services and ramp up the account. Second, we could gain domain knowledge and move from being a low-end, discreet service provider to a value-based solutions provider. Third, I saw this as a quick way to expand our medical practice and win new clients. Our strategy bore fruit and the model was a runaway success. It became a milestone for Infotech's medical technology business.

As we worked with customers, both developed and emerging markets presented opportunities with differing needs. While developed markets grappled with more stringent regulations and the need to align to value-based care, emerging economies demanded locally relevant products. To stay ahead of the curve, MedTech firms needed to embrace innovative approaches to design and development. Moreover, the medical technology business is a highly regulated industry. We noticed that device companies preferred associating with partners who had good domain knowledge and a fair understanding of the evolving regulatory practices (for class 1, 2, 3 devices). More importantly, they favoured partners capable of handling the business life cycle of their products end to end. We had noticed a similar trend in the aerospace business as well. We perceived this as a great opportunity to build our design-led manufacturing capabilities. It was a value proposition hitherto unheard of in the industry.

At the same time, we decided to focus our energies on building domain knowledge in four specific areas. First, in diagnostic imaging, which constitutes X-ray, MRI, CT scan and ultrasound machines. This segment was akin to aerospace with long product life cycles. These machines involved large R&D, mechanical and electronic engineering effort, product refresh and obsolescence. We built up our expertise in this domain through our work with customers.

Next, we chose in-vitro diagnostics (which include clinical chemistry analysers and pathology analysers used in all pathology laboratories). Our existing customers offered several opportunities in this area. Our third point of focus was patient care monitoring, which involved systems and software engineering. Devices in this segment fall under the easy box-build assembly category, which allowed us to design and manufacture. Together, these three areas constitute 50–60 per cent of the overall medical devices industry, hence the rationale to focus on them. Orthopaedics became the fourth area of our focus, and we got involved in orthopaedic product design and regulatory services.

We acquired good logos, established ourselves as a design and manufacturing company and ramped up our capabilities by aggressively catering to the emerging requirements of our customers. This meant we built deep digital capabilities as we saw big shifts in medical device companies developing high-tech equipment. Companies started embedding artificial intelligence, the Internet of Medical Things (IoMT), big data analytics and augmented reality into the devices to provide customized patient care and improve healthcare outcomes and affordability. Wearables, additive printing and robotics became increasingly mainstream, creating exciting prospects for mass personalization of patient care. These devices were connected, their data was shared and communicated between patients, doctors, hospital administration and insurance providers. As a result, medical device companies evolved into software companies. They started producing digital health technology solutions that brought software platforms, data and analytics subscriptions along with hardware/devices. This, in turn, created new service avenues for companies such as Infotech.

We quickly pooled the software and digital capabilities distributed across the organization and built a robust practice. Along with core product development, we began helping customers to apply advanced analytics to improve healthcare outcomes, monitor device performance and enable predictive and preventive maintenance. Through our solutions, the company supported its customers to reduce costs and identify new revenue streams.

We leveraged the AnSem acquisition to step up advanced engineering capabilities and designed, developed and manufactured custom ASICs with lower-power RF connectivity required in product development, especially for class 3 implantable medical devices such as cochlear implants and endoscopy pills. The sophistication is such that the ASIC often constitutes the wearable and is nothing short of a state-of-the-art ultramodern technology that involves an enormous amount of intellectual property in its design and development.

With the industry under tremendous cost pressures, extending the life of existing products gained focus instead of investing in newer equipment. This was critical to protecting revenues and, in some cases, improving margins. So, we began offering a market-driven execution model to sustenance engineering. By leveraging value engineering concepts for design, bringing commonality in bill of materials (BOM), using proprietary in-house tools and process implementation, we helped customers run sustenance engineering programmes so that they benefited from mature product lines. We also expanded our corporate venture capital portfolio for medical technology by investing in two innovative technologies, one in point-of-care (PoC) diagnostics and the other in wearables. During COVID-19, our teams got involved in respiratory care, a major concern during the pandemic. They supported our customers to deliver three different ventilator prototypes in a very short time span in 2020.

Our services and solutions across the design, build, operate and maintain life cycle in key medical technology segments and our end-to-end value proposition started resonating in the marketplace. We simultaneously took the partnership and coalition route to incubate and scale technology-enabled healthcare solutions and minimize the time to take products from lab to market.

Big Bets on Design-Led Manufacturing

In my youth, entrepreneurs started businesses or entered new markets more by instinct than strategic research and analysis. But in today's environment, new business decisions are based on in-depth market intelligence and strategic rigour. Moreover, one should never be hung up on a single business idea or get stuck with a solo customer. Expanding deliberately into new markets, often not adjacent, is imperative to creating sustainable growth and Infotech was always on the lookout for new markets.

Product companies typically outsource to service providers for design engineering and box-builders for manufacturing. But as companies (such as Hamilton Sundstrand, Honeywell, Thales, Bombardier) got bigger and outsourcing became more complex, they started looking for partners who could handle the sub-system end-to-end. They wanted to outsource work that was not core and critical to them while retaining the IP, algorithms and data. This, they saw, could potentially reduce the time and effort of their engineering teams in guiding and managing additional manufacturing suppliers. Seeing us design the components over the years, customers began to nudge us to manufacture those components as well.

We paid no heed to their suggestions for two years as manufacturing was not part of our core competence. Instead, we offered engineering guidance and programme management services, but customers wanted us to do more.

The services business model is replicable, has relatively low stickiness, and revenues can be cyclical. On the other hand, manufacturing is an annuity-driven business and brings a fair degree of predictability. Once a company starts developing a product for large multinationals such as the Pratts and Boeings of the world, it creates stickiness and ensures business continuity. From a business model standpoint, manufacturing started making good business sense.

We contemplated extending our product design capabilities to manufacturing products, as early as 2008/2009. The company had strong mechanical engineering capabilities that delivered a significant portion of its revenues. It seemed like a logical progression to buy a mechanical manufacturer and get a jump-start in manufacturing. To this end, we identified a family-owned German manufacturing company and were all set to acquire it when Infotech's board vetoed the decision.

Paul Adams, Pratt & Whitney's representative on the board, explained his reasons over dinner. He said, 'Mohan, I know you're upset that the board stopped you from buying the company, but do you realize it is a mistake? Manufacturing and services are completely different industries, each with unique operational models. Infotech is good in the services business, but I don't think you're cut out for manufacturing. There are several pains in manufacturing, especially mechanical manufacturing. It is extremely asset-heavy and requires high precision. Besides, manufacturing is blue-collared work, while the services business is white-collared. I don't think you'll be able to manage that workforce. You'll end up de-focusing yourself and this will impact both the businesses.'

It was a compelling argument, so we shelved the idea—for a while.

Infotech's board often brought varied perspectives and experienced insights around the growth and strategic direction that we, the management team, may not have visualized for the company. The board is not a decision-making body but acts as a corporate conscience-keeper in decision-making. This was one of the few occasions when the board's advice and counsel led us to reconsider a management decision. Paul made us understand the nuances of mechanical engineering manufacturing and our ability, or our lack thereof, to handle businesses that were poles apart. It was sage advice at the time.

The reality of the engineering business is its cyclicality, especially in the verticals we operate. Most products in these verticals have a life cycle of typically seven to ten years while some, like aircraft engines, far longer. Companies design, manufacture and market a product for a few years before they plan the next version (the exceptions are consumer electronics such as smartphones, where companies release new models every quarter). This requires service providers like Infotech/Cyient to wait until the next design version.

Product design may take only three to four years in a typical product life cycle, but products such as an aircraft or rolling stock, once manufactured, lasts for 20–30 years. We wanted to explore the other areas of this 20–30-year life cycle. This would include product optimization, aftermarket, product manufacturing, product maintenance and obsolescence management, which presents a huge addressable market. It was also a stable and predictable business that could get us out of cyclicality.

When a customer or company designs a product, it is at a cost, and it falls into their cost centre. Whereas when they sell the product, it is revenue. It was important for us to get into the customer's revenue cycle by taking up maintenance, repair and operations (MRO) of engineering work to ensure continuity of engagement.

We then analysed the economics of manufacturing and started exploring segments of value-added manufacturing that were engineering-intensive and involved relatively low capital expenditure. The answer to our search was electronics manufacturing. Also, the mechanicals of a product do not get a significant uplift for years, while the electronics subsystems inside get frequent upgrades and have to take obsolescence management into account. The real value-addition is inside the product.

When we brought these three elements together, we found electronics manufacturing at a convergence. We essentially understood the industry as it existed, identified the dynamics that would affect our business, especially those beyond competition and the industry, asked critical questions, identified opportunities and potential threats and created a baseline strategy.

One thing we intuitively understood was that electronics manufacturing was industry-agnostic. If we were given the design and bill of materials, we could manufacture for aerospace, rail, industrial, medical or telecom. Similarly, we figured, we could address the needs of most of our customers.

By this time, the company had reached a pivotal point in its growth and needed a unifying brand narrative to represent its diverse offerings. Infotech was rebranded as Cyient.

The next question we asked ourselves was whether we could build manufacturing capabilities organically. That would mean losing a few more years to develop the required pedigree. And that would leave us quite behind in terms of market opportunity. To accelerate our entry into manufacturing, we decided to take the acquisition route.

We evaluated several options before acquiring Rangsons Electronics, a Mysore, India-based electronics manufacturing services and system integration company, and its high-precision machining subsidiary Techno Tools in January 2015. The acquisition enabled us to position Cyient strongly and expand into high-technology and high-value, design-led systems and solutions in line with the company's S3 (services, systems and solutions) strategy.

This time the board was sanguine that this was a great strategy and gave us a unanimous mandate to acquire Rangsons. Even as we completed the acquisition, we knew that while new markets were fascinating, discovery and surprises were common in them. We would have to contend with operating models and margins that would be very different from our traditional services business, manage a blue-collar workforce and deal with supply chains and material inventories. Our naivete in the new market made us prepare for a 'parallel play'—focusing on building new businesses and figuring out what worked on the go—as we progressed toward our goals.

We acquired Rangsons and started operating it as a new entity called Cyient Design-Led Manufacturing (Cyient DLM) to substantiate our 'design and make' value proposition. It took a good amount of time to integrate Rangsons with Cyient, understand the manufacturing business, build synergies between design engineering and manufacturing teams, and instil Cyient's values and culture. We needed to ensure the teams collaborated effectively to address, win and execute build-to-spec (B2S) projects.

The acquisition strengthened our capabilities in prototyping, testing, sourcing, manufacturing and system integration. It not only gave us entry into a new market but also provided a good market presence, domain expertise and customers. We began manufacturing using an integrated product development plan (seamless product life cycle support from concept through manufacturing). The market recognized us as a leader in high-mix, high-tech, low-volume electronic and mechanical manufacturing services in the aerospace, defence, rail transportation, medical technology, telecom and industrial business segments.

In many cases, we also supported our customers to competitively deliver value-engineered products to market through a combination of efficient design, sourcing and production processes. We sharpened our strategy by developing specific industry solutions and capabilities and creating a distinctive engineering, digital and design-led manufacturing capabilities ecosystem.

The one element still missing from the product management life cycle standpoint in the Cyient portfolio, especially for the aero-engine industry where we had and still have a strong presence, was aftermarket support. We did considerable work in analysing the market and decided to opt for another acquisition. In July 2015, we acquired Global Services Engineering Asia (GSE Asia), based in Singapore, from Pratt & Whitney Services Pte Ltd. This site provided repairs, development and validation for aero gas turbine engine components in support of Pratt & Whitney throughout the region.

GSE Asia's acquisition helped us grow our aerospace aftermarket services in the region and expand our reach into other industries within Singapore. Simultaneously, this transaction further strengthened our long-term partnership with Pratt & Whitney and marked a significant step forward for Cyient in shaping our vision in full-cycle product management.

Following these acquisitions, the company continued to invest in manufacturing capabilities, specialized infrastructure such as labs and prototyping facilities, and expanding capacity. We integrated Industry 4.0/Smart Factory concepts into manufacturing operations to remotely monitor machine and line performance in real time, providing a single window on manufacturing performance from disparate legacy systems. Cyient DLM uses real-time information to improve productivity, precision, efficiency and quality of assets, including staying connected with remote factories and supply chains.

We further acquired mechanical manufacturing units in New Britain, Connecticut and Jupiter, Florida to create locational proximity with key customers and also built a new greenfield electronics manufacturing facility in Hyderabad—a state-of-the-art Industry 4.0-enabled facility that is larger than the combined capacity of our Mysore and Bangalore (now Bengaluru) plants.

The Rangsons acquisition was a big gamble for Cyient. Many industry competitors watched us with scepticism when we bought the company. As a mature business, we always stayed on the side of caution but did not shy away from taking risks. We made a strategic choice with DLM, and it fit our risk appetite. The opportunity it created is, in some ways, very unique to Cyient, and is not a strategy that one can replicate easily.

By entering manufacturing and aftermarket, we created a new market segment—of end-to-end design to manufacturing and aftermarket capability. In a market where traditionally either engineering outsourcing or manufacturing companies work in silos, we declared that we provided end-to-end solutions.

New markets do not emerge on their own; firms and their activities create them. Organizations sense, by accident or design, a latent need that is perhaps not even felt and develop products or services that can address that need. By launching design-led manufacturing, we implemented an idea and brought together resources and capabilities to address customers' unmet needs. That is our value proposition and a big differentiator.

There are no proven navigational tools in any new market and no easy answers on where to play and how to win. Cyient had its share of hurdles. The company faced a degree of uncertainty about customers' needs, the most keenly desired products and services, and the best configuration of activities and technologies to deliver them. We had to fine-tune our business model, pick and choose the services that created value in the given space and provided it at a reasonable cost.

In hindsight, we may have probably oversimplified the entire solutions play and the market's openness to award both product design and manufacturing to the same supplier. We probably over-estimated our competence and underestimated the complexity.

The work cultures in manufacturing and engineering services are poles apart. Inventory management is complex and involves huge discounts on volume purchases and yet forecasting the volumes is actually like Russian roulette—one can end up shooting either a blank or a bullet. Component obsolescence is very high, making the problem a lot more severe. Dislodging current suppliers who build products from print is no mean task as they have already recovered their initial investments and can afford to be ruthless in pricing.

The mindset in service-oriented companies and their investors root for high double-digit margins while reaching a double-digit margin in manufacturing is literally impossible. But we course-corrected and hauled ourselves back on track in many of these areas. I do not think we are out of the woods yet, but I see the light and hope it gets us to the end of the tunnel. It may still take a couple more years, but design and manufacturing are poised to become a huge part of the Cyient story.

PART TWO

10

In Pursuit of Excellence: Processes and Quality

I was in class seven and my report card was out. I had scored poorly in all the subjects. I was quaking at the thought of the impending scene with my mother. She was sure to throw a fit when she saw my grades. Scared half to death, I tried to conceal my mark sheet from her. It was an attempt doomed to fail. With the omniscience peculiar to all mothers, she somehow managed to lay her hands on it. And she was furious! It was my first and last encounter with her temper.

She speared me with a gimlet eye and waved the report card under my nose. 'What's this?'

'My report card,' I mumbled in a barely audible whisper.

'Have you seen your marks?' She asked grimly.

Of course I had. But I thought it more politic to maintain a studied silence rather than proffer a defence. The anger in her eyes was sufficient warning.

My report fluttered in her hand as she reprimanded me in a voice that was cold enough to freeze the Arctic. 'I didn't expect these marks from you. Aren't you ashamed of yourself?'

If I hadn't felt any shame earlier, I was certainly feeling it now. Those marks were really disgraceful. There was no denying it.

She unleashed her final weapon. 'Your *akka* (elder sister) is doing so well in her studies. What happened to you? What stopped you from studying and doing well?'

There were no rational answers, no excuses I could offer. I bit my lip and remained silent.

Seeing that no answers were forthcoming, my mother issued an ultimatum. 'You'd better make amends and improve your marks in the next exams. If you don't, I'll stop your schooling and send you to the village. You can join your grandfather and spend your life farming. It's the only choice you'll have with these kinds of marks.'

I could see that she meant business. The prospect of being dispatched to the village to live my life out as a farmer was so unpalatable that it prodded me, as nothing else could have, to get my act together. I realized that change was not difficult as long as I was willing to transform. I focused my attention on my academics and, sure enough, my marks began to improve. I found that the harder I worked, the more I excelled in class. It was at this point that I made a life-changing decision. 'I'll be the best in everything I do, and nothing less than excellence will be acceptable to me,' I vowed. It was a serious pledge and the pursuit of excellence became the cornerstone of my existence from then on—whether in my studies, in sports, in my career or Infotech.

The path to excellence does not always run smooth. For instance, in the early days of Infotech, we encountered challenges in consistently meeting quality standards that gave me sleepless nights. We were providing digitization services to Pepco—Potomac Electric Power Company—a power utility in Washington, DC. We digitized its distribution asset maps. As soon as we sent the digitized output, Pepco staff took them to the field for verification. If the digital data was not dispatched in time, the scheduled field visits had to be cancelled, resulting in an idle field crew, adding to cost and time overruns for the client.

Indian outsourcing services were cost-effective and had a competitive advantage over several global outsourcing destinations. But sustaining and ramping up the business was no easy feat.

Indian technocrats could win repeat business from customers only when they delivered the prescribed quality in a sustained manner. When suppliers missed delivery schedules, customers experienced numerous challenges that increased their operational overheads. I saw several start-ups folding up because of their inability to deliver at scale on time.

I was unwilling to let Infotech go down that path. This meant Infotech had to be affordable and its deliveries had to have the prescribed quality. We had to complete our work on time—not by luck, but through systematic and predictable planning, followed by flawless execution. It also meant that we had to build operational excellence to differentiate ourselves from the competition and scale operations. In other words, Infotech had to become a byword in excellence.

We worked on dense, complex, intricate drawings and maps and adopted a heads-up digitization technique to digitize them. Raster images were converted into intelligent data that accurately represented customer assets (primary and secondary electrical networks, pole numbers, etc.) and the base geography (streets, street names, points of interest etc.) Once the digitization was complete and the maps passed quality checks, we used edge-matching techniques to snap and stitch map sections together. The maps also contained a lot of textual data and capturing them without error was a challenge.

The intelligent digital maps we returned to customers found use in diverse applications once the graphic data (maps) and associated structured data developed a smart geographic information system (GIS).

As long as the team was small, well-trained and skilled, maintaining a high-quality output was not a problem. But as the scale and number of projects grew and we expanded our hiring, keeping our quality consistent became a struggle. This was a tricky problem not just for Infotech but for the digitization industry as a whole.

As quality issues proliferated and we raced to meet deadlines, tempers erupted on the floor and the pressure started to tell on the team. We spent long hours checking and rechecking the digitized files. None of us knew when we would complete the day's work and return home. I often found myself completing the quality checks well past midnight to ensure we could dispatch the consignment the next day. We had increasingly tetchy conversations with our partners who had sourced the projects. Much of my energy went into writing long, apologetic emails to them and spending time taking corrective action.

Occasionally, the team made ridiculous mistakes. In one instance, a leaky coffee cup placed on the source map left a circular imprint on the scanned image. For reasons still unknown, the team blindly digitized it. It was literally: 'what you see is what you get.'

Before FTP servers and the Internet transformed the global delivery model, customers sent us their source material via courier, which took three days to arrive. We then digitized the drawings, plotted out hard copies of the maps and loaded the soft copy on floppies (a large map/drawing typically occupied 10–15 floppies) before we were ready to ship them out to the customer. This continued till at least 1994.

Every day, the courier came by at 5.30 p.m. to pick up the package that needed to be put on the late-night flight to Mumbai (then Bombay) for its onward journey on a connecting flight to the US/Australia/Europe.

As soon as the courier boy arrived, I would go to the shop floor as a matter of course and ask, 'Sunil, is the shipment ready for dispatch? The courier boy is here for the pick-up.'

'Mohan, our best CAD/GIS engineer took time off today. So, we're running behind schedule,' Sunil replied more often than not. He would then proceed to list out the challenges faced by the team on the given day without ever repeating an excuse. 'The consignment will be ready for dispatch in an hour,' he would then promise in all earnestness.

If a skilled, proficient and competent engineer was on leave, the quality would inevitably become questionable. We encountered several expected and unexpected challenges, delaying our shipments almost daily.

At 6.30 p.m., I would conscientiously go inside again to check on the status of our consignment. 'Sunil, is the shipment ready?' I would ask, not very hopefully.

'We've found some more errors, Mohan. We need some more time before we can dispatch,' Sunil would blithely inform, reducing me to near despair.

I would emerge from my encounter with Sunil and resignedly entertain the courier boy till the shipment was ready, fearing that if I did not, he would take to his heels and leave us with an unshipped consignment. There were times when I took this all-important individual to a nearby restaurant for dinner to buy some extra time for the team.

He was quite an impressive young man and I admired him. Not being from a moneyed background, he worked part-time to pay for his education. Despite the difference in our ages and finances, we never ran out of conversation. The first time I took him to dinner, we discussed the importance of education.

'Ignorance and poverty are the biggest curse of our country,' he told me in all seriousness.

I was amazed. I had never come across such wisdom in one so young.

Our conversations were not always serious. Sometimes we discussed the latest movies in town. One tete-a-tete was devoted to *Shiva*—a Nagarjuna-starrer with Amala playing his love interest. It was a typical Tollywood potboiler and the plot was not much to write home about. It was basically about student politics and campus gang wars. But my young friend was a die-hard Nagarjuna fan and treated me to a scene-by-scene account of the movie. I was fascinated, particularly when he went on to lecture me on the hooliganism that was rampant in colleges at the time. I had clearly led a very sheltered life. For a few short seconds, I envied him for the richness of his experiences.

But there were times when these dinners did not do the trick. On such occasions, members of the team headed straight to the airport late in the night and managed to put our shipment on the flight just before take-off! The day's objective was to ensure that we sent the digital files to the customer on schedule and we managed to do that, although admittedly with great difficulty.

As the volume of work increased, managing quality and daily schedules became increasingly stressful. The risks around quality emerged as the biggest threat to the survival of the company. I finally told myself, 'If I have to continue in this business, I must find a solution to this problem.'

As with any first-time product/service scale-up, especially where few industry standards exist, we were reaching a tipping point. A point where the product/service misfires, timelines are missed, rework leads to cost overruns and teammates experience burnouts. Scaling up a business is 10 per cent strategy and 90 per cent execution. The growing customer base and staff added complexity to our operations and amplified these issues. The fluid and flexible environment notable in start-up organizations was becoming unwieldy. We were failing under the weight of our initial success.

We had not anticipated these issues, but it was now time to audit the situation and identify the gaps. To achieve competitive scale and establish a sustainable market presence, we needed a better structure, process and discipline—foundations that would determine whether Infotech could continue to provide high-quality services to customers as it grew. It had become imperative to introduce the right tools, technology and training, motivate the team, boost their morale and ease the pressure before the gaps turned into chasms that posed existential risks.

Do It Right the First Time

I discussed the challenges with our partner Mickey Fain of SmartScan. He advised me to get the digitization work done by two people simultaneously. The cost was still low and it did not impact the bottom line. We started taking two databases and comparing them. Wherever there were discrepancies, the system alerted us and we fixed them.

But there were numerous false positives and false negatives as we lacked a benchmark for comparison. We were comparing two newly created databases, neither of them 100 per cent correct. It was an uphill task as we did not know if it was engineer A or engineer B who had made a mistake. And what if both of them had erred? It was becoming more complex than I had anticipated.

We ran this process for a while, but it became impossible to manage the number of errors the system hurled at us. We then adopted the age-old data entry technique—the double-entry process—using software and introduced it as a maker-checker concept in digitization.

After this, we developed stage-wise process flow charts for each project, taking into account all relevant parameters and customer-supplied specifications, including the quality of source documents and required quality acceptance criteria defined by the customer. We refined the process further by bringing one more concept from industrial engineering—the manufacturing plant's assembly line fundamentals. We broke up the process flow into clearly identifiable process steps and assigned engineers who were specialized in them, adding a few industrial engineers to the team to support the process definition.

After finalizing the process flowcharts, we prepared checklists for each step. Every person on the job followed the checklists and ensured that a digitizer would not miss anything or create something that was not on the map. People who were good at linework identified the roads and electric poles/lines. People who were proficient in English cross-checked names and addresses. We eventually built quality-control measures at every stage of the process.

Once the internal software tools were in place, we introduced another element. If a digitizer made a mistake, the keyboard got locked, a buzzer sounded, and all work stopped. The error had to be identified and rectified before the keyboard could be unlocked and work resumed. It built peer-level pressure to avoid mistakes, leading to enormous consistency in quality. Everyone improved. It led to a culture of 'do it right the first time'. This approach helped us maintain high accuracy (99.5 per cent and above), brought high predictability to deliveries and dramatically reduced rework costs.

Sometimes help walks your way just when you need it. While I was working hard to streamline our digitization business, I got in touch with S.A. Lakshminarayanan, popularly known by his initials SAL. He was heading the hardware maintenance group at OMC Computers and had acquired quite a reputation for his systematic approach to all issues. He was immaculate in documenting every transaction, activity and communication with customers and came to meetings thoroughly prepared, often holding about ten files, each 2 inches thick in the days when laptops were uncommon. SAL knew little about digitization or GIS/geospatial technology. But that did not stop me from asking him to join the company and bring process orientation to the business.

Things began changing after SAL was onboarded. Three shifts were introduced and a formal handover-takeover was implemented every time a shift changed to ensure there was continuity in work. Every customer communication was numbered to make sure there were no gaps between their expectations and our response. Every movement was mapped, computerized and measured so that we had a clear understanding of every workday. It was a transparent system.

Each person's performance and productivity were measured daily, shift after shift. At one stage, the productivity of each individual on a project was displayed every Monday morning. This created peer pressure as no one wanted to appear at the bottom of the list. As a result, everyone wanted to improve, not merely the unfortunates in the bottom percentile. This moved up the average productivity, week after week. A constructive competition ensued.

Along with the right people, tools, techniques and training, process excellence is fundamental to the building of operational excellence. Mickey gave us a model, and we created our own set of processes for the entire organization. After that, we introduced macros, automated several processes, and created digital workflows and checklists at every stage which gave us 100 per cent efficiency. We told the team that our highest priority was quality, and if we got the quality right the very first time, it automatically improved productivity. Wherever enhanced productivity was spotted, the teams involved were rewarded with special incentives.

We measured everything that could be measured, compared it with past data and if there were any deviations, we went through a relentless root cause analysis and executed a fix. We started viewing our processes as assets that should be systematically evolved, diligently managed, maintained and improved upon over time while simultaneously insisting that they should be clear, simple and well-documented. This brought process consistency and helped streamline the operations without unnecessary complexity.

Processes improved accountability, demonstrated a track record of success and established that we were reliable suppliers. At the same time, we facilitated flexibility so that work did not become boring and uncreative. The process still allowed people to innovate and we institutionalized them as process improvements. It facilitated replication, which in turn became the key to our expansion. The approach became a virtuous circle and the company soon became famous for its process orientation.

People believe processes lead to bureaucracy. While there is some element of truth in the belief, the benefits far outweigh the drawbacks. In our case, processes facilitated checks and balances in the hierarchy and were essential in making the enterprise efficient and stable.

In the initial years, when I ran the operations, I reviewed project progress with each manager on our makeshift conference table. The agenda of these meetings was simple—reviewing what we had planned for the previous day as against what we had achieved. These were generally on the following lines: Did we accomplish the goals that had been set? If not, why did we fail? How could we rectify them systematically? We also addressed other allied tasks such as people issues. In those days, our review meetings would begin sharp at 9.30 a.m. and finish by 10.30 a.m. every day (six days a week) till the first shift came for a lunch break and we had to vacate the table. They always went like clockwork.

After SAL joined the management team, I stepped back and let him take over the operations.

'The digitization business is going great,' I told him. 'But converting paper maps into intelligent digital files will not take Infotech far. At some point, this business will flatten. We need to move up the value chain and start looking laterally. I want Infotech to be a sustainable company. And I want you to spearhead the operations so I that can focus on business growth.' SAL was quick to grasp my vision and the needs of the organization. He rapidly took charge of the digitization business operations.

Quality Certifications: The Big Shift

Whenever we met a new business prospect, one of the first few questions that was shot at us was, 'Do you have any ISO certifications?'

ISO certifications gave customers confidence that we possessed the required knowledge regarding documentation and had the necessary processes to ensure cent per cent quality. Early on, we realized how crucial these certifications were to winning new contracts.

To make sure processes received due attention from the teams, we announced our decision to adopt accredited standards. We worked hard on the ISO 9002 guidelines to set up the essential processes so that we could achieve ISO 9001:1994 certification for quality assurance. It entailed setting up systems to ensure quality in all functions.

We followed it up with ISO 9001:2000 in 2001 for GIS/geospatial services and software development. Infotech became the first company in the Indian GIS/geospatial services market to acquire the certification and joined a select few Indian IT companies that had achieved the same. We then began implementing Six Sigma practices in our projects, which continued to drive and strengthen services quality. With the BS7799 accreditation, we eased customer apprehensions over Infotech's ability to handle their data and intellectual property, securely and thereafter upgraded BS7799 with the ISO 27001 information security management certification.

Shortly after acquiring the ISO 9001:2000 certification, we decided to try for the CMMI (Capability Maturity Model Integration) certification. The initiative was not greeted with any great degree of optimism. One of our more outspoken engineers in fact responded to the announcement with the comment, 'Infotech doesn't possess the capability or maturity as a company to get the CMMI certification. It's going to be an impossible task.'

This lack of faith riled me and I took up the task of getting the CMMI certification as a personal challenge. We made rigorous endeavours to implement strict process adherence, immaculate process documentation and relentless analysis on escapes. All eyebrows went up in the company when we managed to obtain the CMMI Level 4 certification. An additional feather in our cap lurked in the near future; we jumped from CMMI Level 4 to Level 5 (the highest SEI-certified quality process) in less than six months. Within a year, we were successfully appraised at the CMMI Level 5 Version 1.1. It became yet another affirmation of Infotech's commitment to continuous process improvement. The certification also reinforced the company's philosophy in its core values statement—outperform and scale new heights, only to beat it next.

The rigours of the CMMI and ISO programmes made us more disciplined as a company. Initial apprehensions and short-term challenges notwithstanding, they saved us time and money while improving our credibility and brand equity with customers. Standardized practices allowed us to move people around based on project needs. Standardization simplified workforce training and they began developing a specific vocabulary, sense of pride and personal commitment to quality.

Additionally, they ensured uniformity in documentation, allowing shorter learning cycles for new resources and better management of project health. The structured frameworks also provided project managers with information and processes to make evidence-based decisions without relying purely on gut feelings.

Over the years, quality and process improvements were no longer knee-jerk reactions to problems but a continuous practice running throughout the organization. After each project, we looked for ways to do things better and faster the next time.

We made quality consciousness the highest priority in the organization and mandated quality certifications for our global businesses and operations. We obtained every conceivable standard and certification in the industry, including domain-specific aerospace and rail transportation certifications. Infotech was honoured multiple times at a pan-India level for its quality excellence. Quality became a way of life, part of our DNA and, in a lighter vein, we started describing the certificates that adorned our walls as 'our exquisite artwork'.

Quality beyond Certifications

In aerospace, if a component fails, the outcome can be fatal, leading to loss of lives. Even the smallest mistake can turn out to be a catastrophe. When Infotech started working with Pratt & Whitney, everyone—right from its president down to its project managers— underscored the criticality of the work we were doing for them. Quality became even more crucial to our business; suddenly it was no longer just a matter of providing output on time. We inculcated quality consciousness in associates by relentlessly communicating the anticipated business challenges we would face if our quality did not match customer expectations. Understandably, quality issues could be a serious threat to the customer's business continuity and inflate its operational costs.

Pratt & Whitney shared some of its standard templates to strengthen our processes and quality even further. Our software team developed an engineering standard work (ESW) template for the company to facilitate process control by documenting proven tasks and procedures involved in design/product development.

This helped our teams to execute projects without errors. It also allowed us to use our creativity to suggest a better way of performing a specific task. We went back to Pratt & Whitney with a mistake-proofing solution that ensured better results quicker. The company liked our solution and revised its ESW.

Pratt & Whitney uses its business operating system—Achieving Competitive Excellence (ACE)—extensively across its organization. ACE has four levels of maturity—Qualifying, Bronze, Silver and Gold. Each sub-group or cell—combustors, compressors, turbines, externals, aftermarket—had to have an ACE certification. They expected us to comply with ACE quality processes.

Initially, our teams expressed reservations about following ACE guidelines as it required several additional hours of work. Project managers educated them, patiently explaining that: 'Complying with customer requirements is part of the job and not additional work. If you follow the process, there is no scope for mistakes.' ACE has several valuable tools to identify the root cause of an issue, perform root cause analysis, certify a process and conduct customer feedback analysis. These tools helped streamline our aerospace processes tremendously.

Pratt & Whitney took the ACE journey seriously and we embarked on it in May 2002. When I met the company president, Louis Chenevert (who later went on to become the chairman of United Technologies Corporation, the holding company of P&W), I informed him that we were committed to earning the ACE certification.

Louis laughed out loud and asked, 'Are you sure you'll make it happen?'

'Give me three months, Louis. I'll make sure Infotech earns an ACE certification,' I asserted.

'Mohan, if Infotech gets an ACE-Gold even in one cell, I'll visit your office and have dinner with you at your house,' Louis promised.

'Louis, I look forward to having dinner with you at my home,' I riposted with a grin. He still looked sceptical.

I got back to my team, created a plan, communicated the importance of ACE, articulated the business benefits and motivated them to implement it. One of the cells—Heat Treatment—was most enthusiastic about embracing ACE. In a short time, it was certified with an ACE Gold. Pratt & Whitney has several thousands of suppliers, and Infotech became the first among them to comply with the stringent ACE Gold parameters. This surprised Louis. He kept his word and not only visited our offices in Hyderabad in 2005 but also had dinner with us at home. It was a special milestone, a recognition of the credibility we had built with the customer.

Subsequently, several of our cells bagged the ACE-Gold. Finally, our delivery centre in Hyderabad became an ACE-Gold site in October 2007, which meant every cell in Hyderabad was ACE-Gold. Steve Finger, then president of Pratt & Whitney, visited us to inaugurate our new facility in Hyderabad and presented us with the ACE-Gold site plaque.

We were quick to realize the value that ACE was bringing to us. We had previously talked only about quality, while ACE added several more dimensions to assess an organization's position in its business ecosystem matrix.

Despite consistently upgrading our processes, we identified some level of customer dissatisfaction in a few projects. I went through another bout of self-questioning. 'The quality certification journey is going great, but what can we do to bring an "ACE-like" standardization across the business units?' I asked myself. This was when we coined the slogan—Quality Beyond Certifications.

Infotech decided to reinvent Pratt & Whitney's ACE (with their permission) and adapt it more purposefully for the business. Christening the home-grown tool 'BESt'—Business Excellence and Standardization, we started rolling out BESt across the company in 2011. It became Infotech's (and later Cyient's) business operating system, not merely a quality standard. BESt made the associates focus on the business side of the metrics. It talked about revenue growth, margins and measured the satisfaction levels of customers and associates. These two metrics became key performance indicators for the company. We took their feedback seriously, developed satisfaction improvement plans and implemented them with favourable and measurable outcomes. This was augmented by monitoring the engagement levels of associates and integrating their feedback into evolving inclusive policies.

Win–Win with Processes

Process excellence has been a major contributor to Infotech's success. But as the company embarked on a rapid growth journey, we realized that 'scalable process excellence' would be critical. The firm increased its focus on building robust, integrated and scalable processes and systems. A range of systems aimed at internal process excellence were rolled out, including SAP, standard costing, project profitability, asset tracking and utilization.

Another set of processes aimed at performance excellence like project management methodologies, automation through technology deployment and developing reusable solutions became increasingly important in every customer engagement. We licensed a project management system and the linkages that ensure that all the systems were in sync and derived exponential value. While implementing them, we continued our investments in industry-specific standards and certifications. We knew that they were the critical differentiating factors for Infotech/Cyient as we sought to deliver system/sub-system level engineering services.

Infotech rolled out organization-wide initiatives to strengthen its finance, delivery, human resources and sales processes. For finance and accounting, the firm implemented SAP across all its global locations. Salesforce.com was helpful in customer relationship management. After a detailed study of our delivery processes in different centres of excellence and vertical units, Infotech implemented a unified delivery management system called e3 (Enterprise Execution Excellence), to support its business and operational requirements worldwide. The company invested in a global HR management system, Workday, to ensure one global platform for recruitment, transfers, training, separation, performance appraisal and planning. This helped enhance our sales automation system for the accurate and timely forecasting of sales data and sales performance monitoring.

If I have to single out one trait that drives me, I would have to confess that it is the pursuit of excellence. I am uncompromising when it comes to measurement, processes, quality and ensuring value-creation for the customer and a win-win situation for both parties. I have seen it transform companies from mediocre to outstanding and it is as morally sound as a management system can be. Investing in scalable processes is investing in the future of the business itself. At Infotech, I insisted that we, as a team, develop a mindset for operational excellence and saw these investments as essential opex to create sustainable improvements in the enterprise as opposed to a one-time capex.

11

Customer Centricity: Delivering Delight

It was the year 2003–04. I received a call from Paul Adams, vice president, Pratt & Whitney. After an exchange of pleasantries, he said, 'Mohan, I want you to do something for me.'

'Sure! Tell me,' I invited.

Needing no further encouragement, Paul plunged into the heart of the matter. 'I'm quite impressed with what you are doing for Pratt & Whitney in India. I want to replicate the model in our export control (US defence) business. We need a low-cost sourcing centre for it. We believe Infotech is our best bet for the job.'

'Sounds good,' I said to fill in a short pause, wondering where this was leading. 'At least so far,' I added cautiously.

'Well, there's a catch,' he blurted out. 'Our export control business is tied down by restrictions on location, so we can't outsource to another country. It has to be an on-shore operation (on US soil) and it has to be low-cost.'

It took a few seconds to understand what Paul was talking about. When the penny finally dropped, I said, 'Paul, I'll be there with you in three weeks. We can sit down then and discuss the details.'

'No, this is urgent. Let me start from here. I've got the report done. We've already worked out possible locations. We can't drag our feet on this,' Paul insisted.

We debated various models. One option was to house the project at a university campus to keep the real estate cost down. We could hire fresh graduates straight out of university. We zeroed in on the University of Minnesota, Minneapolis, as a possible location.

The other option was to set up the project in Albuquerque, New Mexico. It was out in the boondocks which would help keep our costs down. Paul came up with yet another alternative, one that had not occurred to me. He suggested Puerto Rico, a Caribbean island and an unincorporated US territory.

Puerto Rico, an erstwhile Spanish colony, had been acquired by the United States following the Spanish American war in 1898. Puerto Ricans have been US citizens since 1917. Together with the Puerto Rico Industrial Development Company, the US government launched a series of economic projects to develop the territory into an industrial high-income economy beginning in the mid-twentieth century.

Looking at it as an opportunity to build on the trust the customer was expressing in us, I decided to accept the proposal. We kept the discussion rolling and, within two months, Paul and I were in Puerto Rico to finalize things. Infotech set up shop—as Infotech Aerospace Services Ltd. (IAS)—in San Juan, Puerto Rico and entered into a joint venture with Pratt & Whitney in which it had an equity of 49 per cent.

Apart from the lower cost of wages and real estate, the project received a major incentive from the Government of Puerto Rico. It promised to reimburse the capital expenditure within six to nine months of launching the operations. Pratt & Whitney helped us with the recruitment and the business model worked well. Puerto Rico did have engineering capabilities but it did not have aerospace engineers or a track record in building an aircraft engine.

We entered into an understanding with the University of Puerto Rico system, which had about seven to nine colleges. The government assured us that it would fine-tune the curriculum to suit Pratt & Whitney's requirement, so we would have a steady pool of capable youngsters coming in. This apart, we could attract islanders who lived on mainland US and mainlanders who loved the Caribbean island's sun, sand and rum.

As the business scaled, Pratt & Whitney wanted to take control of the company. We switched our shareholding and Infotech became a minority partner with a 49 per cent stake. In a few years, Pratt & Whitney came under pressure from different directions and wanted to divest the company. We said we were willing to buy it, but the company wanted to give us a five-year contract instead. It was an attractive proposition, both on the top line and bottom line. Then, all hell broke loose with an entirely unrelated event.

Pratt & Whitney defence projects were high-security projects and it took every conceivable step to make sure that its technology never breached its secure walls. However, in this instance, the company discovered a small non-conformance and launched an organization-wide audit to make a voluntary disclosure to the regulators. While this matter was amicably resolved with the government, the audit exposed an unrelated incidence of a minor non-compliance by an Infotech associate, and our credibility came under stress. But the strength of our relationship, painstakingly built over the years, helped us tide over the crisis. We resolved the issue by repatriating the concerned associate back to India.

While the incident made no impact on Infotech India's Pratt & Whitney business, the customer did pull back from the Puerto Rican deal. The entity remained as it was at 51–49 per cent. After 12 months, Pratt & Whitney came to me with another proposition—to buy out the Puerto Rican entity. We divested it in 2013 and received handsome returns on our investment. Pratt & Whitney funded us substantially and we gave the firm dividends every year. It was a very involved transaction.

It took an insane amount of effort to build trust and confidence— with Pratt & Whitney, the local government and the islanders. One could say Infotech was lucky to have a large multinational like Pratt

& Whitney as its customer. At the same time, we strove energetically to build the relationship. When the opportunity arose, Paul of Pratt & Whitney thought of only one person to solve the problem: me.

Our Puerto Rican adventure is a fine example of what good customer relationships can do for a company. The function of a business is to create and keep customers. Customers are not merely brick-and-mortar organizations that get us to do their work; they represent a set of people who come to us to solve problems that matter to them or their clients. Simultaneously, they help to shape and expand a company.

I believe in an interdependent social ecosystem and relationships based on human values that sustain the social fabric. And when I realized this human value was helping me build the business, I adopted it with even more zeal, each day that I spent in erecting the Infotech/Cyient edifice.

The difference, between building a good company and a great company that lasts, lies, among other things, in the way the enterprise serves its customers. Nothing predicts organic growth like the strength of customer engagement. An engagement that proactively shapes customers' experience, both at rational and emotional levels, influences buying behaviour and elevates the relationship to a synergistic level where the client perceives you as a valued partner and not just a tactical supplier. This occurs only when there is mutual trust and customers see value for money.

Most of Infotech's early business forays took place through partners. After a few years, we realized that as a result of the model we were suffering from acute customer disconnect and this was limiting our ability to understand their business context, expectations and feedback. We struggled to strengthen our domain expertise and create value proactively. Moreover, our partners were undercutting our profits to accommodate their margins.

This limitation is a given in a partnership business model. It worked well in the initial years, and we used it from time to time. However, we reached a point where it became evident that we could no longer rely on this model alone if we intended to build a sustainable company. We needed to stand on our own feet and not on partner crutches. We needed to be closer to customers— both geographically and professionally. A transactional relationship with customers was no longer enough. We needed to build and maintain lasting and value-creating relationships with them. This institutional view demanded that we review our go-to-market and customer strategy. It prompted us to launch Infotech's operations in the US and acquire companies in Europe at the turn of the century.

Winning Customers, Keeping Customers

In the 1990s, even as we worked with partners, our efforts at business development brought us a few customers directly. I ran into Matt Pichon, VP (Operations) of Etak (a Polynesian word for navigation), on the floor of the USGIS exhibition in Charlotte, North Carolina, in 1994. Etak was a Menlo Park, California-based automotive navigation systems, digital maps and mapping software company. I pitched Infotech's capabilities to Matt as we walked around the aisles, and it aroused his interest. 'Can you digitize, update, edit and validate US road maps to enable navigation? Matt asked.

While we were discussing the feasibility of Infotech picking up work from Etak, Matt made a disclosure. 'Etak produces its data in "Tiger file format" using Sun workstations, UNIX operating system and proprietary DWS software to ensure data security.'

This was a showstopper. It meant Infotech had to buy expensive Sun workstations with UNIX and train its engineers on the proprietary software. I was keen to grab the opportunity, so I quickly devised a way out. 'I'm willing to make investments in training,' I told Matt. 'If Etak loans the hardware and software to Infotech, I'm certain we can deliver to your requirements.'

I sweetened the deal by reducing the hourly rates to factor in the fact that Etak would be loaning the infrastructure. Matt appreciated the flexibility I offered and also our ability to size up to the challenge. He agreed to my proposition. In the next three months, we signed the deal and started serving Etak with three workstations and six trained associates.

Keeping the long haul in mind during every customer interaction, we focused on the key drivers to enrich the customer experience, including proactiveness, speed of response and quality deliverables at an affordable cost. We trained our associates on technology and at the same time ensured they developed the necessary professional etiquette to pay close attention to customer needs. We consistently delivered to Etak's satisfaction and ramped up the account to about a hundred people in the first year.

When we began working with Etak, Rupert Murdoch's News Corporation owned the company (News Corp bought Etak in 1989). Subsequently, in 1996, Sony Corporation acquired it and sold it in 2000 to Tele Atlas, a Belgium and Netherlands-based digital mapping and location-based services company. We continued our relationship with Etak throughout these ownership changes.

Infotech began working closely with Alain de Taeye, co-founder and CEO of Tele Atlas, and his team in developing a digital map of the world. The new contract helped us to lay a solid foundation for a process-driven relationship, emphasizing database and engineering innovation. We built infrastructure and technical competence through a 500-person centre of excellence (CoE) in Hyderabad, kept to our quality and affordability promise and soon came to be seen as reliable partners.

Tele Atlas had built a 600-person offshore production unit in Noida, India (TeleAtlas India Pvt Ltd) to service their European requirements. But Infotech's deliveries were superior to its Noida captive on many parameters. We served Etak/Tele Atlas North America with 100 per cent on-time delivery and 98 per cent quality, while Tele Atlas Europe, which maintained the Noida captive, mustered lower delivery commitments and quality standards. That apart, the unit faced some HR and administrative challenges.

When I met George Fink, president and COO, in Boston in 2004, I amiably took up the issue with him.

'George, you're an expert in managing operations in complex emerging markets and I'm sure you understand the business imperative of TeleAtlas' lower quality deliveries in India,' the straight shooter in me pointed out.

George nodded in agreement. 'Map-making has traditionally been a manpower-intensive industry,' he conceded. 'It has recently become highly competitive with rapid technology adoption. I agree, we need to revisit our operational strategy to secure the captive unit's bottom line.'

'That's true, George,' I concurred. 'The market is on an aggressive wave. In my view, the TeleAtlas India captive requires local leadership and an entrepreneurial mindset to thrive.'

George looked encouraging, so I proceeded to make my point. 'It might help to have strategic relationships with Indian entities which can improve your overall delivery parameters,' I proposed.

'Any suggestions?' He asked.

'If you give us an opportunity, Infotech could lower the captive unit's costs by 10–15 per cent and take strict service-level contracts,' I replied, aggressively mooting the idea that Infotech intended to acquire TeleAtlas's India captive.

Being a long-time customer, TeleAtlas had full confidence in Infotech's highly specialized offshore services. I built on that confidence to convince George that Infotech could replicate its delivery model at its Noida captive. George seemed to like the idea and promised to discuss it with his management team before taking the conversation forward.

This off-the-cuff conversation led to the strategic acquisition of Tele Atlas India by Infotech in March 2005. Servicing the customer through the years helped us understand the intimate, causal relationship between client loyalty on the one hand and cash flow and profits on the other. So, we not only acquired, but also entered into a long-term services agreement to provide database and software solutions. This helped Infotech to achieve non-linear, long-term growth.

We moved from the time and material pricing model to a fixed-cost model within three months of the acquisition and offered a discount on our rates. Such was my faith in Infotech's capabilities and processes that we further promised to deliver 5–10 per cent productivity gains year on year. We brought down costs and kept up with our productivity promise by bringing innovation and automation into our processes. We did not lay off a single employee. Back then, it was a one-of-its-kind transaction where a supplier acquired a multinational's captive in this country, with its blessings!

It took about eight months to completely integrate the captive into Infotech's culture and bring its systems and processes at par with our own, thereby reducing operating costs. From the ninth month onward, the unit turned around and the quality of its map content and on-time delivery improved. From the second year onwards, we passed on the productivity gains to TeleAtlas. We trained the team, optimized the operations, increased business value and gave the unit back to the team to manage in just two years. The team's learning was rapid and the transformation conspicuous and tangible.

The executives who came to Infotech as part of the Tele Atlas acquisition had a great understanding of the mapping world, especially Tele Atlas databases. This inside information, which had become part of Infotech, helped us evolve several innovative processes to enhance productivity. We built a number of tools to improve the cost per hour of work, which became a key reason for the strong bonding between Infotech and TeleAtlas.

At the same time, we strengthened our global delivery model, expanded our service footprint, and our position in the GIS/geospatial data and technology services market. The acquisition served as a high-return investment. We gained scale and expanded skillsets that helped us remain competitive. Several leaders from the concerned captive moved into different parts of the organization and flourished in their careers.

We made sure the Tele Atlas management, too, was comfortable. We allotted equity to its parent company and made it a strategic investor. Along with the stake, Tele Atlas gained a board seat.

George Fink, William Henry and later Alain de Taeye represented TeleAtlas on the Infotech board. Even after Tele Atlas was acquired by TomTom, another Dutch map-making and location technology company, in 2008, our association continued.

The two companies nurtured trust at the senior executive and operational levels, enabling an environment in which we could openly discuss irksome issues to create win-win situations. We actively sought customer feedback and responded to their suggestions with detailed action plans. We were mindful that partners typically grow dissatisfied as the relationship ages. So, we made sure we aligned and realigned with them. We constantly kept up with the evolving complexity of mapping needs through database and engineering innovation, process orientation and domain expansion to fulfil the customer's unmet needs. In every project, we went above and beyond a typical sales-customer relationship to create deep engagement. Furthermore, we acquired a 10 per cent stake in Tele Atlas Kalyani (India) Limited (TAKI) which focused on the Indian market. This strategic investment improved the synergy with Tele Atlas/TomTom, which had by now become our largest geospatial customer. The firm subsequently bought Kalyani and Infotech stock and it became Tele Atlas/TomTom's fully owned subsidiary.

Our business relationship with Etak stood the test of time, ownership changes and leadership transformations, strengthening the relationship each time, even as we improved our service proposition and remained their supplier of choice. We earned corporate trust, not just the confidence of a few individuals. There was a collective belief that Cyient was the right partner for its growth. We scaled the account year on year and grossed a cumulative revenue of over $300 million—a testimony to the rewards of a long-term committed partnership. Etak/TomTom's investment in Infotech/Cyient appreciated handsomely. But more than serving as a purely financial investment, its stock served as an anchor to the relationship itself and enabled sustained value-creation for both partners.

Values such as fairness and integrity that are true for Infotech/ Cyient are true for TomTom and Tele Atlas and this has been the driving force behind our long-standing relationship. This match made the relationship much stronger and there were hardly any difficulties we could not resolve. While we did business, we always kept an eye, a big eye, on the human aspects of doing business, and the relationship never stopped growing. Loyal customers such as Etak/TomTom became the most valuable assets for us.

Servicing Large Corporates

When we clinched a five-year contract with Pratt & Whitney, it presented a huge business opportunity for growth-hungry Infotech. But it meant that we had to bring a step shift in our customer strategy and create distinctive value and experience with our offerings, channels, operating models and capabilities. To accomplish that, we needed to know our customers at a granular level. We could not live with one helpful connection in the entire hierarchy. We needed to operate along a continuum of intimacy and trust. So, we began fostering deeper multi-point multi-level contacts across the firm.

For instance, during our first meeting, I interacted with Jyoti Purushottaman, India champion and CFO of Pratt & Whitney (and subsequently of UTC). Once we signed the contract, Jyoti and I worked to strengthen the relationship. Jyoti routinely inquired whether Infotech associates had the right skills, training, domain expertise and assured all possible support from his company. He brought everything—from the smallest quality issue or team problem to the biggest strategic concerns to my attention.

While we worked to iron out issues and deepen trust, we also got to know each other at a personal level. Our personal values and family cultures were similar and we bonded over our shared interest in temples and holy towns. Jyoti would invite me for dinner at his house every time I was in East Hartford. Over the years, the relationship turned into an enduring friendship between two individuals who were not fettered by professional affiliations and customer-supplier equations. At the same time, we had the maturity to demarcate our professional and personal relationship.

While I maintained good ties at the CXO level, my team and I worked closely with our end user—the vice president of engineering at Pratt & Whitney. In the initial years, Ed Crowe headed the engineering division and led the delegation which signed the contract with Infotech. He played a crucial role in strengthening the relationship.

Within Pratt & Whitney, we had multiple stakeholders, customers and touchpoints at various levels, often with differing opinions and agendas. These touchpoints changed over time. Ensuring a sync and understanding different divisional, cross-functional needs of the customer account, being flexible and creating an open feedback mechanism at all levels in Pratt & Whitney was critical. So, we kept a holistic and intimate contact with the customer in real time (or near real time) across our organization and never lost sight of its changing dynamics. At the same time, we ensured consistency in communications and interactions across those touchpoints. This 360-degree view of the customer was essential for us to deliver superior customer experience.

Joe Adams succeeded Ed Crowe. After him, we developed a strong professional relationship with his successor Paul Adams, who later became the COO and president of Pratt & Whitney. Paul served on the Infotech board.

We did everything to become successful, but always within the guardrails of my values. We did nothing unprofessional, illegal or antisocial. Instead, we invested an enormous amount of time and effort to occupy certain space in customers' minds. But we were always cognizant that we occupied that space only when we delivered on our promises consistently.

Building deeper customer relationships and winning customer trust gave us a little more margin for error and brought us benefits from unexpected quarters. For instance, George David, Chairman and CEO of UTC, who was not part of our relationship, surprised us with his decision to invest in the company. He did not know us, but our excellent relationship and top-of-the-class performance positioned us well in the eyes of Pratt & Whitney's decision-making hierarchy, prodding it to take a stake in Infotech.

When Paul Adams got promoted, Dave Carter took over. We had a great relationship with Dave as well.

While we built strong relationships at the senior executive level, we also developed and maintained healthy relationships at the operational level. Pratt stationed a director of outsourcing, in India. He played a key role in building the Pratt business ground up and acted as an influencer in deepening the relationship. It was not easy to maintain a smooth relationship at the operational level when we had to work together on the quality, timelines, systems, security, teams and recruitments. But our operations team meticulously managed the relationship for years.

While we had good days and bad days with Pratt & Whitney, I often heard snide remarks from our competitors who quipped that 'I cook for Pratt & Whitney and I cook the best chicken in town for them'. It did not matter. I kept the Pratt & Whitney account and they kept their jealousy. To win business, suppliers often promise the moon, stretching their capabilities and costs. Over the years, we learnt to push back on customer expectations that hurt our profitability. This prompted Pratt to entertain competition. It did not hurt us, and counterintuitive as it may seem, our business with the firm kept flourishing.

We enhanced our value proposition for Pratt & Whitney by energetically taking on a significant design engineering role in their state-of-the-art NGPF engine programme. It transformed aviation by delivering game-changing economic and environmental performances. Pratt & Whitney's faith and proactive disposition allowed us to take significant risks and experiment with reducing the weight and cost of many NGPF engine parts. Today, we are proud of the fact that Cyient contributed to over 22 per cent of its engineering effort.

When I started distancing myself from operational responsibilities at Cyient in a planned succession, I ensured that it included relationship-building with key customers. The new leadership took ownership of the UTC account and fortified it further. With a cumulative revenue of over $1.5 billion in more than twenty years of our association, Pratt & Whitney continues to be Cyient's flagship customer. It is a fine example of how we won and scaled a large account and built a long-lasting relationship. We successfully repeated this approach with several customers over the years.

Customer First

In the early years of outsourcing, apart from technical competence, Western multinationals preferred enterprises that could give a sense of comfort and safety in the business relationship. Infotech adopted this critical aspect of outsourcing and turned it into its brand promise.

We set up independent centres of excellence (CoEs) with requisite infrastructure, skills, leadership, training, systems and processes. We bettered our output, improved accountability, and secured customer privacy and confidentiality. Our customers routinely inspected the development floors and interacted with our engineers. While these stopovers improved customer confidence, they also allowed our teams to build up a rapport with clients and gain a deeper knowledge of their business, requirements and objectives. As a result, customer satisfaction improved. We hammered home the message that customers paid for our salaries and we therefore needed to understand their expectations; these were delivered right down to our newest associate. 'Customer First' became our mantra and we enforced it rigorously across the business units.

We reviewed our customer strategies, began tapping into the intelligence of the project teams and measured every project parameter. We solicited ideas from associates and implemented them, going beyond the statements of work. A majority of Infotech's business is annuity-based through repeat customers. And it became harder to transfer benefits year-on-year consistently and match customer's newer expectations for the same or similar kind of work. It demanded a consistency of innovation, purpose and action over a long time.

Customer experience, journey and feedback became the heart of Cyient's growth planning. We adopted a three-pronged approach to measure customer experience. First, we solicited 'transactional or project feedback' quarterly or on completing a project. We measured quality, on-time delivery, budget, communication, customer support and overall satisfaction. As a second lever, we sought 'periodic feedback' at the executive level on a quarterly/half-yearly basis to understand programme engagement, programme level budgets, challenges, risks and mitigation plans.

At a third level, we launched an annual customer satisfaction (CSAT) survey using the services of an independent firm to maintain confidentiality and objectivity. We included every customer with whom our yearly revenues exceeded $0.5 million in this survey to cover approximately 90 per cent of our revenue. Each year, the survey interfaced with a minimum of three respondents for every million-dollar revenue account across North America, Europe, the Middle East and the Asia Pacific.

We measured customer perceptions and benchmarked business dimensions on overall satisfaction, value continuum, expectations, improvement areas and brand perception, apart from performance feedback on project management, delivery and people skills. These annual surveys helped us gauge customers' experience with Infotech and the strength of engagement at the tactical level.

Every customer is different. We analysed their feedback and developed a customer satisfaction improvement programme (CSIP) for each customer at delivery, operations, account and geography levels. Individual CSIPs allowed us to address key gap areas and define our priorities to improve the outcomes.

Recognizing that account growth could only be achieved by making the right investments, we identified a set of key accounts and created forward-looking key account plans (KAP) by integrating structured and unstructured customer feedback along with customer, competition and industry intelligence. We created account-level strategies in the immediate, short and medium term and aimed to 'run' the core/current business at peak profitability in the immediate term and 'change' the account by creating business value through innovative technology solutions in two to three years.

In the medium term, Infotech intended to become a strategic partner and 'transform' the account by creating new revenue opportunities and expanding customer market share through new services and products. We not only planned, but also developed action plans and reviewed the progress periodically to monitor and measure progress. We captured customer intelligence and mapped white spaces and adjacencies. Account teams were encouraged to launch joint innovation projects, leverage cross-industry capabilities, expand capabilities through acquisitions and partnerships, and design future-ready solutions through novel pricing/business models. These activities also helped us to evolve our business development roadmaps, either by validating or course-correcting the direction we took or intended to take.

We constituted a board-level committee to oversee and strategically guide our customer engagement activities at both organization and business unit levels. The committee reviews the annual CSAT results and the responsive actions taken by the management. Its periodic recommendations reinforced the process, improving the surveys and the ability to use the findings to develop organizational and business unit strategies.

One of the questions we look out for in the customer survey is: Do you think Cyient will act on your feedback? In the first few years, we scored terribly on this question. But over time, we improved the effectiveness of our response with meaningful actions and consistent improvement and began scoring well. Customers tell us the truth and partake in shaping the business when they know we value their opinions and act on their recommendations. At the same time, we take on the concerns raised about associates or delivery and deal with them professionally.

One might argue that Pratt & Whitney stayed with us for more than twenty years because of high switching costs in the complex aerospace engineering design domain. However, the account witnessed steady growth despite the maturity of the aerospace services ecosystem. It testifies that our ability to retain the customer was not forced loyalty but a result of the consistent value we offered.

Beyond Business

Right from inception, my utmost focus has been on my customers and their needs. Whenever a customer visited our facility in Hyderabad, I received them at the airport (till at least 2010) and did everything I could to make them comfortable in the city. We invested in building professional relationships with customer teams within the business ethos of the company and simultaneously, struck up a personal rapport as well. We often hosted customer parties at home. A business accomplice rarely gets invited to someone's house in the West. This made our dinners at home a special honour for our international customers. We delighted our customers with home-cooked gourmet meals that were tailored to their taste. 'If you want the best food in town, come to my home,' used to be my slogan. They enjoyed coming home, while my family and I loved hosting them.

As we threw open our home and regaled our customers with the best of Indian hospitality, they started trusting us more. I moved on in life, so did several customer executives. Yet to this day, whenever any of my associates or I bump into them, they fondly remember the get-togethers at my house and the various delicacies that were spread out for them. Moreover, maintaining a personal connect with the customer became the basic hygiene to nurture and scale the accounts, and the practice continues in a number of different ways in the company to this day.

We introduced another practice to honour our clients and do our bit to preserve the environment at the same time: we invited customer executives to plant saplings on our campuses, christening the plants with their names. For us, a sapling is the symbol of a budding relationship and our aspiration to nurture it. Standing true to our sentiment, many of these saplings have grown into well-cured trees, adding to the green quotient of our campuses while we continued to foster new relationships and young saplings.

I made sure that every customer encounter was a pleasant exchange. Even when the issues under discussion were tricky, I went out of my way to ensure that cordiality was maintained and that each interaction culminated in win-win solutions. I never minded giving up a bit in a negotiation as long as I got what I had set for myself. As long as the customer was happy, I was content.

This frontline obsession and founder's mindset helped us to attract, delight and retain customers. The company has the distinction of retaining 99 per cent of its customers. We have grown from strength to strength by aligning and realigning with customer needs amidst dynamically changing market realities. We speak their language, breathe their aspiration and have become their extended arm and partner of choice. This unbending predisposition to vigorously advocate for the customer has become a deeply ingrained part of the company culture.

12

Developing People

Dear Chairman,

I would first like to thank you for inviting me to 'Interaction with our Chairman'.

I am a proud member of the 25-year-club. I started my career at the age of nineteen while I was still in college. Later, I moved on to a company called Wellsco Inc. in 1993, which Infotech/Cyient bought in 2010. Today, I am an important part of the company, helping 5G fiber optics roll out to the entire New York City from my home here in Illinois.

I just wanted you to know it was a privilege to hear you speak this morning. I found your words inspirational. We share many of the same values and beliefs. I didn't get a chance to share the three words that guide my life—but you touched on all three—delight the customer, diversity, and success.

I am proud to work for a company that supports women. I am lucky to be surrounded by strong women. My supervisor DZ and her supervisor RD do a fantastic job of allowing me to lead tasks and provide me with all the support I need to do my job as best I can! There are a lot of women here in North America, making Cyient what it is today! My girlfriend, who works for a hospital and is in contact with COVID-19 patients every day, is another strong woman in my life.

My goal each day is to win the 'Chairman Award'. Everybody in my office knows that I have been trying for this prestigious award every year for the last 10 years. I didn't nominate myself this year because I didn't want to feel disappointed and let down again. I regret doing that now because this could have been my year. I will nominate myself again next year, win or lose.

I just wanted to let you know a little about me, and express my gratitude for giving me the opportunity to work for your company. I look forward to our interactions in the future.

Jan Logan

I received this email after a recent interaction with members of our twenty-five-year club. It was touching in the extreme and brought to mind the evolution of the people practices at Infotech/Cyient—the challenges that had threatened our existence in the early years, the conscious effort to create an inclusive, equitable and empathetic culture and the labour that had gone into building a sustainable institution.

Now, consider this mail from the viewpoint of a visible demographic: in the thirtieth year of our operations (August 2021), we had 380 associates who had put in twenty years or more, and about 20 per cent of the organization were under the age of twenty-five! For a technology enterprise like Infotech/Cyient, knowledge is produced, disseminated and co-created in an environment nuanced with employees who are at different stages of their career aspirations. It is in this vast continuum that we kept trying to build and rebuild the people systems over the years.

Talent Takes It All

Entrepreneurs experience a wide range of people needs as their start-ups transect different phases. At the launch, the company had no brand to attract talent, there was only me acting as brand ambassador and flagbearer. Like any other start-up, I had to sell my vision to the local hires who knew me as the ex-CEO of one the largest computer companies out of Hyderabad—OMC Computers.

That's when I discovered Sunil Kumar Makkena. He was working with Suri Computers when I approached him. Sitting on the patio of my home, I made my pitch to Sunil, offering him all the reasons I could think of to get him to work with me.

'Sunil, my dream is to make Infotech into a sustainable global business,' I told him. 'There will be no dearth of opportunities for you. I promise you a fantastic career growth in the company. We'll give you clear responsibilities. It will not be a family-run firm because I want to build a professional business and to do that, I need good people like you.'

I laid out my aspirations for Infotech before Sunil, stressing on the values it would stand for as I wound up my proposal. 'I'll try my best to share the company's wealth with wealth creators like you who'll be striving for the company with your sweat and blood.'

Two days after the conversation, Sunil agreed to join Infotech. People like Sunil acted like talent magnets, attracting more people with their influence and professional networks. Six months into the operations, more resources were needed. Digitization skills were in short supply, so we went for campus recruitments and scouted for graduates with adjacent skills, offering job guarantees if they qualified after the training.

When we launched Infotech, there were only a couple of digitization companies in Hyderabad. Since the sector had low entry barriers, within a few years competition built up. They set their sights on our resource pool and started poaching our highly trained personnel. A Department of Electronics official summed up the situation accurately with the following quip in an open meeting: 'New start-ups in services businesses always targeted their neighbour's customers and employees to start their business.' He was absolutely right, so much so that even prominent players entering the local market made Infotech a part of their 'must poach' target. This led to high attrition levels.

Employees are assets that walk in and out of a technology enterprise every day. The organization invests in them, trains them, treasures them and develops them, even though it does not know if they will return the next day. Yet, an enterprise grows and succeeds only to the extent that it nurtures talent and turns it into a competitive advantage. Adhering to this belief, we continued to invest in training. We created a 'CAD and GIS Academy' to institutionalize training. This was the first in the GIS/geospatial industry and it helped us build one of the largest geospatial expert pools in the country.

By this time, I had figured out that PPT (People, Processes, Tools, technology and training) was vital to scale the company. In the 'people' part of the model, I had introduced the 4Rs—recruit, retain, reward and finally retrain—so the team kept up with the changing business needs.

As digitization provided the economies of scale and training expanded the resource pool, it presented a new situation—a lack of role excitement and job satisfaction. Our process compliance rigour created a lack of job satisfaction, especially among engineering graduates. Understandably, they began to cast about for opportunities that allowed higher-order work. This, too, contributed to attrition.

In the 1990s, Infotech lacked the brand recognition of established companies, so attracting and retaining talent was an uphill task. At one point, quality and attrition became the biggest threats to the company's business sustenance despite our best efforts.

The outflow of people added direct and indirect costs to the company. We lost employee knowledge to competitors and spent significant time searching, screening, hiring and replacing lost associates, which inflated our direct costs. At the same time, we lost productivity as it took time to train the new hires and make them productive. This added to our indirect costs, impacting delivery timelines and customer satisfaction. Attrition also affected the morale of the existing staff as they had to take on the additional burden of the associates who had exited.

Our desire to build careers hit roadblocks at every turn, pushing us to continuously reflect on our people practices. It was time to live and perpetuate our values even more vigorously. This made us introduce multidimensional initiatives—to create an even more professional work environment, giving associates challenging tasks and paying commensurate salaries, making sure they saw progress in their careers, all the while creating a culture of empathy. Infotech's revenue growth made these initiatives possible and its scale allowed us to create career paths for hundreds of associates over the next few years.

At the dawn of the new century, our engineering services picked up momentum and that proved to be a different ball game altogether. We now needed to acquire talent with engineering skills and domain knowledge. This was also the time when Pratt & Whitney had started entrusting us with complex projects and preferred to recruit engineers with ten to fifteen years of aerospace expertise to jump-start the operations.

We discovered that Indian public sector units (PSUs) had a vast amount of skilled and experienced talent waiting to jump ship and take on roles that offered better career prospects and commensurate salaries to boot. Companies such as Infotech presented them with just the kind of opportunities they were yearning for.

We recruited scores of highly competent professionals from PSUs and complemented their domain knowledge and engineering orientation with the freedom to develop a number of practice areas at Infotech. In an informal conversation, a senior practice leader who had spent twenty years with us chuckled over how he was hired. He told me: 'Initially it was confusing when I received the job offer. In the follow-up discussion, the hiring manager asked me to develop an organization chart that was best for the practice. It was great fun. I had never imagined that I'd be able to decide my own area of expertise and develop the team.' The individual concerned ended up building a team of over 600 people.

Some of these hires cited interesting reasons for joining Infotech. One of them, who joined us in 2001 and is still with us, shared his feedback: 'In July 2001, I was offered a position of project manager in Infotech. By this time, I had a similar offer from GE. Both the offers allowed me to work for global leaders in aircraft gas turbine engines, which I always aspired to. While GE was the fifth-largest company globally with $130 billion revenue, had an enviable reputation of being a great engineering company and joining it required no relocation, Infotech was a little-known SME in India with a modest $20 million revenue and required me to relocate to Hyderabad. The contrast of the choices could not have been sharper.'

'During this time, I was invited to visit Infotech in Hyderabad on a fully paid trip to see the work being done and interact with key leaders. I took the free tour. As I was wrapping up my visit, I met Gopal Krishna Tadanki, the then vice president of HR. Sensing my dilemma of GE vs Infotech, he offered his wise counsel. "Raj, it's not important how significant the company is to you but how significant you are to the company and what opportunities you have to make a difference. This should help you make the decision."'

'By the time I reached home in Bangalore (now Bengaluru), the decision was made. I joined Infotech in October 2001 and have never looked back since. I am fortunate to witness the company grow 33X in twenty years and derive immense personal and professional satisfaction by being part of it. I am not sure if I could have achieved the same had I picked the safe choice twenty years back.'

This new breed of aerospace recruits competed fiercely in all the seven module centres (each handling one engine sub-system) of the Pratt & Whitney account, vying to head them and its delivery function. This set a healthy template for performance and percolated to the rest of the organization.

Pratt was a big brand, and it definitely helped to attract the best talent in the country, but our recruitment story did not end there. Every time we launched a new vertical business—rail transportation, nuclear power, off-highway vehicles or medical technology—we had to entice domain experts from established enterprises in the sector.

Even as our reputation as an engineering-oriented outfit grew, we had to give a unique thrust to our core skills. Whilst other employers converted engineers from every specialization into coders, we built specializations in geospatial, mechanical, aerospace, medical technology and electrical engineering. Infotech stopped hiring generalists and started recruiting specialists and subject matter experts.

We cross-trained associates so that they could switch between projects in various domains. For instance, one of our managers took rotations through six engagements even as he moved up the vertical hierarchy. He started as a senior engineer and became operations lead in a period of fifteen years! The gentleman then pushed a rotational model that trained mechanical engineers across domain areas. As a sponsor of such rotations, he demonstrated credibility. Along with automation, these initiatives resulted in impressive outcomes, especially around efficiency and quality, and our staff compared with the industry's best. We created a continuous pipeline of resources, and our projects never suffered from a shortage of skilled workforce.

Once we had people on board, we started sharpening role definitions in line with the company's mission and goals, cascaded them as SMART (specific, measurable, achievable, reasonable and timely) targets and introduced the 'measure to manage' concept in our people practices. Associate assessment was rigorous, process-oriented and mature. Even though our salaries did not match multinational remunerations, we continuously benchmarked ourselves against competition and reworked our compensation and rewards model. We focused on cash and non-cash methods to recompense our employees, which brought about a positive change in how the job market perceived Infotech. Retentions improved, particularly when people spent three years or more with the company. But we continued to witness a drift at the lower levels, particularly as newer players entered the market.

Undeterred, we always acknowledged associates were pivotal to the company's success, and ushered in stock option schemes immediately after we went public as an expression of our fairness. We were one of the first few companies to do this in India.

In 1999, the company set up the Infotech ESOP Trust and allotted shares to it. We evolved a scheme to issue restricted stock units (RSU) at face value instead of market value, writing off the difference as cost to company. We implemented several stock-option plans thereafter to retain and reward associates for their performance and contribution. On the eve of our twenty-fifth anniversary in 2016, Infotech again issued RSUs to all eligible associates. More recently, in 2021–22, the company launched another RSU scheme by purchasing shares from the market, banking them in a separate trust and issuing them therefrom. Infotech/Cyient has spent Rs 900 crore over the years under the ESOP schemes.

These schemes resonated with many managers and added to the population that has completed ten to twenty years. This apart, we encouraged re-training, subsidies, salary advances and sabbatical options as reward mechanisms. Our consistent emphasis on 4Rs (recruit, retain, reward and retrain) gave birth to the twenty-five-year club.

But keeping associates happy is more than just providing them with incentives to stay on—it is also about viewing them as fellow humans and watching out for their needs. Take the case of Neeraja Vejendla, who joined the company in November 1995. Married in May that year, she was three months pregnant when she joined. Our office was on the sixth floor of Maitrivanam and her reporting time was 6 a.m. The elevator in the building was often out of order and there was no security around to help. I bumped into her once on the staircase and noticed her difficulty. I was appalled—even more so—as there was no easy way out. Elevators in Maitrivanam fell under government preserve—which meant cutting a swathe through endless bureaucratic barriers.

But I was on the warpath. There was no way I would allow an expectant mother in my employ to endanger herself and her future child walking up and down six floors! I took the matter to the Director, STP (Software Technology Park) Hyderabad, J.A Chowdary. Apparently, he was not equipped to deal with it at his level either, but he raised it with the Secretary, Department of Electronics (now Ministry of Electronics and Information Technology), Government of India, who helped us resolve the issue. It took weeks of chasing, but the building finally had a functional elevator!

As for Neeraja, she kept up with our business needs and continued to better herself. She had come to us straight after completing her diploma. Thereafter, she pursued BTech, MBA and Six Sigma Green Belt while managing work and her family that included two children. Throughout this period, she sacrificed all her weekends to improve her education and skillset. As she gained new skills, Neeraja was given a range of opportunities such as project management, customer management and resource management. She is currently working as a lead analyst in the business excellence team and is a proud member of the twenty-five-year club.

'I want to be a role model for my kids,' she once told me. Both her children followed her footsteps. Her son and daughter completed their engineering and interned/worked with Cyient before leaving the country for higher education.

While we rallied around associates who were loyal to us, we also opted to hit refresh and bring in lateral talent whenever we felt in-house expertise was absent or did not measure up to the opportunity. A standing example is how we got PNSV Narasimham (Nam), our current chief human resources officer (CHRO). By 2014, the company had morphed into a large organization, expanding into new verticals and locations and clocking revenues of over $350 million. The HR function needed to level up to be in sync with the transforming needs of the organization.

Ashok Reddy, who had been heading the HR function for about fifteen years at around that time, was inching towards his retirement, requiring us to plan the transition carefully. We had one of our business unit heads, Anand Parameswaran, head the HR function for two years before we brought Nam, a seasoned HR leader with extensive experience in establishing, growing and stabilizing large and complex workforces.

At the same time, Cyient was mindful of being flexible and inclusive in its hiring. When visa regimes tightened, we turned to local recruitments while many companies struggled. We hired from local community colleges to staff our requirements in areas like New England on the East Coast of the US and Tupelo in Mississippi. Unique apprentice programmes attracted local aspirants to work with us. We were one of the few companies that embraced the regulatory guidelines to ensure the business growth was fuelled by strong localization. In a way, not only did we correct our earlier approaches, we also set an example for much larger competitors who subsequently followed suit.

Employee Satisfaction: Crucial Conversations

Creating a great customer experience began at home, and an engaged and energized workforce was a powerful lever for a satisfying customer journey. Moreover, associate engagement was a vital link for company reputation and overall stakeholder value.

To underline the criticality of associates in accomplishing our mission, we communicated our aspiration at every internal platform and channel and established trust and alignment. The moment the company's strength crossed 100 associates, we started soliciting their feedback. Our first associate satisfaction survey took place way back in 1995 when I remember collecting 112 hand-written feedback forms at an all-hands meeting. They were pleased that the company was managed professionally, their salaries and benefits were paid on time, they were provided upskilling opportunities, and managers ensured personal connect. Some even stated that Infotech treated them as an extended family. The act of soliciting feedback and responding to it improved engagement as associates felt that they were being heard and acknowledged.

We took associate engagement a step further by introducing an integrated framework, INFOTOUCH, to facilitate holistic attention and support for associates. It brought in several initiatives through Internal communication and branding, such as New adventures, Fun@work, Outperform (high-performance work culture), Talent development, Opportunity (career growth), Unique work practices, Connect with managers and Health and wellbeing. Many of these initiatives were taken in response to associate feedback.

Several honours such as the Excellence and Chairman awards were instituted to accord recognition to associates whose contributions to the company had been extraordinary. Rigorous processes were put in place in the nominations, evaluation and selection of winners. The administrative load on the organization notwithstanding, transparency in conferring recognition to associates was tracked closely. They soon became Infotech's most coveted awards.

As the organization matured, we adopted more structured and nuanced approaches, seeking associate feedback during employment and after exit. To garner candid feedback and improve transparency in the process, we launched a third-party managed associate satisfaction survey (ASAT). This provided us with an accurate perspective of employee attitude. While we learnt from them, we also made them self-reflect, align with our values and change their behaviour and opt for objectivity while assessing the organization and their managers.

Response to associate feedback was initiated at three levels—team, function/CoE and corporate. These surveys became the essential stimuli in evolving policies, creating an inclusive culture and bringing about location-specific, business-specific and country-specific programmes. More importantly, they became the lead indicators for customer satisfaction and attrition and spurred us to take proactive measures. Our initiatives created a virtuous loop to improve ease of operations and levels of comfort for employees; today our associate surveys have response rates touching 85-90 per cent.

Management wisdom recommends formalizing structures as an enterprise expands, but in my view, having a semi-structured form often works well, as we experience better connect and greater responsiveness. Even today, with our increased employee strength and presence across continents, we adopt a policy structure that allows human interface. Exceptions to policies, and at times their lack thereof, are instrumental in making us face ground realities that are essential to understand the drivers of employee satisfaction.

'Fertile Training Ground'

Technology companies deal with rapid and sweeping changes in the business ecosystem. Uncertainty is part of the territory. Acceleration in globalization and emerging technologies continuously propelled us to acquire new and diverse skills and adopt new models of working. Moreover, as the organization moved up the value chain, our needs matrix changed. We added several capabilities across technical, project management, finance, marketing, HR and administrative functions. Adopting a growth mindset and focusing on learning and development became critical for continued business success.

At the turn of the century, Infotech was spending 13 per cent of its operating costs on training. Compared to many other organizations, this might have been small. However, the focus was to invest in training from an early phase (a practice that many organizations emulated much later). We were so successful that online feedback on employment portals started pulsating with discussions that revolved around Infotech being a 'fertile training ground'. To this day, Infotech alumni mention these trainings on social media.

As becoming a technology partner of choice for customers turned into a priority, defining an enabling employee framework became an imperative. We created a learning ecosystem to support high-performing individuals and exposed them to challenging opportunities. We recognized a continuous learning aptitude not as a 'nice to have' but a 'need to have' associate characteristic.

In every customer project discussion, apart from technical staff, we involved sales, marketing, finance, legal and HR associates right from the first day until project closure. The team's complementary skills and cognitive diversity enhanced our ability to solve complex customer problems.

Our teams had furious disagreements, but in closed rooms. When they walked out and got into execution mode, they proudly represented a united front to the customers. This approach helped associates appreciate business sensitivity in a way that was important for decision-making. They developed a sense of ownership, celebrated project success and took pride in customer delight. The team gained hands-on experience on the softer aspects of relationships, customer engagement, professional etiquette, collaboration, commitment and co-creation. This inclusive and participatory approach acted as a learning fuel for the teams. More importantly, this approach helped nurture sustainable innovation and made it the organizational fabric and culture.

For instance, we were once awarded an important multi-year project by a major aerospace client to architect, develop, test and deploy a piece of safety-critical software that controls the loading functions of a modern aircraft under development. This was a complex and challenging technical problem.

While executing the project, we followed our key precept of involving and empowering all relevant internal stakeholders at every stage. In one of the reviews, the client expressed concern that the aircraft programme was experiencing unexpected delays and asked us to accelerate and deliver the project ahead of schedule. Our team sprang into action and worked out innovative ways to accelerate the project delivery.

They did not stop there. And this is where I believe the collaborative power of an empowered organization kicks in. A young lady who handled the relationship management asked, 'What else can we do? Can we look beyond the project? How can we make a difference to the customer?'

The team proactively sought permission from the customer to review the entire control system in the aircraft programme. They discovered that the customer was working on a similar software development project for multifunctional display, but in a classic, time-tested, linear approach. During brainstorming sessions, the delivery team suggested that alternative models should be explored; the research team came up with a recommendation to consider a model-based automation platform for safety critical applications; and the finance team helped with the RoI calculation. Collectively, the team made a new pitch to the customer, and came up with a good case to accelerate the schedule of the programme. The customer was impressed beyond belief.

The team won the project and it remained a proud moment in their memory when the aircraft was finally delivered and certified. When I now watch these aircraft streak the skies delivering critical missions, I feel proud that our multi-stakeholder driven, inclusive, innovation-led approach has made a difference. And a long-lasting contribution.

Such continuous learning is as vital to individual career success as it is for company growth. For this reason, creating success paths for the professional development of our associates became a priority. We created numerous avenues to facilitate this. On-site opportunities became one such method. We gave opportunities to work at customer locations on a rotational basis and encouraged associates to move laterally into different functions and roles, especially at leadership levels. For instance, I encouraged Rajendra Velagapudi to cross over into an account management/business role after he spent a number of years in delivery function. 'If you wish to see yourself leading a business someday, you should be in front of the customers,' I told him. Having worn several hats thereafter, Rajendra currently leads Cyient's design-led manufacturing business as its MD & CEO.

More recently, we offered Pierre Carpentier, a high-potential associate leading a large delivery function for Pratt & Whitney-Canada, a chance to lead the delivery function of our newly carved out digital business unit. Such actions always have a domino effect. Pulling Pierre out of Pratt & Whitney Canada meant we had to identify someone within the group to take on his role and so on. We, however, managed to create a positive cycle out of the situation.

Professional development soon became an employee benefit that increased engagement and retention. Such interventions, although risky for the company, are done with the intention of imparting multidimensional skills. These well-rounded professionals took their learnings to their respective teams and over the years, expanded our capabilities and created a leadership pipeline in every business unit.

Developing Leaders

I have always wanted my successor to rise from the ranks of the company and have sought to ensure that all senior leadership positions, not just the top job, are taken over by eligible home-grown leaders who understand our ethos. As our engineering practice grew and spanned several industry verticals, we continuously discovered new roles and higher capabilities to fit in. While the existing leadership pool toiled to keep pace with our evolving needs, we recognized that a shortage of leaders could undermine our future growth ambitions. Developing new leaders and refreshing the capabilities and mindsets of those who were already associated with us was pivotal to the company sustaining speed and preserving its core while stimulating change and progress.

To this end, a leadership development framework—Infotech Leadership Qualities (ILQs)—was evolved to produce a pipeline of senior executives and a cadre of entrepreneurial leaders. We identified twelve desirable leadership qualities—four external-facing (adaptive to change, creating collaborative partnerships, customer leadership and global strategic mindset), four internal-facing (innovative thinking and acting, ambition for excellence, business acumen, self-confidence & decisive) and four personal traits (integrity and leading by example, technical/domain thought leadership, entrepreneurial ownership, building talent and teams). Internal communication and numerous workshops to create awareness enabled associates to imbibe these twelve qualities and their constituent desirable behaviours at proficiency levels that were impressive.

Recognizing first-time managers and managers of managers as the next-gen leaders, we invested in the expansion of their skill matrix. Structured leadership development programmes for every leadership layer were created, some in partnership with top business schools, to facilitate transformational learning and develop leaders capable of taking responsibilities in strategic roles across business units, functions and geographies.

All our leadership programmes were aligned to corporate strategy and challenged the assumptions and practices of participants to educate them on the nuances of new-age business. Individual career development paths and upskilling avenues for each senior executive were laid out. This, too, yielded great results.

While I endorsed and championed these L&D (learning and development) programmes, I was keen to ensure that these investments made business sense. As a consequence, our people champions constantly fine-tuned programmes to keep them closely aligned with our evolving business needs. I insisted on measuring the outcomes of these programmes. While it is never easy to quantify their results, we measured the directional outcomes to gauge the returns on investments.

For instance, we monitored the global and executive programme cohorts to gauge whether they developed into leaders who could handle P&L roles after completing the programme. Besides, these associates registered higher levels of engagement, satisfaction and retention.

Moreover, these programmes enabled a higher internal fulfilment rate for senior positions. A solid second and third line of leaders emerged from our ranks—successors who did not mirror existing capabilities. We fanned their ambition, even as they grabbed opportunities to run small businesses within the organization or moved on to senior roles.

For instance, N.J. Joseph, who joined Infotech as marketing manager in 1998, grew from challenge to challenge. He held diverse positions in sales, marketing, business development and P&L ownership and was closely involved in the company's acquisition and integration of businesses in the US, Europe and India. As chief strategy officer, he is currently helping Cyient execute 'services to solutions' growth and investment strategy.

Leadership development took on a new dimension when we consciously nurtured women into managerial and leadership roles. Acting on gender disparity reports, we started reviewing gender representation in the outcomes of appraisals. The HR team reviewed all promotions and in instances where there were obvious misrepresentations, we provided the necessary feedback to managers to reassess and correct the imbalances. We are gently trying to weed out what may be an unconscious bias against women. Industry players recognized and acknowledged the organic way in which women leaders began to take on organization-wide positions. Even as I write this, we are targeting a 10 per cent increase in women managers/leaders.

While leadership development has been a critical and continuing priority, some imbibed the learnings and found opportunities outside the organization so much so that we started questioning the soundness of the strategy. Were we justified in investing so heavily in learning and leadership development, only to lose them to others eventually? We ultimately faced the truth: continuous people development is an essential business imperative for technology companies and the reality is that there will always be people who will look for new opportunities.

While we recognized and rewarded high performers, the truth is that an organization cannot run only on them. Corporates and teams are also made of associates who may not be A+ players and do not have the ability to stretch or upgrade themselves. However, they are the loyal champions of the company and understand the pulse of the organization. We trust them and entrust them with roles that match their skills and compensate and reward them according to their performance.

Values FIRST

Entrepreneurs often presume that the success of a business venture is contingent on hitting the right idea, developing a good business model and putting certain fundamentals in place. But often, it is not the mission statement, next fundraise, top line and bottom line or employee handbook that guarantees long-term success. Enterprises are living organisms pulsating with the actions and emotions of the people who make them. It is their behaviour with fellow colleagues, customers, investors and society that underpins the organization's success; it is the value-based culture encouraging performance and an ownership mindset that defines the reality and quality of organizational life.

This philosophy guided my actions at Infotech. And I deemed it my responsibility to create such a culture right from the outset. Together with Infotech's stakeholders, I believed I could co-create something larger than I could alone. We communicated this aspiration relentlessly, drawing a significant alignment from associates in terms of their attitudes, actions and language. Values such as fairness, integrity, respect, sincerity and transparency (Values FIRST), which buttressed the beliefs, attitudes, behaviours and ultimately the organization's culture, became Infotech's lingua franca. Our actions were clear, consistent and visible with no scope for debate or compromise. There was no room for grey areas. I was prepared to give up profits and, in fact, did sacrifice them multiple times to stay within the contours of the values I believed in.

Since culture is shaped by the beliefs and actions of leaders, we made sure managers and senior executives reflected the company's values and became its strongest advocates. At Infotech every new associate undergoes an orientation on the values and expected behaviours.

I hold integrity and trust as key values in a relationship. There were instances when I walked senior executives out of the office when I found undeniable evidence that they had compromised on our values. On the other hand, I walked the extra mile on numerous occasions to support associates and their families caught in difficult circumstances. More recently, as COVID-19 assailed and disrupted our work locations, managers and leaders at all levels stepped in to assist colleagues to mitigate some of the hardships they endured along with their families.

Yet, at the end of the assessment period, what spoke for an associate was the results they produced and the company's numbers. One of the organizational values that is not so explicitly stated in Values FIRST but implicit in our actions is 'performance'. We reward performance, and plain loyalty has never scored over it, although it has provided our associates with a long rope. This virtue improved our sustainability quotient.

At the same time, we didn't stop at associate accomplishments. In the course of building up Infotech, associates became my extended family. Till the company's strength hovered at about 500 people, I attended the nuptials of all the associates who invited me even if I did not know them personally. We organized Infotsavs, our annual cultural get-togethers, bringing associates and their families together to express our gratitude. These most-awaited celebrations were a lot of fun with song and dance routines. Besides this, associates also performed skits, a number of them featuring Bill Gates in mythical situations. One amusing plotline was centred around Gates's marriageable daughter (again imaginary), with several software engineers vying to woo her to hilarious effect. One enterprising character changes his name to Thalupulu (doors), arguing that 'doors' would be the perfect fit for 'Windows' in building a strong future for Microsoft. This particular skit, naturally, was a runaway hit. As the organization expanded, Infotsav attendees ran into thousands. Logistics became a challenge but it was well worth it as it helped us maintain a personal connect with our associates and their families.

Organizational empathy also manifested as inclusivity with regard to gender, culture, race, and nationality. We were ruthless about nipping objectionable behaviours and unethical practices in the bud. At one point, a section of our associates complained about the growing clout of a particular language community in the company. I snubbed them and asserted that we recruited professionals for their merit and skills and valued their contributions without prejudice. While I have little tolerance for politicking and inefficiencies, language and gender are no measure of performance.

Working with a long-term and institutional view in an export-oriented business made us realize that diversity and inclusion (D&I) are business imperatives and growth drivers. Even when we were small, we managed a global workforce that reflected a mix of cultures and races. They came into our fold as partners first and later as associates through our acquisitions in Europe and the US. We demonstrated that diverse teams could leverage their varied knowledge and network benefits to improve performance and project outcomes. Even as D&I became a practice, Cyient created a board sub-committee to provide guidance and seriousness to inclusion efforts.

We promoted awareness on issues related to LGBTQ, specially-abled, generational/demographic diversity, unconscious biases and wellness. Inclusive policies such as paternal leave, expanded maternity benefits, free childcare facilities, healthcare and community services interventions fostered a more egalitarian outlook across the organization.

To ensure our D&I initiatives are effective, we created tangible goals and announced incentives and recognition for highly inclusive teams, leading to improved innovation, engagement and, more importantly, camaraderie and a sense of belonging. Values are not those that are splashed on posters. Employees have to relate to them on the ground and validate them. Letters such as Jan's reiterate my confidence in the values Cyient lives by—values that serve both the individual and the organization. In the course of my journey as an entrepreneur, this was one dimension I never overlooked. Values and people have been at the heart of my success in every venture I entered, every crossroad I took.

13

Strategy and Business Transformation

At the heart of every strategy is a string of choices, well-thought-out decisions and a number of actions to be undertaken to shape the desired future outcomes. For an entrepreneur, strategy begins with the idea or a concept for the new business. While this may help an entrepreneur to launch a start-up, a winning strategy is not solely an individual's choice or something that is done once in the life of a company. It is expansive, evolves over time, re-emerges periodically, involves countless decisions, some emergent and others deliberate, and affects several stakeholders. Strategy has varied ramifications and impacts all aspects of a business—product/services, customers, technology, capabilities, investors—and is influenced by the external environment of markets, trends and competition.

Expanding Footprint, Embracing Customers

When I incorporated Infotech in 1991, though my vision was to create a global engineering services company, we ran into a blind alley even before launching operations. The hurdle was not market potential or resource availability but market readiness—the engineering services market was not yet open to outsourcing.

I saw that I had three choices before me: to wait and watch; to start something completely unrelated; or choose a segment that was related to my vision. I decided to adopt a fit-for-purpose strategy that would enable me to capitalize on the market opportunity.

I had figured out that although engineering/CAD drawings and cartographic maps belonged to different disciplines and their representations and applications were distinct, the fundamental elements for building databases were similar and the software used was the same. I reckoned that if I built digitization capability and capacity, it would help us to build both engineering/CAD and mapping/geospatial competency at a later point. I opted for the road less travelled and began pursuing digitization of paper drawings/maps. This gave the company a strategic entry into the geospatial business and enabled it to bring scale to the enterprise fairly quickly.

When the partnership model gave us the initial business momentum but limited our value proposition and impeded our ambition for rapid growth, we contemplated our imminent priorities and questioned—How could Infotech improve its value creation. How could it own the customer relationships? How could it transform itself into a global business that was not susceptible to the vagaries of partners?

We weighed the choices before us—Should we make or buy? Should we launch sales operations in the markets we operated in and build from ground zero or embark on an inorganic strategy to gain a geographic footprint?

Weighing the options before us in each geography, Infotech thereafter set up a wholly owned subsidiary in the US in July 1999 to primarily engage in computer software and related services instead of GIS/geospatial; this was to ensure that the move did not threaten our partners but help us get our boots on the ground. At the same time, we pursued the buy route and went on an acquisition drive between the years 1999 and 2005. Infotech acquired Dataview Solutions in the UK in August 1999, which gave us a foothold in the UK geospatial business. We quickly followed it up by buying Advanced Graphics Software (AGS), a mechanical engineering software and services company specializing in 3D CAD/CAM, in Germany in 2000. These two investments gave us access to the European markets.

As these were the first acquisitions for me and the company, integrating the diverse cultures of these companies was taxing. Dataview had a very English, friendly, small and cohesive team. We had to struggle to move the team away from small commercial geospatial projects to large AM/FM mapping projects. This involved revamping the team with the right sales people to suit the new go-to-market strategy. AGS, on the other hand, was very German, closed and genitive. Martin used to be friendly and cooperative but gave no access to anyone below him. Language was a big barrier. Local regulations were an oft-repeated reason against change. We patiently tailor-made strategies to integrate Dataview and AGS. Dataview's integration into our fold was much faster than AGS but eventually both teams came around and became big contributors to Infotech's success.

By 2003, our experiences with our partners in the US made us believe that it was critical to acquire a local GIS/geospatial company to establish a stronger foothold. Moreover, our subsidiary team did not have a good understanding of the market or the domain. We bought VARGIS, a geospatial services business, in January 2004. The company brought us additional capability in cartography and photogrammetry and doubled the existing run rate of the geospatial services business. It released critical management bandwidth in the US, enabling us to increase focus on engineering services.

Subsequently, Infotech capitalized on TeleAtlas' confidence in its highly specialized offshore services partner and pitched to take over its India captive in 2005. By promising to replicate our own successful model in its Noida captive, we bought it and strengthened our global delivery model and expanded our services footprint; the move also helped us to fortify our position in the geospatial data and technology services market. The acquisition served as a high-return investment, Infotech gained scale and an expanded skill set that helped it to remain competitive.

These small, synergistic and successful acquisitions and alignments in a short window of six years gave us early beachheads, considerably improving Infotech's global visibility. They set the company up for growth. We maintained consistency in direction through this inorganic play with a clear understanding of our desired goals and a keen awareness of how to manoeuvre ourselves into a position of advantage.

Growth through Diversification

Entrepreneurs use a variety of techniques and processes to arrive at strategic decisions. While some rely heavily on instinct and intuition, others follow a highly formalized, rigorous and deliberate process using internal resources or external consultants. In the early stages, entrepreneurs may find themselves taking decisions reactively or reflexively. For instance, I did not know much about Pratt & Whitney when its team visited Hyderabad in 2000, nor had I envisioned becoming an aerospace services provider. This was also the case when Bombardier Transportation visited us in 2003 and awarded us a project in rail transportation instead of the expected aerospace assignment. We just laid out a grand vision for the company on the eve of Infotech's IPO in 1997 and said, 'Let us build an engineering services company.' We had limited domain knowledge and barely understood engineering services in aerospace or rail transportation, but we rapidly built our domain capabilities as we aligned with these anchor customers.

But as Infotech scaled the engineering business, witnessed rapid growth and grasped the huge potential in the sector, we were hit with a new realization: the company needed a more formal and structured method to define its identity and make decisions. To this end, we worked closely with Prof. Mrityunjay Athreya, a Delhi-based management consultant and professor at London Business School, in 2004–2005.

We asked existential questions such as who we were and what was our purpose, what we mean to our customers and what could make our businesses distinctive. We debated and distilled complex information, market dynamics and organizational merits to arrive at Infotech's vision, mission and goals. We articulated our vision statement of being 'a global leader in expert technology solutions'.

This forward-looking vision statement gave the company direction for its growth and allowed it to deliberately chalk out a set of aspirations that could motivate the management team and inspire associates while simultaneously elevating its brand value with customers and investors. It also generated commitment and drive by setting up what Jim Collins and Jerry Porras call in Chapter 5 (page 91) of their best-selling book *Built to Last* 'big, hairy, ambitious goals'.

The intent behind the vision statement encouraged us to explore the product design market and strategically expand the portfolio into new verticals such as nuclear power, automotive, off-highway vehicles and telecom in the next few years. Besides, we closed the gap between our resources and ambitions and created several new competitive advantages.

Scaling these vertical businesses again meant Infotech had to chalk out well-informed strategies. While we organically built the nuclear power business with Westinghouse as our anchor customer, we shelved the automotive sector when we recognized that we were late to that market. On the other hand, we built the medical technology and healthcare business organically by providing differentiated services and solutions. When lead generation and opening prospective customer doors became akin to clawing up a wall and every trick in the book had been exhausted, we chose the acquisition route in off-highway vehicles and telecom. Through our acquisition of Daxcon, the company gained domain capabilities and Caterpillar as a customer, while our investment in Wellsco won us AT&T as a client.

Our desire to build a diverse and sustainable business beckoned us into the high-tech/telecom sector, which could complement our highly successful mechanical engineering business and move us into the system-level product design space.

However, this was not a simple go-no-go decision as both the risks and rewards involved were substantial. We had to brace ourselves for a steep learning curve irrespective of the decision: to make or buy. We chose the buy route and acquired Time To Market just as the world witnessed the fall of Lehman Brothers and stared at the prospect of economic recession in 2008. We had to hold on to our new baby and nurture it to stability and eventually to growth.

We simultaneously embraced a number of organic approaches. These included identifying potential markets, building domain expertise and delivering to delight customers. A combination of organic and inorganic strategies, emerging and proactive strategies put the company on an accelerated growth trajectory between FY2002 and FY2012 when we averaged a growth rate of 35.5 per cent, year on year.

Our strategy to foray into electronics manufacturing with the acquisition of Rangsons Electronics in 2015 was not simple either. While it was imperative to address the complete product life cycle for our customers, we recognized that build-to-specification value proposition was challenging, while build-to-print was relatively easier. Sales cycles were longer and needed a lot of effort to gain customer confidence. Margins were thin and managing inventory was tough. We roped in an external consultant to evolve the growth strategy. It contributed in defining industry value propositions, evaluating internal capabilities, designing the go-to-market approach and helping to build initial momentum in an identified set of accounts. The capability made us industry-agnostic. Whenever we were given the design/specifications, we could manufacture for aerospace, rail, industrial, medical or telecom. We complemented this further by entering into aftermarket MRO services by acquiring GSE Asia from Pratt & Whitney. While the verdict awaits, this pivot positioned Cyient as a unique player in the market, providing end-to-end solutions.

Gaining Competitive Differentiation

The critical requirement for a company's success is its ability to create a competitive advantage. For this reason, enterprises often prioritize business strategy over corporate strategy. Yet at the same time, the two are intertwined. The scope of a firm's business has implications for the sources of competitive advantage, and the nature of its competitive advantage determines the range of businesses it can succeed in.

Infotech complemented its diversification strategy with appropriate operational strategies to compete in each industry and market it played. It implemented robust processes to execute organization and industry-level strategies. More importantly, the company communicated its objectives across the organization and created a pipeline of committed and aspiring leaders. Effectiveness of decisions has a high correlation to financial performance, so the firm continuously monitored performance and revisited these guiding statements several times, refining its strategy and sharpening its goals. Infotech also evolved meaningful ways to improve stakeholder involvement in each business vertical.

In the early years of the Indian outsourcing story, mature practices were few and far between. Customers preferred relationship-based business models. Quality, affordability and on-time delivery were primary expectations. Customers preferred vendors who could create a sense of comfort and confidence in the relationship. Back then, scale reflected in the size of the centres of excellence (CoEs) built for customers, whether they were board-level, strategic or single-source partners.

But business models were rarely single-source. One outsourcing vendor would be pressed into service for engineering, another for products and a third for product maintenance. Back then, product companies outsourced mechanical work to one vendor and electronics to another. We had many clients who took our support for the mechanical part of a product design, while sourcing electronics design from our competitors and executed the system integration themselves. Over time, customers began looking for partners to own the system integration piece.

As the client-side and vendor-side ecosystem matured, customers measured the value and return-on-investment (say, a 5 per cent or 10 per cent improvement in operations) outsourcing partners delivered. Long-term sustenance of business relationships became contingent to the value outsourcing companies passed on to their customers year after year through innovation in the product, process and service. Contracts were signed based on competence and not primarily on relationships. Relationships still mattered, but business models had changed.

The next step shift came when companies began operating in an environment underpinned by accelerated technology changes, intense competition along with volatility and uncertainty in the market. That demanded new business models to be a greater source of innovation along with products and services. Moreover, it became contingent upon enterprises to be flexible and redefine strategies continuously, and find new ways of gaining competitive advantage.

As the outsourcing scenario changed, Infotech demonstrated its value and differentiated itself in five ways. The first was trust. Infotech proved, time and again, that we were a trustworthy partner to our customers. Winning customer confidence empowered us to explore adjacencies that allowed us to move up the value chain, and in some cases even challenge the customers in spirit. Our ability to protect intellectual property (IP) and allow customers to keep the IP generated further enhanced customer trust.

The second was our ability to invest. Once we saw an opportunity, we went all out and invested in building or acquiring infrastructure, technology and laboratories. We set up development centres in East Hartford-Connecticut, Dallas-Texas and Clearwater-Florida in the US, and Prague in the Czech Republic. We expanded our geographical footprint within India to tier-2 and tier-3 cities including Visakhapatnam, Kakinada, Warangal, Mysore and Noida. We acquired companies in North America, Europe and the Asia-Pacific.

Third, we recruited world-class talent and managed our global workforce well. Even when we were small, we thought and excelled as an international company. Our global integration experience was a critical factor in our transformation. If we were a purely Indian company trying to grow organically, it would have taken us twice as long to achieve what we did.

The fourth element was our ability to build up relevant domain expertise. We hired subject matter experts who shared their knowledge and worldview with techno-savvy young engineers. When we brought domain and engineering expertise together, it created an explosion in value momentum. Tying these aspects together helped us move up the value chain rapidly when the opportunities arose. Along with an intense customer focus, we built a defendable moat that made us thrive against the competition—both domestic and outsourcing players who did onshore business.

Fifth was the intense focus on quality and innovation. Early on, quality deliverables became part of the DNA of every employee. I used to say that I hate this word called 'quality control' for I see quality as every associate's responsibility. In recent years there has been an enormous effort to bring innovation into every individual's DNA. Starting with a mundane concept called 'ideas tree', we introduced several initiatives to be innovative in every area.

This drive to differentiate ourselves gained momentum with Krishna taking on leadership roles, first as head of strategy and subsequently as president of engineering and chief operating officer. Through these roles, Krishna gained an extensive understanding of the business and envisioned end-to-end product development cycles with many customers. He strategized to push the company towards providing higher-order services.

On a Transformation Continuum

The economic recession that hit the world in 2008 had a massive impact on several verticals, especially between 2009–11. The aerospace sector remained an exception. Infotech's aerospace business which constituted about 50 per cent of revenues continued its growth until 2011 but witnessed a sudden dip in 2012. This forced us to review our over-reliance on the sector and revisit our long-term strategy.

I called a meeting of senior executives, Krishna among them. Desirous of creating a business that endured market fluctuations and industry cyclicalities, I deliberated the issue with my senior colleagues. 'We are creating and revising business strategies in the verticals periodically. But we seem to be missing the long-term portfolio approach to strategic decision making.' I paused, gazing around the table for a response.

'Yes, that is true. It's time to start looking across all Infotech's businesses, to analyse how they impact each other so that we can determine how to create the most value five or seven years ahead,' Krishna concurred.

'So, how do we create most value? How do we make sure Infotech is resilient and future-ready?' I shot back, encouraging my executives to articulate their ideas on the subject.

'We need to create an entity within Infotech that brings a holistic view of all the businesses. Such an entity can work to optimize human capital, organizational structure, governance, while balancing the trade-offs between risk and return across the firm,' Krishna responded.

'There are a number of teams within Cyient that are working every day, every month to achieve the quarterly results. The new team should focus on the long-term without worrying about monthly/quarterly targets. The team should have the ability to visualize the technology market, evolve a blueprint in line with our mission, create enabling action plans and guide the entire organization,' I said, giving a directive. This was when we decided to create a corporate strategy function within Cyient under the leadership of N.J. Joseph.

The next step change in the journey came when we set ourselves the task of sensing the changing expectations in the market. Our external consultant pitched in to undertake market assessment, determine Cyient's right to play/right to win, prioritize industry-specific opportunities, determine investments, etc. Customer insights, experience and engagement at multiple touchpoints with several customers across different industries made us understand that customers were looking for strategic partners who could help them conceive-design-develop-deploy great products in a global environment. We brainstormed and asked: Can we bring new ideas and innovation to product design and development? Do we have the right to manufacture the products we helped to design? How can we support the performance and reliability of those products in the field? We deliberately began to envision changing customer expectations as new growth opportunities.

These reflections set us on the road to transformation. We knew we could not be everything to everyone while moving up the value chain. Even within one industry there is considerable segmentation and many differentiators, and an insane amount of domain knowledge is required to gain maturity. For instance, the domain knowledge within aerospace is hugely different between fuselage, engines, interiors, etc. We segmented the verticals and consciously decided to play in distinct specializations within them. We began to take on significant risks by engaging in value-based and shared risk-reward pricing models. We invested upfront, took complete ownership of the projects and got paid only when clients delivered the products to the satisfaction of their end customers.

This work culminated in articulating the Services, Systems and Solutions (S3) strategy in 2014. We acknowledged the opportunity to expand from core ER&D services to design and develop sub-systems/systems and thereafter support product manufacturing and aftermarket requirements to deliver integrated life cycle solutions. In effect, S3 allowed us to engage customers across the continuum of services, systems and solutions.

S3 offered customers a three-fold value proposition—our design, development and system engineering expertise to help them bring outstanding products to the market. Our electronics, mechanical and additive manufacturing expertise to build complex parts/products to specification. And our aftermarket solutions to support the quality, reliability and performance of their products, assets and services. S3 became an inflection point in the company's growth and a big part of our strategy to build a sustainable business.

Infotech developed capabilities across the S3 continuum in the aerospace, rail transportation and heavy equipment verticals, both organically and inorganically. The company adopted the plan-build-operate model in the networks and operations space and leveraged its track record of network planning and design, supporting network roll-outs to manage the S3 continuum. Between 2014 and 2017, the firm acquired three companies—Softential, Inc. (service management and service assurance), Invati Insights (data sciences) and Certon Software, Inc. (full product life cycle engineering services)—to expand technology capabilities. Thereafter, the company acquired IG Partners and most recently, Grit Consulting, both specialist consulting firms in energy and mining sectors to strengthen its technology consulting practice.

This strategy set the company on a business transformation continuum. First, we transformed Cyient from being a delivery-led service provider to a practice and domain-led company. Next, we differentiated ourselves as an end-to-end 'concept to solution' firm by creating an ecosystem with distinctive engineering, digital and design-led manufacturing capabilities. Further, the company strengthened its position as consulting-led, industry-centric, technology solutions partner that could lay out transformative roadmaps for its customers and execute the same skilfully.

This shift is visible in our investor reports too. Before 2015, we would report onsite-offshore revenue mix, utilization, free cash, and receivables. Today, our investor updates additionally report the nature of our solutions, solution to services ratio and number of patents filed, among other metrics.

The transformation to solutions is crucial since businesses become commoditized over time. With the commoditization of lower-end services, we moved into higher-order work to differentiate ourselves. At the same time, it was important to deliver commoditized work efficiently because it gave continuous scale and volume. The higher end of the value chain drives the lower end and not vice versa.

Over time, our higher-end capability became vital as it allowed us to make a difference to the customer and win credibility in double measure. Getting this combination between volume and value right was key and, as an organization, we performed this balancing act fairly well. Today, we follow a 70:20:10 rule. About 70 per cent of our work is volume- and process-driven, while 30 per cent is high-end and value-driven (20 per cent sub-system design and 10 per cent solutions). This keeps our pyramid and cost in control. The key lesson of S3 is not to lose focus on what we are good at. We are good at services and will continue to strengthen them while simultaneously expanding into solutions.

This transformation is both a natural progression and a well-thought-out strategy. The key was not to jump the gun. We did not want it to be a purely natural progression because competition could eclipse us. At the same time, we did not want to be a domain expert too soon because credibility is only built over time. It turned out to be an unprecedented need as well as an opportunity for the company.

Executing the Blueprint

Early on, we understood strategy is not a one and done effort. The real value emerges by building competitive advantage and enduring change through flawless execution. Business leaders often regard strategy execution as the tactical side of the business, something they can safely delegate. I differ with this perception. Execution is not just tactics, it is a discipline and a system. It is a set of behaviours and techniques that companies must master to gain a competitive edge. Leaders must engage in it deeply, or else, enterprises will experience a widening gap between the set objectives and the results delivered over the years.

While we were rigorous in implementing the strategy blueprint, I must admit in certain instances we were not meticulous enough. For instance, we embarked on our digital journey in 2014 with the acquisition of Invati Insights. But we did not move aggressively to implement an organization-wide digital strategy. By 2020, digital technologies had become the mainstay of every business as the world shifted dramatically during the pandemic and we found ourselves playing catch up. But once we cottoned on to the shift in the macro environment, we swiftly gathered the digital pockets within the organization and created a suite of digital solutions (IntelliCyient).

We ramped up our capabilities to accelerate the digital transformation of customers with Industry 4.0 technologies. Our decades-long engineering and geospatial experience across design, build, operate and maintain value chain in asset-heavy industries positioned us uniquely to create a non-linear value for our customers.

While S3 laid out the direction and goals, the AGILE framework gave us a scheme of actions to achieve predetermined outcomes year on year. AGILE clarified our strategy (Ambition), goals (Growth) and operating levers (Investment, Leadership, Execution). We also recognized the importance of becoming an 'AGILE' organization that embraces new ways of delivering value. Management cannot take centralized decisions and declare that the organization is culturally ready to work on the strategy. We acknowledged the need to deepen our culture of values and empower people. We needed a culture that was open to change, willing to take risks and accept ownership and accountability. We had to make the strategy clear and real, get stakeholder buy-in, identify and manage risks, learn from failures and reward success. Communicating the strategy was as important as making it. We grasped that explaining the strategy repeatedly and keeping people informed on how it was working would convince them of the company's intention. So, Joseph, Krishna and I spent the first few years relentlessly communicating to internal stakeholders about the long-term strategies, simultaneously imploring them to continue achieving quarterly targets. We put in significant efforts in realigning the culture to the evolving strategy.

While the business unit heads were upbeat about the S3 strategy, it was not an easy job to percolate the message to the 14,000-plus associates across the organization. Yet, we persisted in pushing the envelope with weekly strategy cadence calls in which we brainstormed, welcomed new ideas and created a culture of openness and inclusivity.

The biggest challenge, we realized, from an execution standpoint is always about how we balance the organizational capacity, the teams' capacity, structural capacity between what is to be done today, this month, next quarter, and yet continue to envisage the future and build capabilities. Take the case of the aerospace customer Pratt & Whitney/United Technologies. While a large part of our services to them constituted the mechanical side of aircraft design, the firm's vice president of engineering enlightened us that the aerospace industry was fast embracing the fly-by-wire (semi-automatic and computer-regulated system for controlling the flight of an aircraft) technology and that there was an imminent need for Cyient to ramp up its capabilities in the area.

It was a huge transformation—ensuring a large Pratt & Whitney team that was mechanical-focused was reskilled and prepared for the embedded electronics world! Yet, it was pertinent that we feed the voice of the customer into the strategy, and execute it to scale within eighteen months to make the business future-ready. The teams acted on the customer input in all earnestness and urgency. We convinced our engineers that products needed multidisciplinary skills and, consequently, there was a need for them to acquire additional skills. We embraced NASSCOM's 'Future Skills' platform to reskill/upskill/multiskill our engineers and this soon became an ongoing exercise.

As we launched ourselves on to the next growth phase with S3, we realized that Infotech as a brand offered no competitive differentiation. Our diverse offerings needed a name that tied everything we did together and created a distinctive brand image that was crucial for our success. So, we adopted the name 'Cyient'—a name that is truly representative of our character. With a new name, we sharpened our value proposition, established a visual identity, and nurtured our brand personality with consistency. We packaged our offerings and created sub-brands such as IntelliCyient (digital solutions suite), CyientifIQ (Innovation platform to develop new IPs and solutions), Cyient DLM (Design-led manufacturing) and Cyient Consulting to improve their positioning, overall brand recall and trust. Several initiatives such as branded merchandise, event branding around Cyient were done with great vigour. It was a very challenging transformation since Infotech was a very strong brand for the common people and replacing it with Cyient was not easy. But we have come a long way.

Another important aspect of S3 are our people and leadership. While reskilling the existing staff, we also hired extraordinary talent from the industry. People who aligned with our values, whether in sales, general management or operations. These people understood the business, were close to our customers and spoke their language. This reinforced our behaviours, culture and energy. We aligned our sales group with the vertical industry dynamic. Traction followed.

To bring vigour into strategy execution, Infotech expanded the scope of people initiatives, stepped up its engagement, introduced inclusive policies and leadership programmes, and continuously matured structures and processes to enable collaboration. We broke down organizational goals across functions and business units and evolved measurable outcomes for executives, which became part of their annual KRAs. It enabled AGILE to work as an anchor, increase ownership at every level and help align the organization to a growth mindset.

Infotech then established a customer innovation centre and launched a 'New Business Accelerator (NBA)' to incubate leading technology solutions. Its purpose was to innovate and develop new products and solutions at the 'edge of the organization'. We brought in Dr Jan Radtke (a customer whilst at Bombardier Transportation) to head NBA. Working with the business units, Jan identified customer demand that could be addressed by investing in emerging technologies. The opportunity to innovate and become internal entrepreneurs attracted associates from across the organization who came to NBA to help translate ideas into market reality. Those ideas included drone/LiDAR-based asset inspection and precision agriculture solutions, transmit-receive modules for radar systems, dual USB charger, 3D geospatial platform, AR/VR based inspection and maintenance and (in collaboration with a leading eye institute) a portable vision-screening device.

By placing resources and investments in a dedicated unit, we could focus intensely on innovation and R&D that would deliver new technology-led offerings. As it evolved, we also had to think about the path back from NBA to the business units and customers. While innovating at the edge was fundamentally the right approach, we realized we would eventually have to fold NBA into the core organization structure to ensure ownership, accountability and results. With that in mind, NBA was integrated with the digital business unit in 2020.

This strategy gave us a proper structure to address evolving opportunities and increase our relevance and value with customers. We strengthened sales from new clients and adopted a 'large deals' approach to create scaled, multi-year engagements with customers. Large deals reflect multi-sector and multi-threaded themes that combine several core horizontal capabilities into offerings across many verticals. For example, our asset management, location-based solutions and enterprise network offerings bring together digital, communications and geospatial capabilities that focus on the utilities, telecom, mining and energy verticals. Large deals are enabled through a go-to-market team structure that brings together the solutioning, sales and delivery resources to engage around specific customer opportunities.

This resonated at many levels across the stakeholder community. Cyient began to be viewed as a company that helped in 'designing tomorrow together'. We reinforced our long-standing commitment, worked closely with our customers to develop innovative solutions and solved complex problems. By doing so, we have positioned ourselves as a strategic partner and industry leader.

Strategy is about thinking inside-out and outside-in. An inside-out strategy is contextual to the organization, its competence, customers and experience. When applied to an existing vertical, it limits the enterprise's ability to think through all the implications. The outside-in brings unfettered, dispassionate insights about the market landscape, macro environment and the competition that helps assess what a firm has, what it can build on, how it can find adjacencies and expand. In most cases, Infotech/Cyient discovered and played at these two intersections.

It became an effective game plan that defined the organization and performance.

Ever since we articulated the S3 strategy in 2014, the board committee guided us on strategic planning and execution (subsequently expanding its charter to include customer engagement). Whilst not a statutory requirement per the Companies Act, the strategy committee provided valuable 'outside-in' perspectives and guidance.

For instance, Alain de Taeye of TeleAtlas/TomTom, who was a member of the strategy committee since its inception, made Cyient visualize the future auto industry and the trends in mapping. Alain said, 'The future belongs to advanced driver assistance applications (ADAS) and autonomous vehicles, which means the vehicle becomes the driver. When that happens, mapping decisions become a lot more important. Maps need to be high-definition to precisely localize themselves and to accurately navigate on a lane-level basis. They need to have inch or even centimetre-level accuracy and a high environmental fidelity—showing the exact positions of pedestrian crossings, traffic lights/signs, barriers, vehicular traffic and more. This makes it imperative for Cyient to focus on building automation that uses deep learning and machine learning techniques.' Alain's pitch made us revisit our geospatial strategy and make course-corrections.

John Paterson, CEO of Rolls-Royce Marine Engines, UK, another member of the strategy committee, spoke passionately about the future of the product design market. He said, 'Tomorrow is all about maintaining existing assets and not creating new ones. If an aerospace OEM builds 60000 engines, each lasting for sixty years, a service provider like Cyient must focus on the 60000X60 years lifespan of the engines and how to optimize their efficiency.' This made us deliberate even further about asset optimization, MRO, Industry 4.0 and technologies such as IoT and AI.

The beauty is that the strategy committee diligently meets the Cyient teams every quarter before the board meeting to debate on issues that are critical to Cyient's growth aspirations. Since its inception, all the board members and the business unit leaders adhered to this cadence in spirit, not just because it is one more meeting. The committee engages in brainstorming sessions and intense debates while reviewing the strategy execution by the business units. Through constructive confrontation and valuable guidance, the committee influences the teams' thinking and approach to find solutions.

Alain encouraged our team to build a long-range financial model (LRFM) to calibrate the progress and outcomes of S3 execution. Explaining the concept, Alain said, 'While formulating a strategy, companies often make growth forecasts that are too optimistic. It is prudent to adopt a "strategy-financial model-budget" approach to ensure budgets are in line with execution and remain aligned as the company continues to revise and improvise the strategy over time.' Designed as a three- to four-year rolling plan, LRFM helped us capture various growth scenarios, weigh the risks and adapt the growth model to evolving market realities.

Another strategy committee member, Som Mittal, who has held several leadership positions including chairman and president of NASSCOM, got us to ask some hard questions about our inorganic strategy. 'View inorganic growth as a strategic option and not as an opportunistic one,' he encouraged. 'And don't forget to focus on targets that fit the S3 strategy.'

Drawing on his own experiences, Som cautioned us. 'A team involved in an M&A transaction can eventually cross a threshold where an emotional need to get the deal done tends to replace its initial objective assessment. Red flags in due diligence become less of a concern, and the team tends to defend them as problems that can be managed post-acquisition. Valuations are justified even when they seem generous to industry multiples, he warned.

Som advised us to bring a more independent and dispassionate view to target evaluation, wherever it was feasible. We heeded Som's counsel and involved a reputed consulting firm when we wanted to acquire an aerospace ER&D services company and a wireless communication service provider. Its objective feedback influenced our decision to exit those transactions.

Vision, mission and strategy are about business ambition and a belief system an entrepreneur builds into the organization. In the year 2000, when we made our first overseas acquisition (Dataview Solutions), it was with a strategic view to build a global business and not rely on subcontracted work from our sales partners. We wanted to be the masters of our universe.

It is this belief system that we bring to the organization as Cyient undergoes yet another significant transformation, even as I write this memoir. What is our reason for being? To apply technology imaginatively to solve problems that matter. Cyient's vision is bold and clear, and it is deeply committed to living its purpose.

And strategy is about creating a blueprint to live that purpose. Cyient imagined a few things in 2014 when it articulated its S3 strategy. Between 2014 and 2022, the world had witnessed shifts in globalization, digital disruption, business model disruption, COVID-19 and the work-from-home paradigm.

Undeterred, our strategy function continuously evaluated the unfolding business reality and course-corrected the action plans to make the organization more resilient and future-ready. If someone asks me, 'Is Cyient better placed in 2022 than it was in 2015?' I would vociferously say, 'Yes, Cyient is more resilient in 2022. Organizations are living entities that continuously evolve, grow, change, scale, realign and transform. And today, there is a visible shift in the energy of the company, and it is more robust in terms of talent, technological competency, customers, market awareness, financial vigour with focus on profits, predictability, risk management, and ability to respond quickly—essential characteristics that assure the sustainability of the enterprise.'

14

Money: Thrift Is a Good Revenue

It is rare to find me flying business class on domestic flights or first class on international flights. At home, no extra lights are switched on. We even have a stringent protocol for driveway lights at dusk. I live and swear by the old adage 'waste not, want not'. In all my meetings, it is customary to serve just tea and biscuits. I invest or spend when I am convinced, and not to keep up with the Joneses. I spend where I spot optimum returns, long-term functionality and a very comfortable living. I prefer simplicity and elegance to ostentation. I respect the wealth I have built so painstakingly since I learned early on that money does not grow on trees. One has to earn it, in the right way, without cutting corners and by staying on the right side of the law.

I learned this philosophy of monetary prudence from my mother and maternal grandfather. They hailed from a middle-class family and were honest, religious, God-fearing, caring and, most importantly, law-abiding people. They lived frugally, were generous to charity and were not given to avarice. They did not covet property that belonged to others preferring instead to invest carefully and created family wealth on their own terms. Their way of life shaped mine.

Raising Capital

Vulture Capital: I carried this outlook to my workplace every day. I took a huge risk when I became an entrepreneur. I invested Rs 20 lakh, my entire savings at the time, as equity to launch Infotech's operations in 1991. Some friends and a few members of my family pooled in another Rs 5 lakh. Some start-ups successfully bootstrap (self-fund) themselves, but they are the exception. I certainly needed more capital.

I prepared a financial plan, approached the venture capital (VC) arm of the Industrial Development Bank of India (IDBI) and managed to convince the bank to extend a loan. IDBI sanctioned Rs 97 lakh as venture debt, but it came with stringent conditions—to the point of being punitive.

I agreed to an 18 per cent interest, which was the norm for short-term borrowing in the early 1990s. To cover its risk, IDBI charged another 3.5 per cent of revenue (not profit) as royalty. On top of that, it pegged Rs 67 lakh as a floor (with no ceiling) on the royalty, to be paid over five years. If I fell short, the balance would convert into debt. Dealing with such uncertainty and risk must be second nature to an entrepreneur, I thought, ready to embrace both. I accepted all the conditions set by IDBI after prolonged negotiations, convinced I could not wait as I needed to get the business off the ground and had very few alternatives. 'I'll just go along with IDBI. I'll miss the opportunity if I spend too much time trying to raise funds,' I told myself.

When I explained IDBI's terms to my friends and well-wishers, they quipped, 'You seem to have misunderstood the word "venture". This appears to be "vulture capital", and not "venture capital".'

There are numerous avenues to raise capital today. But in the early 1990s, capital markets in India were not mature and lacked variety. Private equity, as an asset class, was conspicuous by its absence. Banks had a low-risk appetite, while the venture capital industry was nascent, short on funds and expertise. There were only two VC funds in the country—one led by IDBI and the other by ICICI.

Fundraising is always arduous, complex and often humbling. It devoured all my time and creative energy. But that is the path all entrepreneurs must tread to build a company unless they have deep pockets. This experience taught me that an entrepreneur should never raise capital in desperation. Investors ride roughshod with unpalatable terms and conditions. I implemented this early lesson all through my journey as a businessman.

The seed capital helped me kick-start the business, with software exports as my primary focus. Though Infotech began gaining traction, I held costs under control, so the company was profitable and had enough cash for IDBI's quarterly pay-outs. I paid seven instalments and Rs 67 lakh in royalty and built the company's creditworthiness. At the same time, our business success exposed the flaws in the deal structure. Since IDBI was entitled to a percentage of Infotech's sales revenue, the unanticipated growth in sales resulted in ludicrously high payouts to it.

This was in the nascent days of early-stage investing in India, and IDBI seemed to have taken the view that Infotech was the rare stud that had to make up for the other duds in the IDBI VC portfolio. After several discussions, I subtly threw a googly and communicated the 'possibility' that this structure could force Infotech to float another company.

I wound up my meeting with the general manager of the VC Division of IDBI saying, 'By signing the (earlier) agreement, you locked me in your floor (twelfth floor) and all but asked me to find my way out of the building. The only way out is to jump from the twelfth floor, which, by the way, will lead to unintended consequences not only for me but also for you. You can't afford to let the goose which is laying all those wonderful golden eggs for you quarter after quarter, disappear.'

Good sense prevailed and IDBI agreed to merge the floor and ceiling and remove the royalty. It wanted me to return the favour and asked Infotech to convert Rs 15 lakh of debt into equity. I agreed without a second thought. I put forward a counter request for an additional Rs 1 crore debt for business expansion. Since Infotech's credibility was high, IDBI saw it as a good risk and obliged me while bringing down the interest percentage by 150 basis points. This helped the company clamber to the next stage of growth, seamlessly.

When I apprised my financial advisor Mahesh Madduri of IDBI's proposal to convert Rs 15 lakh into equity, he made me understand that a debt was less expensive in the long run than giving up equity. 'Equity costs a portion of the business forever,' he warned and added, 'You'll be sacrificing future profits indefinitely to meet a short- to mid-term need. If the opportunity is right, a debt is often a better choice as the interest cost reduces taxable profit and, naturally, tax expenses also go down for the start-up,' Mahesh coached me.

I realized my folly, but not being a person who could renege on a promise, I converted the Rs 35 lakh retained earnings into equity and broadened the equity base from Rs 25 lakh to Rs 60 lakh. I then extended the Rs 15 lakh equity over the Rs 60 lakh base.

I learnt a few things the hard way.

Capital needs are inevitable in a start-up journey. This experience taught me to be prudent and study how much money to mobilize, in what format (debt or equity), from whom and under what terms only after analysing the business need. Besides, I learnt to be mindful of the fact that fundraising events create commitments that I, as the founder, must honour irrespective of the funding instrument. This made me accept the wisdom in inculcating financial discipline and prioritizing all financial obligations.

By 1995–96, Infotech had surplus cash. We started entertaining inter-corporate deposits in bundles of Rs 25 lakh each. A few of them defaulted on repayments. I thought it was poor judgment on my part, so I forfeited my salary until the principal returned.

Infotech Goes Public: In the second quarter of 1992, several irregularities in securities transactions of banks and financial companies came to light. Also known as the Securities Scam or Harshad Mehta Scam, the fraud shook the Indian stock market and the banking system. In response, the government acted swiftly and promulgated the Special Court (Trial of Offences relating to Transactions in Securities) Act with several draconian provisions. Stock markets panicked and the index fell sharply, representing a market capitalization loss of Rs 1 lakh crore.

The government put economic liberalization and banking sector reforms on hold temporarily. SEBI (Securities and Exchange Board of India) deferred sanctioning private-sector mutual funds. These developments acted as catalysts for stock market reforms, policy changes and strengthening of rules and regulations. The government empowered SEBI to launch a series of initiatives to regulate listed and unlisted companies, IPOs, fraudulent trading activities and collective investment schemes. It established the National Stock Exchange (NSE) in 1993, which commenced technology-based trading and dematerialized shares, introduced several investor-protection measures and brought in much-needed transparency.

Since Harshad Mehta had milked money from public issues, new ones that were floated were regarded with suspicion. Publicly traded companies came under severe stress, often attracting undue indignation from regulators. In many instances, there were no takers for public issues and they had to be devolved. As law enforcement agencies unearthed new facts, the scam, it turned out, was much larger. By 1996, speculation was rife that the government might forbid new IPOs for five to seven years.

By mid-1996, Infotech was profitable quarter on quarter and not hamstrung for cash. We were repaying IDBI promptly, often ahead of time. We did not require funds for the existing GIS/geospatial and CAD business. Nonetheless, we needed growth capital to foray into engineering consultancy and double software and product development capacity.

By then I had figured out that the fresh growth capital would have to be sourced from another avenue. Those days private equity funds did not exist in India. The handful of VC funds such as IDBI facilitated limited financial and strategic support. I weighed my options. Initially we thought of going through the OTC exchange based on the advice of one of our auditors. But we dropped the idea after a friend recounted the bad run he had had with OTC. The only viable option that remained open to us was public markets and the IPO.

We assessed the benefits an IPO would bring to our start-up—greater visibility, improved trustworthiness and an enhanced corporate image. We knew international customers would find it safer to build a relationship with a public company. Improved trustworthiness would attract better talent and business partners.

Infotech had hitherto made a limited impact working through partners in various geographies. An IPO would undoubtedly mean robust financials with improved liquidity to chalk out an overseas expansion plan. Going public would also enable us to benchmark our operations against other public companies in the industry.

While we recognized the benefits, we were conscious that the public-company status had a downside. First, we had to consider the enormous effort, management time and cost of going for an IPO and the recurrent overheads post-IPO. IPO also entails increased disclosures, loss of privacy and accountability to a much broader universe of stakeholders, analysts and regulators.

It warranted disclosing our top-line, profitability, capital structure, workforce and infrastructure details, process and quality certifications, customers and business prospects. We also had to open up about the company, including the risks associated with the business. Among other things, we had to disclose that Infotech was in litigation with BayState Technologies in a Boston–Massachusetts court. We deliberated if we were ready for such public scrutiny.

Apart from the loss of stake in the company, we had to brace ourselves to deal with the burden of shareholders' expectations without hindering the management's freedom to make decisions, especially for the long term. It is always a trade-off between diversification gains versus the benefits of private control. The decision to go public calls for more than a straightforward comparison of immediate costs and benefits.

We reviewed our strengths and weaknesses. Our core GIS/CAD business was strong; Infotech had a consistent record of growth and could sustain growth and shareholder value in the future. It had a strategic vision to become a globally recognized engineering services company. We also assessed our operational readiness. Our management teams, processes, accounting and auditing systems, and governance structures were stable enough to live under the constant pressure of meeting investor and regulator demands.

It is a highly complex exercise that has no foolproof formula. Moreover, those were the days when people believed that if entrepreneurs could take their company to the public, they had arrived! Only a tiny fraction of entrepreneurial companies reached this bar post-independence or reached a point where an IPO was necessary or even feasible.

Another big question we contemplated was whether it was too early for our five-year-old start-up to go public. Often, if a company files for an IPO too soon, it may not make the most of its potential. And if it is too late, it may miss a bullish investment market. IPO is a transformational process, not just a financing event.

Added to this dilemma, the Congress Government headed by PV Narasimha Rao had been voted out in May 1996 and had been replaced by a rainbow coalition of multiple parties headed by the relatively unknown Deve Gowda. The political and economic situation in the country had turned gloomy and by December 1996, the BSE Index had hit a three-year low. Capital markets faced liquidity crunch and, consequently, corporate performance turned poor.

To me, IPO remained the only way to raise money so that we could proceed with our growth plans (and also gain chalk for my own destiny in a more independent manner, i.e., by moving past the IDBI era). So, I laboured on and cajoled IDBI to enable Infotech to embark on its IPO voyage. Convinced that it had to back an asset which had a robust financial run in the past and had good potential, IDBI launched the process despite the volatile markets. After intense deliberations, we decided to raise Rs 4.65 crore through an initial public offering (IPO). The issue was scheduled to open for subscription on 17 March 1997.

Despite thinking through ahead of time, the public-issue process was not easy. We had significant surprises in store, not all of them pleasant. People did forewarn that it would distract me from business, and I agreed. For our lean finance department, it was a huge undertaking. By the time we recognized the magnitude of effort that an IPO warranted, it was too late. So, we persisted and forged ahead.

We secured approvals from SEBI, the regulatory authority, and prepared the IPO prospectus and filed it with the registrar of firms. We convinced the bankers that the Infotech IPO merited a premium of Rs 10 and set the issue price at Rs 20. Considering the prevailing scepticism against IPOs in the country, IDBI offered a safety net option to subscribers, with monthly buy-back rates, for fifteen months from the date of allotment and protection against any downward risk. This was the first time in the history of an Indian IPO that an investment banker gave a buy-back option to subscribers.

We reserved about 25 per cent of the public issue for institutional investors. IDBI claimed the entire stake and kept other potential institutional investors at bay. When they sought IPO application forms, IDBI staff claimed that it had run out of them!

Fortune favours the brave and P. Chidambaram presented his dream budget at the end of February 1997 and the markets boomed temporarily. Infotech's IPO opened on 17 March and was oversubscribed (1.56 times) despite the challenging capital market conditions. The issue closed on 24 March and was listed in three stock exchanges—Hyderabad, Chennai and Ahmedabad—as per the prevailing regulations (delisted after a few years due to change in regulations and low trade volumes). Infotech was listed in BSE thereafter based on trade volumes and finally in NSE. The valuation at the time of listing was about Rs 11 crore. Soon the markets plunged again as political instability worsened, eventually leading to Prime Minister Deve Gowda's resignation in April 1997.

IDBI tracked us each month and monitored if the stock price grew by 12 per cent annually. If the stock price was lower and someone turned in, they could approach IDBI for the guaranteed returns. Infotech stock price always traded higher than the threshold. A few people even tested the safety-net option to know if IDBI would pay them back.

In hindsight, the IPO was a bold move. While we certainly benefited from the fundraise, one question that often nags me to this day is—'Did we go in for public issue too early?' Had we waited for a few more years, we could have gained a better valuation and premium. From one standpoint, we diluted too early. But I never felt unnerved in taking the company public. Public companies are under constant pressure to see their stock price move up. I do not disagree. But I never worried about Infotech's price fluctuations because I never intended to sell the stock away. An entrepreneur can only ensure that the company's stock is profitable for investors by focusing on business and reporting remarkable growth and performance. We single-mindedly aligned with our strategic vision and never compromised on it for stock market gains.

Once the public issue closed, the company became debt-free and our relationship with IDBI started slowing down. In 1999–2000, during the dot-com bubble, Infotech's share price sharply rose to Rs 1860. IDBI dumped significant Infotech stock and made big money. By FY2007, IDBI had divested completely from Infotech Enterprises. The handsome returns absolved the IDBI Venture Capital Fund from its previous poor investment decisions.

This fundraise enabled Infotech to take a leadership position in providing CAD/GIS solutions in all five continents. Close on the heels of the IPO, we launched engineering services and also diversified into business software solutions by acquiring a local software company (SRG Infotech). Soon after, we made two overseas acquisitions—Dataview Solutions in the UK and Advanced Graphic Software (AGS) in Germany. Infotech's IPO augured well as it marked the beginning of a long-lasting growth phase.

Private Equity: The first decade of the new millennium presented many macro and microeconomic changes that refined and redefined how enterprises did business. The perception of value creation continuously evolved with the rising importance of emerging markets and the movement of skilled workers, capital and technology. Investment began flowing into countries and asset classes where value is created and can scale.

A couple of years after Infotech went public, Ernst & Young (E&Y) approached us in 1999 with a private equity recommendation. Private equity partners bring in additional experience, influence and even market connections to fuel a company's growth as they have a vested interest in its success. Infotech was in no need of money, but I gave it a thought. I finally relented on the condition that the strategic investors would get business along with cash. This led to GE Capital, the financial arm of GE, investing Rs 16.40 crore in Infotech. Walden International joined GE. The latter opted for a convertible instrument with a clause to convert into equity within eighteen months. We agreed but asked for some guaranteed business in return. GE refused to make a commitment but assured us that it would do its best.

While the funds came from GE Capital, the business had to come from GE's operating divisions—GE Aerospace, GE consumer products, GE Power, etc. Individual GE divisions were already in multi-year service agreements with several Indian IT companies. We soon realized there was no scope for new business until the commitment cycles (three years typically) were complete. I made numerous trips to the GE headquarters and operating plants, hoping to win new business, but faced a dry run for eighteen months. The relationship went south for both parties.

I decided to return its money. GE was shocked. Infotech had enough receivables and given the strength of our balance sheet, Andhra Bank was ready to give us a line of credit. I borrowed from Andhra Bank and closed the investor relationship with GE.

By this time (in 2000), Pratt & Whitney was in town, shopping for an outsourcing partner. Infotech entered into a multi-year contract with Pratt & Whitney. The icing on the cake came within a few months when the firm cemented our relationship by acquiring a 15 per cent stake in Infotech and becoming a strategic partner. We went cash-rich and immediately repaid the outstanding loan.

This experience taught me that an entrepreneur should never borrow or raise capital from anyone eager to invest. Instead, one needs to be sagacious in onboarding investors, and bring in strategic investors who are likely to help scale the business by bringing volumes of work, best practices and mentoring (which was the case with Pratt & Whitney). Nonetheless, one had to be careful that strategic investors did not try to steer the company's direction and control pricing (which was not the case with Pratt & Whitney).

After Pratt & Whitney, we explored the strategic partner route once again in 2007 to support our expansion plan. This time we were a lot more prudent, and ensured there was a heightened focus on profitability and shareholder returns. We roped in General Atlantic Global as a strategic partner. In its selection, design of engagement and subsequent dealings, I persisted in making sure there were no compromises on long-term retention of associates as well as servicing of customers. There were times when the pressure to give more to investors and not leave enough for customer investments was intense, but we usually managed to side-step it with some dexterous handling. While General Atlantic's investment lasted only for about five years, we received promising customer breakthroughs and gained IBM and others as clients. That was the last instance we raised money in the thirty-year history of the company.

Raising money takes enormous bandwidth. It requires time and effort from entrepreneurs and their teams which they can otherwise invest in building their business. I consider fundraising a diversion from a company's core activity. We never mobilized funds as an ongoing exercise at Infotech. But when we did go for it, we ensured that business did not suffer.

Often, the financial comfort entrepreneurs gain after a fundraise makes them splurge. Entrepreneurs tend to change salary structures, upgrade offices and increase discretionary spending. The moment a public issue is complete, I have seen instances where a brand-new Mercedes-Benz is parked in front of the entrepreneur's house. This is a big no-no for me. The lifestyle of an entrepreneur or that of a company should not change as a consequence of raising capital.

Once entrepreneurs infuse capital from external sources, the company no longer belongs to them. They become custodians of public wealth. Whether funds came through IPO or private equity, I have always viewed new capital as an increased responsibility to investors. I used the financial comfort brought about by the funds as a lever to leap forth to higher levels of growth. It gave us opportunity and improved our risk-taking ability to build the business.

We made several promises to investors during the IPO. Adopting a long-term view, we became intensely focused on driving growth and exceeded investor expectations before expanding our salary structures, offices, or lifestyles. I took no salary or just a nominal amount in the first nine years of Infotech. From the year 2000 onwards, a substantial part of my salary came as a percentage of profits and not as a fixed salary. My priority was to preserve cash and continuously invest retained earnings in the business. We created detailed budgets year after year and made them our holy grail. My team often found a million reasons to cite why they would not be able to hit a budgeted number. Rather than worrying about the whys and wherefores, I preferred to unearth one compelling purpose to meet the targets.

Cashing In on Frugality

Launching a new business involves a host of decisions every day. Paramount among them is knowing what to spend on and how much. In the initial years, I had to provide for technology, salaries, infrastructure, marketing and several other aspects of the business from limited resources, often requiring trade-offs.

I chose to be a watchful spender. We shifted office from my home to Software Technology Park, Hyderabad, only after seeing clear signs of business growth. We conservatively forecasted the timeline for expected revenues and managed our costs accordingly. This enabled us to stay cash-positive.

We executed the projects without a glitch and made sure operations ran in a watertight manner. If the project estimated a requirement of fifteen persons, I would ask the manager to run it with a team of thirteen or fourteen to improve productivity. Senior executives understood the vision and values of the organization and cascaded them to the managers. Even in the boardroom, we maintained a sense of frugality and tradition. I am a purist when it comes to my values.

My sense of thrift, however, never led me to compromise on business needs. We got Price Waterhouse to undertake the enterprise's risk assessment multiple times in the first decade of the new millennium. Based on its findings, we brought about changes in the organizational structure and strengthened our Management Information System (MIS). Infotech was a small company but it implemented the best systems and processes with a long-term view to make the organization systems-driven. Co-workers were informed about the key strategy costs that were essential to stay competent and grow the business. They were also told how the returns would justify the investment.

As we scaled the business, expanding our people's capabilities and having specialists became important even in corporate finance department. For instance, N. Lakshmipathi, our finance manager, had been with the company since its inception. As we grew, we thought the company needed to upgrade its finance function. We brought Nataraja Seetharamaiah as general manager, Finance. As we scaled further, we created a CFO position and brought in Mohan Krishna Reddy. He worked for about six seven years before Nataraja took over as the CFO.

By 2010, we needed a strong CFO who could manage the company's next phase of growth. I was keen that the incoming CFO should possess the highest levels of integrity at par with his (or her) predecessors. I wanted someone who had strong process regimentation, was techno-savvy and people-centric.

The audit committee chair, M. Murugappan, and I found Ajay Aggarwal, who had considerable expertise and possessed all the requisite qualities. He brought in an excellent understanding of investor relations, consolidation of overseas subsidiaries and technology deployment. His addition to the team strengthened financial discipline, process rigour and cadence.

To build competitive advantage, we needed to be profitable and sustainable. When we emphasized revenues and not profitability, we ended up getting a fairly low-margin business that created employment but no profits at the end of the quarter.

So, we emphasized margins right from the budget planning stage. Margins took precedence in all project discussions with sales executives, business units and geography heads. We created a project costing system (PCS) to assess projects comprehensively and made sure the feedback flowed to the project managers. The granularity of this evaluation was such that we could identify loss-making projects with ease. We worked relentlessly on our receivables and brought down the days of sales outstanding (DSO) to keep a strong free cash flow (FCF).

Many a time, businesses use future cash flows to make purchases today. These obligations to pay short and long-term loans on an ongoing basis restrict free cash flow, which is money available to invest in a growing business. We safeguarded the company from falling into such financial traps by implementing ERP tools.

We made each spending decision and transaction justifiable. This created a cultural expectation of thriftiness throughout the organization. Project heads and business leaders took ownership for delivering 'value for money' in their roles and functions. This discipline set the company up for better margins. Strong cash flows allowed us to be strategic and proactive rather than reactive and defensive.

To create an identity and a brand, we built state-of-the-art infrastructure on our own campuses in Madhapur and Manikonda in Hyderabad, Noida in Uttar Pradesh, Electronic City in Bangalore (now Bengaluru), Kakinada, Visakhapatnam and Warangal. However, over a period of time, we embraced an asset-light model, moving away from capex-heavy infrastructure, and launched a campaign to move our associates to special economic zones (SEZs). Within five years, 50 per cent of our associates began working from SEZs. Our capex on infrastructure became sub-3 per cent from about 5 per cent, and free cash flows improved to over 50 per cent from 10–20 per cent.

Being a services export business, Infotech had to deal with foreign exchange volatility. The dollar grew stronger vis-à-vis the rupee over the years, and that proved advantageous. But between 2003–2010, and especially during the global economic downturn of 2008–09, the rupee became stronger against the dollar. This operating exposure made our software exports costlier, impacting our operating profits. Even as our revenues increased, our profitability suffered.

We responded swiftly and introduced a foreign exchange hedging strategy to protect our bottom line. We covered 70 per cent of our net inflows for twelve months through a plain-vanilla forward contract. We have been following this policy ever since, making us outliers in terms of gains on forward contracts. It introduced tremendous predictability in to the business and business bottom line.

Auditing has always been my priority. It is in my nature to dive into the details of every accounting issue and make sure the team has full support. I even avoided business travel for the first fifteen days of a quarter to be readily available for any problem-solving. This was in the initial years when we lacked processes, controls or a good team to manage the finances. Over the years, we introduced processes and controls, pooled the best-in-class talent who owned the finance function and led it efficiently. Yet, when the Satyam scandal came out in open, all companies headquartered in Hyderabad became suspect. To combat the doubts that were fluttering around in the market, I took a hard stance. Transparency and disclosures would not only be internal, but from now on, we decided to demonstrate them externally to build trust.

We changed the auditors but managing the style of new auditors, that too from the big five, took time. To ensure smooth functioning, I had a direct line of communication with the head of their audit practice. We put systems in place, meticulously outlining that no issue raised with the CEO, audit committee or board by auditors should come as a surprise to CFO. The auditors needed to red-flag problems with the CFO first before others. Such practices resolved many issues quickly without any escalations.

Cash management: I care about every rupee/dollar in the business. Once the organization grows bigger, entrepreneurs think they need not break a sweat over a few dollars. But as a value, I keep an eye on the monetary outflow and the value it brings to the organization. This is one of the reasons why the business succeeded.

Business sustainability has driven me right from Infotech's inception. For this, companies need to have enough funds at any point. Cash reserves indicate a company's robustness and growth potential. It is also crucial for the success of a long-term business strategy. We managed and preserved cash well. Otherwise, the internal and external market and geographic risks we faced would have grounded the company.

For instance, during the 2008 economic downturn, companies had to downsize staff strength. Infotech did not lay off anyone, nor did we force radical changes on the associates. Tough times continued for three years but did not rattle the organization. Though business was sluggish, we survived on our funds and did not have to depend on banks to run the operations.

For this reason, I constantly stress the importance of cash and exercising prudence in spending. Not only in the context of enabling resilience during a downturn but as a source of value creation and capital for future growth—be it new infrastructure, innovation, new technology, more training and development. Capital efficiency and cash flow metrics were as crucial as P&L metrics for us.

Barring a couple of occasions when we had to borrow temporarily, we ensured Infotech always had surplus cash in the bank. There was never a time when we were short on working capital and had to approach a bank. Instead, banks came calling on us on numerous occasions for deposits. That, I believe, is a virtuous culture to nurture in a company.

We routinely set aside part of the profits to fund mergers and acquisitions and other investments and disburse part of it as dividends to shareholders. We followed a conservative policy, focusing on safety rather than on returns to invest the surplus in the best-rated fixed deposits and debt-based mutual funds with minimal risk and zero speculation.

In many enterprises, cash management is the sole responsibility of the finance department and not business units. However, we made certain that business and finance shared ownership for cash performance. For instance, accounts receivable is a shared responsibility of finance and sales, not finance alone.

Automation and finance transformation: In the formative years, we manually consolidated our accounts in MS Excel. We then introduced an ERP system. As the organization grew, we needed tools to recognize revenue accurately. We began infusing IT and automation into our finance function, and strengthened process and systems. For example, we developed a timesheet tool (E3) that required our associates to clock their working hours every day to enable revenue recognition. The initiative faced stiff resistance from associates, requiring us to manage a substantial organizational change. We educated associates and project heads that timesheets and revenue recognition are not about trust but governance. We recruited Sam, who operated from Singapore and came from a large multinational company, as CIO. I ran a weekly cadence call for one year to monitor the successful rollout of E3. We emphasized the importance of having these checks and balances to bring transparency, accuracy and timeliness into reporting.

Infotech embraced technology tools and platforms for enterprise planning, customer relationship management, productivity enhancement and database management, so our finance function was in tune with the rapidly changing corporate world. We made investments knowing that they were way ahead for our size and scale but essential for future growth.

Prudent Mergers and Acquisitions

Entrepreneurs have varied perspectives on risk and different appetites. People perceive me as a conservative risk-taker. It is partly true and is probably a reflection of the society and family I grew up in. However, I am quite aggressive when I make up my mind. Entrepreneurship was unheard of in my family, yet I took the risk of launching Infotech. After all, entrepreneurship is inherently risky.

At Infotech, we adopted a strategic view of every risky proposition and carried out due diligence every time we took a chance, and believe me, we took on fairly significant risks. We dipped our toes first by aligning with business partners in various geographies. But soon, there came the point at the turn of the century when partner-dependence was limiting our customer value-creation. We needed a direct presence in geographies such as Europe and the US. We could either 'build' or 'buy' to have a local presence. We chose the latter, which was riskier and more expensive but a far quicker way to establish ourselves in customer geographies. We bought Dataview Solutions and AGS within a year (1999–2000) in Europe while building the business organically in the US.

When an enterprise is in the growth phase, has a strong balance sheet, sees a good stock run and enjoys access to capital, an entrepreneur tends to go for big-ticket acquisitions. Many an entrepreneur has fallen by the wayside with this approach. Prudence tells me that a company should buy what it can afford. I never considered it a good strategy to raise a huge loan and bid for a company larger than Infotech.

When we acquire an entity by paying a price, it has to bring value through new customers, market access or capabilities. The acquisition is a suboptimal move if it pulls down the margins, impacts the bottom line and earnings per share (EPS), or bleeds the enterprise with project/capex spend without bringing recurring revenue. I can sum up my mergers and acquisition (M&A) philosophy in three letters—MPC—math, physics and chemistry. The math in M&A cannot just be the sum of the revenues of the two companies. In M&A, 2+2 has to be twenty-two, not four. Physics is about synergy. The synergy between the teams in addressing new service offerings, customers and geographies should be vibrant. More importantly, we always looked for chemistry or a cultural match between the companies. We let go of a few good opportunities that did not fit into our value system.

Infotech has done well with this M&A philosophy by looking for smaller yet strategic acquisitions. Some of them worked well, some turned around with persistence and some did not. We persisted with an owner's mindset, learned from experiences, always had a long-term outlook and continued to invest without taking short-term calls.

The traditional perception is that M&A is all about acquiring, but it is also about letting go. We let go of our home-grown IT business and shut down the operations of a few acquired companies after integration. One of the greatest abilities of an entrepreneur is switching quickly, being adaptable and letting go of businesses that serve no more.

At the same time, an entrepreneur needs to think ahead too. When services growth showed signs of stagnation, we had to explore new markets to sustain growth. That's when we bought Time To Market (2008) to enter the hi-tech sector and Rangsons Electronics India (2014) to build a design-led manufacturing practice. We forayed into defence, automotive and digital. These were strategic bets. Most companies cannot take such risks or replicate our actions. Yet, I would say we have been prudent risk-takers.

The risk appetite of the younger generation at the helm of Cyient today is significantly different. It pleases me to watch them take calculated risks while being conscious of the downside. The aptitude towards risk has changed, but the guardrails remain the same. We err on the side of caution but jump at opportunities when we chance upon them.

Risk is intangible, and acquisitions are double-edged swords. I would not bet the entire company on a single acquisition. Nothing is worth putting an entire company on the block, whether it is a single initiative or a combination of initiatives. This is the cardinal principle of our acquisition strategy. Initially, it was an approach based on the conviction of building a sustainable business. Now, it is a combination of conviction and caution.

And Equitable to All

Business leaders who pursue long-term growth strategies understand that a company can best serve its diversified investors when it focuses on sustainable value creation takes into consideration all stakeholders' interests, not just shareholders. This is also the purpose of the enterprise. I never saw being equitable to stakeholders as a lofty ideal or a difficult objective to practice.

We recognized early on that value creation was brought about by associates and we instituted a practice of rewarding them with stock options even before SEBI mandated the ESOP scheme. Infotech shared profits as a percentage of salary and arrived at salary structures by reflecting on the gross margins and maintaining respectable PBT and PAT. It was a balancing act to maintain employee salaries, investor returns and retained earnings that supported future growth.

The company worked with customers with strategic and long-term intent. In business, especially in the B2B space, customers feel nervous if they do not see the supplier/partner reporting growth and expanding capabilities year on year. They worry about business continuity. This made it critical for us to build their confidence by demonstrating growth and financial stability.

I constantly questioned myself, 'How much money is the company making and how do we use it to build it further?' We comforted customers by investing in infrastructure, resources, prioritizing processes, quality standards and creating a value momentum. Customer obsession became second nature.

Publicly traded companies usually get fixated on short-term performance metrics, particularly earnings per share. Companies that conflate short-termism with value creation put both shareholder value and stakeholder interests at risk. At Infotech, we balanced long-term value creation with short-term performance and laid greater emphasis on profitability and cash-flows. Quarter on quarter, we posted good revenue and profits. In the twenty-five years since our IPO, we have delivered a revenue CAGR of 29 per cent and PAT CAGR of 24 per cent. Our stock had a fantastic run. We set high benchmarks for corporate governance, maintained high levels of transparency with investors through our disclosures. We even made sure our board of directors had diverse experiences, skills and interests to reflect the concerns and priorities of a wide range of stakeholders instead of shareholders alone.

Cyient has a significant retail investor base. We created a policy and put a process around dividends to ensure they received payouts year after year. The approach helped us to increase our dividend payouts progressively. This was a good value to maintain credibility before investors. We transformed the pedigree of investor relations function by organizing investors' days, aggressive roadshows, investor satisfaction surveys and found ways to nurture foreign investors. This improved the visibility of the organization amongst the global investor community. Top investors such as Carlyle, Franklin Templeton, Fidelity and T. Rowe Price came on board. Over time Infotech became the darling of investors, not just customers.

We managed the interests of even vendors and took their feedback seriously. Respect to vendors was displayed in small ways such as not making them wait. I used to get quite agitated if procurement personnel made them wait and did not provide them with proper space or give them the attention that was due to them. We started vendor meets, which built trust.

We aligned our non-financial goals and stakeholder outcomes with strategic vision and pursued them with the same rigour and process orientation as our financial goals. We never lost sight of the other stakeholder—society—ever. Community supports an organization in numerous tangible and intangible ways, and we are conscious of our social responsibility. We set aside money to fund education, healthcare and introduced social development initiatives before the government mandated that corporates set apart 2 per cent of their earnings for CSR activity. We never viewed social responsibility as a nice-to-have activity but as an expression of our values and how we do business.

Being equitable to stakeholders and building a sustainable business go hand in glove. For this reason, I constantly ponder over what more I can do to grow the company sustainably. Every financial decision I have made and every business initiative the company has taken this far has been centred around building a sustainable business that outlives the founder. That is my biggest dream, and I am committed to it till my last breath. It keeps the adrenaline pumping. Sometimes, it creates pressure on the teams, but unless we take the route of continuous evolution, the entrepreneur, the enterprise and the teams quickly become irrelevant to the market.

15

In Times of Crises

I met Peter Brooks, vice president of engineering at Bentley Systems, a well-known CAD software player, at a trade show in the US. It was the year 1996.

Several CAD software brands had been floating around in the market but a lack of file format standardization had thrown up major interoperability issues for users. CAD users typically used more than one CAD system and, as a result, often needed to transfer information between the various systems they used. This had created a huge demand for translators in the CAD market, and several companies developed data translators, frequently employing 'reverse engineering' techniques.

While developing MODES (Management of Drawings and Engineering System), Infotech had acquainted itself with the file formats of several CAD software products and had ended up developing some translators of its own. Since the year 1994, it had started counting a few CAD software product companies amongst its customers. CADKEY Inc was one of them.

When Peter learnt about our company's CAD translators at the trade show, he became quite animated. 'Mohan, can I read files created in the CADKEY software in Bentley Microstation?' he asked.

'Indeed, you can,' I told Peter and went on to give him all the low-down on our translator product. He grilled me a little more and our chat ended with a handshake and an exchange of calling cards. Matters rested there for a while.

Although Peter evinced little interest in taking the conversation forward at the trade fair, I knew he was convinced that Infotech held the key to Bentley's problems. A few weeks later, my assessment proved correct. I received an email from him, requesting a proposal for the development of a CAD translator.

He seemed quite keen to develop a CAD translator with Infotech and I was equally eager to close the deal with him. To me, making the translator for Bentley seemed like an appropriate starting point for a long-lasting business relationship with the firm.

But Peter had a caveat. 'Mohan, since you're working with CADKEY already, I'm sure you're aware that its Part File Tool Kit is under copyright and is deemed as confidential material belonging to the company. I hope you realize that if you use the same tool kit for Bentley project, it'll be tantamount to intellectual property violation.'

'I'm aware of the IP laws, Peter,' I replied laconically. 'We'll keep both the projects isolated. We won't assign any engineer who has worked on the CADKEY project to Bentley, or vice versa. We will maintain customer confidentiality.'

Bentley decided to trust us and we bagged the project. Bentley was an established player in the CAD software market and the deal was a breakthrough for Infotech. Taking competitor sensitivities into account, I instructed Dr G.D. Rao, who was in charge of our CAD software division, to keep the two projects and project personnel completely insulated. I trusted Rao and entrusted him with the responsibility of overseeing both the tasks.

The Bentley project progressed well and I monitored it remotely. One day, Rao informed me that he had shipped the translator's alpha version to Peter. I was elated that the project had crossed its first milestone.

A few days later, my phone rang while I was wrestling with some pending work that had piled up as a result of a short trip I had made to Tirupati. It was around 6 p.m.

I took the call. 'Hello, am I speaking to Mohan?' a not-so-familiar female voice with a strong American twang enquired from the other end.

'Yes, this is Mohan,' I replied, mystified. 'Who's this?'

'This is Mrs Bean from Baystate Technologies,' the voice at the other end announced assertively. Something about her tone gave me pause. I smelt trouble.

Mrs Bean was the co-founder of Baystate Technologies, a Marlborough, Massachusetts company, along with her husband Robert Bean. Baystate had acquired CADKEY a few months earlier and the transaction was still in process. As a result, Baystate had obtained all the trade secrets and copyrights associated with the CADKEY product line. It had also assumed CADKEY's rights and obligations of the development project Infotech was undertaking.

Now that the penny had dropped, I remembered the brief conversation I had previously had with Mrs Bean. On that occasion I had told her about Infotech and had expressed our willingness to continue to work on the CADKEY project with Baystate. She had assured me that she would review the deal and get back to me on the subject. I wondered if Mrs Bean was now calling me to pick up where we had last left off. Little did I know that this unanticipated call was about to throw up a business crisis, the likes of which our nascent start-up had not yet witnessed in its short history.

Before I could acknowledge her and engage in the customary pleasantries that normally preceded business discussions, Mrs. Bean went on the rampage. 'You've stolen our intellectual property (IP) and handed it to our competitor,' she bellowed. 'It's a clear case of copyright violation.'

Taken aback, I thought on my feet and interrupted her. Handling irate women was something I had never quite mastered. 'I would never do that, Mrs Bean,' I said trying to calm her down. 'There must be some mistake. Tell me what's happened. I really don't know what you're talking about.'

My astonishment was apparent and it steadied her somewhat. She became a little more coherent and revealed that CADKEY had received an email that said, 'We cracked the CADKEY file format. You can now read it in Bentley Microstation. Here is the code for it.'

I quickly envisioned the mix-up that could have taken place. Rao might have mistakenly sent the alpha version of the translator to Baystate instead of Bentley. My heart sank.

Mrs Bean was still furious and seemed intent on holding on to her anger. 'Infotech has taken our file format and shared it with Bentley. This infringement will wipe out my business. I'm going to sue you for IP violation.'

'I apologize for the goof-up but I'd like to assure you that there's been no IP violation. What can I do to redress the situation?' I asked, valiantly trying to soothe her ruffled feathers.

'Here is the deal,' said Mrs Bean, coldly. 'CADKEY owes Infotech $120,000. Write it off and I'll let you go. I'm giving you thirty minutes to decide. That's all I have.'

'Okay, let me give it a thought. I'll get back to you,' I replied.

I did not know the gravity of the situation but I was not quite willing to let go of $120,000. My first task was clearly to solve the mystery at hand. I went downstairs and called an emergency team meeting to figure out how the email had gone to Baystate instead of Bentley. I did not call back Mrs. Bean within the thirty minutes she had so generously offered me. I decided she could do exactly as she pleased. By this time, I was in quite a rage myself.

A preliminary probe revealed that an engineer who had been previously working on the CADKEY/Baystate project had been moved to the Bentley project. He had access to the old files. With no awareness of customer sensitivities, the engineer had happily carried out a cut-paste of the program schema and had transferred it to Bentley's translator project. Without verifying or validating the source code the said engineer had developed, Rao in turn had dispatched an email addressed to Peter Brooks, attaching the executable file with it. He had clearly ignored the stipulated process and had, moreover, mistakenly sent it to Baystate instead of Bentley.

Infotech was still in its early years, but even then, we had a well-laid out process that clearly proclaimed that no emails were to be sent with attachments. Files that were shared with customers had to be routed through FTP (file transfer protocol: a standard Internet protocol used to transmit files from one host to another). The team had not followed the prescribed process while sending the alpha version. It was a grave mistake and had caused a terrible mix-up, all thanks to a careless non-compliance with the laid-out process.

The next day, I called back Mrs Bean, apologized for the errant email and explained that the translator was incomplete. I offered to terminate the translator project with Bentley to ensure continuity of the business relationship with CADKEY/Baystate. 'I cannot afford to lose $120,000,' I explained. 'But I'm ready to let go of 50 per cent of the sum.'

I thought it was a generous offer; Mrs Bean obviously did not think so. She refused to entertain my olive branch and slammed the phone on me.

A few days later, Baystate sued Bentley on six counts and made Infotech a party to one of the six charges. The petition read, 'Plaintiff, Baystate Technologies, Inc. ("Baystate"), filed a six-count complaint against Bentley Systems, Inc. ("Bentley") alleging . . . (2) copyright infringement in violation of 17 USC § 106.[1]

The petition further stated that Bentley had commissioned a project in India with an outsourcing partner called Infotech Enterprises and its managing director, B.V.R. Mohan Reddy, to develop a translator. In view of Infotech's expertise in CAD products and reverse engineering, it showed clear intent to steal Baystate's intellectual property. The firm even had a summons issued for Peter Brooks.

Bentley invited Infotech to join the legal battle and fight Baystate shoulder to shoulder with it. There was a catch! The deal on offer was that Infotech would bear its costs in fighting the case. If we won, Bentley would assume the $120,000 and award fifty Bentley

Microstation licences to Infotech in lieu of the amount. If Infotech chose not to join, Bentley gently warned, it would pursue us legally for getting it into this mess. Infotech was caught between a rock and a hard place. Unsurprisingly, we decided to join Bentley.

We consulted the top lawyers in the US. Our counsels warned us of the very real possibility of the IP violation charge escalating into a criminal breach, which could lead to serious prosecution in the US.

The trial opened in the US district court, Boston, Massachusetts, in October 1996. The court issued a summons to me in December. We booked several airline tickets to keep my port of entry into the US a secret till the end. I flew to Washington, DC, via New York to meet Karlu and our attorney. After ensuring all the groundwork was complete, we took a flight to Boston and camped in a hotel adjacent to the district court till it was time for me to depose.

I was nervous and spent a sleepless night. The situation tested my resilience to the utmost, straining my nerves to almost breaking point. While such challenges are not uncommon in business, they cause extreme lows and anxiety. They can drain an entrepreneur emotionally and intellectually. My imagination was going haywire as I conjured up all kinds of unpleasant scenarios. I tried to wrestle with my fears and strove to imbue them with a sense of context and reality.

I gave myself a good talking to. 'Worry is a vice in business. Whatever has to happen will happen. Why cross a bridge before you've reached it? If you think there's still something you've left undone, do it now. If you've done all you can, just go to sleep and let tomorrow take care of itself.'

I was still nervous when I entered the courtroom the next day. I sat down, crossing my legs to conceal my anxiety. The judge noticed and admonished me, remarking that I should not sit with my legs crossed before him. I apologized for my ignorance and corrected my posture.

Experts from both parties agreed that 'the data structures at issue were at least similar to some extent'. The expert who was testifying on behalf of Bentley and Infotech told the judge that such similarity was 'necessary'. Other than the similarity in data structures, neither of them testified 'with respect to any similarity between the source code or the object code of the CADKEY program and the proposed Bentley Translator program'.[2]

He said there were only a few ways of expressing an idea; process or fact and copyright protection could not be applicable to them.

When it was my turn to take the witness box, I testified that the name of a file was typically related to its function. A file that controls or creates colour has a name in which the word 'colour' appears. In that case, the name of a file 'colour' merges with the idea or function of the file 'to create a colour', and is not protected by copyright laws. Barring the similarity in the data structures, there was no similarity between the source code or the object code of the CADKEY program and the Bentley translator program.

The right thing to do in any situation is to tell the truth and stay transparent. Transparency creates trust. But yes, one always has to grade it in one's mind and position it in a way that it is convincing. The credible part in this instance was that we had not copied the CADKEY code and Infotech had not violated any intellectual property. The judge patiently heard my deposition, put a few questions to me and let me go.

Annoyed at this turn of events, Baystate then trained its guns on me and decided to sue Infotech. It immediately had a summons issued to me. The statute, however, ordains that a witness who has appeared in court to depose cannot be summoned again until the concerned individual returns to his or her residence (arm's length). That objection was good enough to void the summons against me.

I returned to Hyderabad and got back to business. Infotech was due to go public in March 1997, and we were neck-deep in pre-IPO work. The judgment was due any moment and the likelihood of it going against us played heavily at the back of our minds.

Statutory norms mandated that Infotech should disclose the IP violation case in the IPO prospectus as a risk factor in investing in Infotech. We briefly toyed with a 'what if' scenario, envisaging the outcome in case we opted for the non-disclosure route, but ultimately decided against it and elected to divulge the situation, upfront. Complying with the regulations, we informed IDBI, our investment banker, about the case. We patiently answered all their queries and allayed their fears by enumerating our defences. It was a major risk for the company from an investor standpoint and it took real courage to be transparent. Transparency not only makes good ethical sense but is also good business practice. It is about presenting the company authentically with all its strengths and weaknesses.

We disclosed our legal advisers' opinion that since an identical case filed by Baystate against Bentley, in which Infotech had also been a party, had been dismissed by the Massachusetts court previously, it was likely, if our objection on jurisdiction was upheld, that the present case would also be set aside. We did face some embarrassing moments from potential investors, but it provided us a good lesson on the virtue of transparency.

One morning in January 1997, Karlu informed me that the Massachusetts court had absolved Infotech completely. The court ruled in favour of Bentley and Infotech with respect to the trade secret misappropriation claim related to the CADKEY source code or the Part File Tool Kit source code.

The court observed that I had testified credibly and that Infotech had not misused CADKEY proprietary information at any time. It averred that Baystate had not been able to rebut our claim, adequately. Moreover, there was no evidence that Infotech had ever disclosed the Part File Tool Kit documentation to anyone else. What it revealed to Bentley through the translator source code was the MODES computer program, which was created by reference to such documentation. Although the court found no impropriety on Infotech's part, it also noted that the CADKEY and the Bentley translator projects had not been completely segregated.

The court cross-marked the paragraph for which Infotech was sued. The court acquitted Infotech while the fight continued over the remaining allegations. Once acquitted, we honoured our commitment to Bentley. We forfeited the $120,000 in exchange for Microstation software licences. Infotech went public in March 1997 free from a court-case risk and we were oversubscribed 1.56 times.

In August 1997, Bentley and Baystate came to a mutual settlement on the other five counts.

The word 'crisis' is written in both Chinese and Japanese with two symbols signifying 'danger' and 'opportunity'. While deeply unsettling, the truth is that every crisis also presents the seeds of opportunity. We did prepare an appropriate courtroom response and fortunately came out of the IP violation case, unscathed. While this was the first such situation Infotech faced, we realized it might not be an isolated case. Instead of viewing the situation as a short-term evil that we should relegate to the past, we asked ourselves how to use the situation to speed up long-overdue changes.

We realized we could pre-empt such crises in the future only by improving our operating model and laying even greater emphasis on internal processes, aware all the while that laying down processes was just one step; it was making the teams adhere to them that was far more critical. I had forewarned Rao several times that CADKEY and Bentley were competitors and had cautioned him that serving competing customers was tricky and any mix-up would cost us our credibility. Despite the guardrails and warnings, the error had occurred.

The situation was clear-cut; we needed to adapt boldly. We threw out our existing playbook and introduced policies to strengthen the proverbial 'Chinese Wall' to isolate project teams. These included physical separation of groups, distinct file servers and client-specific virtual private networks. The associate code of conduct was revised to define with precision the usage of conflict mitigation tools, including firewalls and policies for training, audits and enforcement, to ensure that we could serve customers who competed in the same market, ethically. To this end, teams were aligned to a daily dashboard of priorities, and new metrics were established to monitor performance and create a culture of accountability.

No crisis ends without blood on the floor, but this was an exception. The two software engineers who were involved in the mix-up disappeared overnight. Rao thought I would fire him, but I did not. Empathy got the better of me. I preferred to walk in the shoes of associates, customers and their broader ecosystems. Rao was a man of good values and I respected his work ethic and contributions. He served Infotech for several more years.

At the same time, I took a hard, rational line to protect our financial performance from the inevitable softness that often accompanies such disruptions. Our actions may have been reactive, but the silver lining to the crisis was that it made us aware of the lacunae that existed in the firm; we came up with solutions to overhaul existing processes and introduced new ones so that associates could be prevented from making similar errors. I wanted to make sure that the company never went through that kind of trauma ever again.

Terror in Our Closet

The cold truth is that as long as organizations are made of people, there will be mistakes, controversies and crises. While some emerge from under the carpet, others detonate out of the blue. In both cases, they leave the entrepreneur and the enterprise staring at the prospect of serious business disruptions and a highly damaged reputation.

On 30 June 2007, two men rammed a Jeep Cherokee laden with propane gas cylinders and petrol cans into the doors of Glasgow airport's departure area. It was the first Saturday of the Scottish school summer holidays, and 4000 people were inside the terminal. The departure halls were packed with passengers waiting to check-in or board their flights. A concrete pillar at the main door stopped the jeep from entering the main concourse. When the SUV failed to explode, one of the inmates threw petrol bombs from the passenger seat while the driver doused himself in petrol and set the car alight. As stunned holidaymakers began to run for their lives, the duo got out of the vehicle, attacking police officers and passers-by before being pinned down to the floor.[3]

Police called it a terrorist attack and linked it to a car-bomb plot that was foiled in London the previous day. Britain's Home Office raised the national security alert level to 'critical', expecting more such imminent attacks. The world witnessed the shocking incident on television. The airport reopened for business in less than twenty-four hours while investigations were still underway. Police identified the terrorists involved as Bilal Abdulla, an Iraqi doctor, and India-born Kafeel Ahmed, an engineer who had grown up in Saudi Arabia.

After a few days, we received a call from one of our customers, Airbus, alerting us about an article in the *Wall Street Journal*. We hurriedly procured a copy of the report online, in which the newspaper claimed that Kafeel Ahmed had worked at Infotech Enterprises, Bangalore (now Bengaluru). The next day it appeared in the *New York Times* as well.

Giving further details about Kafeel, the newspaper mentioned that he had worked for much of the previous year as an aeronautical engineer at Infotech, which designed aircraft parts for Boeing, Airbus and other original equipment manufacturers (OEMs). It also speculated that Kafeel might have had access to some design secrets of top aircraft makers. However, there was no suggestion that he had done anything untoward while he had been at Infotech. The article subtly pitched against the offshoring of technology business, indicating that offshore service providers could have terrorists on their payrolls, thus putting Western lives at risk.

The article named several Infotech customers, including Boeing, Airbus, Bombardier, Pratt & Whitney and Alstom. This was quite a jolt. An organization is never really prepared for something like this, and we were a hair's breadth away from being labelled as a security threat. I was a deeply worried man. I could just see the edifice I had built with so much passion blowing up in the face of the latest bombshell.

As soon as the *New York Times* report appeared, the Indian press began to explore the story and started snooping around for more details. We had become the meatiest bone for the newshounds in the country! Infotech's Bangalore (now Bengaluru) office was flooded with the media—both print and electronic—bombarding it with endless questions about Kafeel. Journalists wanted to know everything there was to know about him. They wanted to see where he had worked, meet his friends and ex-colleagues, and learn the names of the clients he worked for. We diverted all press queries to Infotech's Hyderabad headquarters.

Crisis management is like firefighting. An unprecedented event of this nature and magnitude can consume an organization in no time. Leaders and their teams are caught unawares and scamper around trying to understand the ground reality. More than anything else, such unanticipated emergencies and developing situations demand a dexterous balancing act. On the one hand, we had to employ every resource and ounce of energy to understand and deal with the crisis. On the other, we also had to ensure business continuity.

Often, organizations tend to narrow their focus in the face of a threat. However, that restricts the field of vision to the immediate foreground. Instead, we decided to take a broad, holistic view of the challenge to affect a well-directed management of the situation. As we gathered details of Kafeel's association with Infotech, we simultaneously kept ourselves informed with the ground situation at all times through associates, customers and other stakeholders. An empowered crisis management team was constituted to tackle the exigency, comprising K.S. Susinder, PR director; Ashok Reddy, VP of HR; Krishna, VP of Strategy; and me.

A black swan event of this nature demands speed over precision. We quickly charted out a crisis management action plan. In any catastrophe, it is quite important to know where one stands. We assessed the situation accurately and were quite certain that the company was in the clear. Aware that in such cases there are no secrets, and everyone will eventually find out all there is to know, we decided to meet the issue head-on without any sugar-coated approach, fighting every instinct to react or overreact.

The company decided to engage with internal and external stakeholders to alleviate their concerns and win back their confidence. First, we agreed that Susinder would be the sole company spokesperson. He alone would address all media queries and no one else would speak to the press.

Once it had been ascertained that Infotech had not slipped up in any way, we knew that the time had come to get our side of the story heard. We reached out to the *New York Times* correspondent who had initially reported Kafeel's association with Infotech, and requested him to listen to our view of the situation before publishing anything. Thankfully, he obliged us. As the investigation progressed and more details emerged, we proactively updated the press and took follow-on questions.

We also took our associates into confidence and informed them of the incident, apprising them of Kafeel Ahmed's involvement in the terror attack and his employment with Infotech from December 2005 to August 2006. The company kept sharing information wherever it was required to quell rumours and misinformation.

We learned from associates who had worked with Kafeel that he had mostly kept to himself and only a few people had known him at a personal level. Associates were requested not to make any comments about Kafeel or speak to the media. It was actually the last of our problems as they understood the gravity of the situation. We then sent a note to the board of directors and took them into confidence.

After that we got in touch with Pratt & Whitney. Kafeel had worked on one of its projects. I spoke to Paul Adams, who was President of Pratt & Whitney America and Canada by this time, and furnished him with a detailed account of Kafeel Ahmed's engagement at Infotech.

Paul listened to me patiently. 'Mohan,' he said. 'I have only two questions. Was there a defined process to recruit people for the Pratt & Whitney project? Was background checking part of that process?'

'Yes, Paul,' I replied. 'Yes, to both the questions.'

'Was the process followed in Kafeel's recruitment?' Paul queried, probing a little more.

'Yes, we followed the process. I have the documentation,' I affirmed. 'We stuck to the agreed guidelines on how he worked. There was no data leakage. The good news is that Kafeel left Infotech about a year before the bombing.'

'Mohan, I trust you. Don't worry and don't blame yourself too much. You've done all the right things. If anyone harasses you, ask them to talk to me. You have our support,' Paul promised. Pratt & Whitney stood by us—unflinchingly.

We connected with all our key customers and handled each conversation responsibly, assuring them that Kafeel did not have access to confidential information of any customer apart from the project he had worked on. We also reiterated that the customer's intellectual property had not been compromised.

The law took care of the rest.

In the meanwhile, each of our clients supported our stance. We opted for transparency and it improved our goodwill with several of them. For instance, our relationship with Bombardier Transportation strengthened because the CEO was directly involved in the conversation. He knew us reasonably well, but after this incident, we earned his respect.

We also released a note to the stock exchanges and disclosed the name of the client Kafeel had worked for. We assured the market that we enjoyed the confidence of all our customers, including Pratt & Whitney. It was business as usual for Infotech's stock after that.

By communicating transparently and prudently to our stakeholders, Infotech emerged out of the crisis stronger, demonstrating the organization's resilience by adapting to the situation rapidly and managing the sudden disruption efficiently. Otherwise, this incident could have severely dented the reputation that the company had built for itself so painstakingly over the years.

Pratt & Whitney's contract stipulated that we run background checks on every employee working on its projects. We obliged every customer requirement, and that saved us the day. Pratt & Whitney's trust in us redoubled after this episode, and our relationship scaled further as a consequence. The wisdom we gained from the incident made us strengthen our HR practices. A process to run mandatory background checks for new hires on all customer projects was introduced shortly afterwards.

Our emphasis on values-based governance helped us to manage the crisis. In Kafeel's case, we could have dodged media questions by saying we had launched an internal inquiry into the matter. Instead, the company owned responsibility, accepted that he was an Infotech employee and disclosed the customer's name he had worked for. Without shirking our moral obligation, we presented ourselves transparently before our stakeholders and the media. We carried no blame as Kafeel had left us a year before the Glasgow incident.

Sometimes, crises explode with a single event, like the Glasgow bombing case, but organizational catastrophes rarely have a single trigger. They are often a consequence of an unexpected amalgamation of multiple small and seemingly insignificant human errors like the IP violation crisis, technological failures or bad business decisions. They grow right under one's feet and may seem like random, unrelated incidents.

These episodes made us aware that multiple near-misses often foreshadow a business crisis. Our cognitive biases may make us misread and ignore signs or accept anomalies as normal deviations. Our biggest lesson was to take proactive measures before such signs seeped in silently and blew up as major eruptions.

16

Building an Institution: The House of Cyient

During my fourth year at OMC Computers, my boss Tobaccowala put the following question to me in a board meeting. 'Mohan,' he said with a gleam in his eye. 'What would happen to the company if a bus stops on you (runs over you) tomorrow? There is so much concentration of power with you. You control everything!'

I gulped. I had a quick vision of a bus running into me and the feelings that swept through me were definitely not pleasant.

Tobaccowala was waiting for my reply and I did not quite know how to answer him. 'I don't know what will happen to the company,' I blurted out honestly. 'But if a bus stops on me tomorrow, it would be a catastrophe for my family. They would be my biggest worry, especially my two young kids.'

In hindsight, perhaps my reply did not belong to the boardroom. It was too emotional. But it did the trick and questions of this nature were never directed at me again at OMC.

Twenty years later, a similar question was posed to me, this time from an investment analyst. 'Mr Reddy, what happens to Infotech if a bus knocks you down tomorrow?' he asked, indicating that the functioning of the company was entirely dependent on me.

This time my thoughts were different. There was no denying that my children were by then grown-up and able to fend for themselves. My absence would not affect their lives as much as it would have when they were younger and reliant on me for their needs. But Infotech had about 5000 associates who depended on me for their livelihood. What would happen to them, their families or my customers for that matter—who relied on Infotech and had vested so much faith in me?

That's when I was struck by an epiphany! If authority and control were vested in a single individual in the enterprise, turning it into a sustainable and lasting institution would be a serious challenge. I realized that I needed to build a team and delegate several functions to competent individuals. At the same time, it was not only incumbent upon me to empower them to perform—it was just as important to hold them responsible for the outcomes.

Entrepreneurs often have misplaced notions of what constitutes an enterprise and an institution. They regard a company as a legal entity that carries out business activities purely for profit while they identify institutions as units with a social purpose. These are popular yet narrow definitions that shape the actions of most enterprises, driving them to maximize profits and deliver shareholder value while paying lip service, if at all, to societal and environmental risks. I realized companies should indeed work to make money, but the institutional spirit holds that they could be more than just money-making entities.

Enterprises should be vehicles to accomplish a larger purpose, while balancing the interests of all stakeholders. When a company also devotes its energies to gauge how it can sustain the conditions that will allow it to flourish over time, it delivers more than just financial returns. Such entrepreneurs build enduring institutions. When the entrepreneur aligns with a larger purpose and institutionalizes the same, the business stands a chance to survive beyond him.

I always wanted to build an enterprise that outlives me. I was certainly not one of those serial entrepreneurs who launch and scale a business only to sell it at a future point to incubate the next venture. It is not wrong to be a serial entrepreneur, but that is not what I am. I aspired to contribute to society through my enterprise—by generating employment at scale, creating wealth for wealth creators, increasing tax income for governments and contributing to nation-building.

I was always driven by a desire to build a sustainable business and transform it into a multinational institution with a global outlook. This aspiration was interwoven into every nerve and sinew of the firm, whether it was strategy, business model, people development, governance or social responsibility. While the company reviewed and reinvented its operational practices and business strategies from time to time, it also ensured that they aligned with its long-term purpose. Infotech aligned institutional logic with economic rationale and balanced public interest with financial returns.

De-risking to Sustain

In the start-up phase, my priority was to bring predictability into the business. We explored and added those service offerings with significant, long-term potential and ignored lesser opportunities that did not match our sense of purpose. Standard operating procedures were developed to perform every task and monitor them. Internal audits, quality and security checks were carried out to ensure adherence to the processes. Our data-driven approach helped us to mitigate all uncertainties involved in project execution, human resource management and technology obsolescence. Several measures were introduced to forecast demand for resources, optimize their utilization, minimize idle time and improve the billing of our associates.

Our intense customer focus turned tactical relationships into long-term strategic partnerships and won customer loyalty. This allowed us to grow our revenue year after year and ensured business sustainability. Further, we constantly monitored costs and contributing factors and put guardrails to improve the profitability metrics.

Business sustainability calls for a robust de-risking approach that recognizes, measures and mitigates risk in many different dimensions.

Infotech continuously evaluated geopolitical and economic risks and entered Eastern and Western markets to curb over-reliance on a single country or a few economies. Several industries the company addressed, such as aerospace and rail transport, were rife with inherent business cyclicality, leading to fluctuations in revenues. Some of these risks were offset by strengthening the industry verticals stemming from the geospatial sector such as communications and utilities. Sustainability concerns made the organization enter new industry verticals such as off-road highway, power generation, semiconductor and medical technology. The firm continued to hone its value proposition, and kept track of market shifts and the competitive landscape; it worked hard to nurture innovation on many levels—processes, services and solutions and business models. There were checks and balances to prevent undue concentration in one service, vertical, customer or geography to ensure organizational sustainability.

Further, Infotech constantly evaluated its risk matrix and executed strategies to safeguard the business as best as possible from known and unforeseen financial, reputational, internal process, legal, regulatory, competition, macroeconomic, employee skills and attrition, and customer concentration risks that could prevent us from achieving our business objectives. Besides, ensuring cyber and information security became critical for business continuity. Such measures sustained shareholder value creation and consequently built the firm's reputation and rating. Our risk management approach has become one of our best practices and aligns well with our institutional perspective/logic.

The larger the size of an organization, the greater are the challenges it faces in terms of cohesion, and collaboration between different service lines and business units. We restructured the organization from time to time and introduced several initiatives to build synergies between teams and encourage collaboration. No single structure can be prescriptive to an organization at all times, it has to change with business needs, availability of leaders and customer compulsions. When Infotech was small, its structure was aligned to the service lines—geospatial and engineering. When the company witnessed growth and needed more leadership bandwidth, we restructured it to verticalize the organization based on business lines—aerospace, rail transportation, communications, utilities, and semiconductor, to name a few. We then realized that the business unit heads were concentrated in India but customers were geographically spread. That made us adopt a more geography-centric structure—North America, EMEA, India, South-East Asia and Australia. When business knowledge became critical to gain traction with customers, we went back to verticalization with some service offerings like digital, geospatial and semiconductor as horizontals. An organization's structure is never carved in stone, and we had to periodically review the same to ensure the structure augmented the efficiency of the firm.

Compliance and Transparency: To the Letter of Law

I often say: 'I believe in God. I never get to see him, but behave with him because of my faith. I see the regulator all the time but I behave with him because of my obligation.' The government is an important stakeholder in every economic activity. It facilitates the infrastructure, introduces appropriate policies, smoothens the ease of doing business, expedites the skill ecosystem for companies to thrive in and expects firms to comply to ensure order and progression. In international business, realizations are high, but the complexity is enormous. We learned to respect and follow the laws of every country we operated in, some even punitive.

We are sticklers for governance and have laid down processes to ensure all statutory and legal compliance in client contracts. We adopted a well-balanced corporate compliance programme to reduce risk, build trust and a positive reputation among employees, customers and the public. Compliance programmes forced us to prepare accurate and timely documentation of activities and expenses, which became critical inputs for informed investment and planning decisions. Soon, our commitment to compliance even became our competitive advantage.

Statutory compliance is undoubtedly complex and it made Infotech teams cringe on occasion. The costs of compliance seemed immense, without any clear-cut benefits. But I always advised all the teams to take it seriously as it was critical to our survival in various countries. The business ramifications would have been devastating if any incidence of non-compliance had ever come to light. 'This overhead can be an organizational virtue,' I said repeatedly. 'It's like an insurance policy.' Among other factors, I can attribute our global success to our determination to navigate the compliance challenges and follow the rule of the land.

In the interest of transparency, we share all mandatory information such as quarterly results, business updates and even some sensitive information that may impact the stock price to keep investors fully updated. Our investor presentation is quite comprehensive and ranks high in terms of transparency. We adopted a liberal corporate access policy and always met investors one-on-one without a bias between small/large or domestic/foreign investors. Infotech is one of the most widely-tracked engineering services companies by analysts. Their underlying perception is that the company may falter on performance once in a while, but it never wavers on transparency and corporate governance.

The Board of Wisdom

In a start-up or a large enterprise, the board of directors is an essential leadership and decision-making think tank. The directors fulfil their fiduciary duty to act in the company's long-term interests. I consider having a powerful, credible, independent and diverse board an institutional virtue. But this function usually receives little attention from entrepreneurs or only inasmuch as is necessary to fulfil the regulatory obligation.

Boards bring new perspectives to the management, demystify the operational fog and are uniquely positioned to help executive teams walk the tight rope of balancing immediate fundamentals while keeping an eye on the long-term.

Right from our early years, I used institutional logic while constituting the board. I looked for integrity, eminence, independence and influence to help me build the business. First, I enrolled M.M. Murugappan as an independent director (Murugappan became executive chairman of the Murugappa Group of Companies in 2015 and chairman of the board of Cyient in 2021).

Knowing Murugappan's high levels of integrity and his strong views on compliance and governance, I made sure he headed the audit committee. With his consistent engagement over the years, we brought several best practices into the audit and governance processes.

We handled several sensitive situations from time to time with the board's support. For instance, Price Waterhouse (PW) has acted as our auditor since fiscal 2001. In 2009, Price Waterhouse was allegedly accused of complicity with the main perpetrators of the accounting fraud at a Hyderabad-based IT services company. SEBI and CBI maintained that Price Waterhouse 'intentionally' failed to apply certain auditing standards in the years of its association with the said IT firm.

Infotech came under stress, as it was another Hyderabad-based company and had the same signing partner. Stock market and strategic investors turned sceptical about our auditing. I was, however, confident that Infotech's accounts had been thoroughly audited and we maintained transparent disclosures. Yet, the unfounded suspicion in the market perturbed us. Our investors were not keen to have Price Waterhouse onboard anymore.

Our board, especially the audit committee chair, Murugappan, who knew our business fundamentals well, took a determined stance, insisting that we change Price Waterhouse. We heeded his advice and decided to transition to Deloitte. Price Waterhouse made every effort and used every possible connection to convince us against the transition. We stood our ground. It was a professionally trying situation, but in retrospect, the right move. A company has to balance the interests of its stakeholders, and that includes the investor. We were confident about the quality of our accounts, but at the same time, we could not ignore investor perception. Our board supported us at every step and we ensured that the quality of our audits remained the same, the change in our audit partner notwithstanding.

Members of the board are also team players. We have our moments of agreements and disagreements. For instance, there were certain decisions on acquisitions where initially some directors were not sanguine. Yet, they chose to go along with the popular verdict. They supported the moves because these acquisitions brought additional growth. The board thought it wiser to leave such entrepreneurial decisions, especially the smaller deals, to the management.

The board evaluated every decision we took, assisted the management in assessing the quality of our choices, and allowed us to make and own our decisions. In reality, not all our decisions were great, some were failures. But this is the essence of entrepreneurial behaviour. We made mistakes, learned from them and over the years our directors championed our entrepreneurial decisions.

We have had customers such as Pratt & Whitney and TomTom invest in Cyient. The investments anchored the relationships, transforming them into strategic partnerships. Paul Adams and later David Carter, as representatives of Pratt and George Fink, and later Alain de Taeye on behalf of TomTom brought significant value-add to the board over the years, while their stock reaped good returns.

We always made sure the Infotech board had distinguished people from diverse entities, nationalities, cultures and stakeholder groups, including key customers, strategic investors and even academicians with unblemished pasts and brilliant track records. We sought professionals who had abundant experience running large balance sheets and P&Ls and simultaneously looked for human resource, organization and leadership-development skills. Another consideration that determined the selection of directors was market access. Directors were not expected to sell for us, but their ability to open doors did have a hand in accelerating sales. The company had women directors who were very independent and made significant contributions. We leveraged the best of the board's wisdom, allowing for an explosion of ideas and a wide range of perspectives while facilitating business network expansion and best practices adoption. This brought a culture of inclusivity, transparency, diligence and a global outlook to the company.

Good governance has always been a credibility scorer for Infotech, especially in winning large contracts. Although they are a time and cost overhead for the company, the benefits far outweigh the efforts.

What's in a Name: Infotech to Cyient

I seldom pay close attention to a company's name. My only consideration is that it should reflect what the enterprise does. When I incorporated the company in 1991, I did not cogitate much about the name and opted for Infotech, as I intended to work in the information technology industry. It was broad enough, or so I thought, to cover all our bases. Brand recognition came after we started attracting appreciation for our work and a time arrived when people spoke well of us even when we were not in the room. Infotech Enterprises grew to become a brand the stock markets loved.

But as technology acceleration transformed the market, 'Infotech' became a bit too generic. We could not copyright it as it was not even a proper noun. We enjoyed the brand equity associated with it, but it often landed us in annoying situations. Customers and investors alike mistook us for other players in the industry who had used the word 'infotech' as part of their brand name.

We made our first push for a brand refresh in 2004. By then, our brand recall was very high and people often referred to me as 'Infotech Mohan Reddy'. At the time, a brand refresh was an expensive proposition, so we decided against it, fearing that we might harm the brand.

A decade later, it was a different story. By 2013, the brand was ageing and offered no competitive differentiation. After building a strong engineering practice, brand Infotech displayed a suboptimal representation of our vision. What had seemed like an appropriate name at the time of the company's inception no longer appeared entirely relevant. We had diverse offerings that needed a unifying brand narrative to increase our effectiveness in the market. While our brand recall was still high, we were increasingly encountering instances of incorrect recall too. We needed a refresh in terms of the logo, and it seemed like a good time to change the name.

Krishna argued for it vociferously, pointing out that we had reached a pivotal point. Infotech had hit about $350 million in revenue and we were launching into the next phase of growth with the S3 strategy. If we were to rebrand, this was the moment to do it. It was a tricky proposition but necessary if we wanted to stay current. It was also a chance to refresh the brand and show our customers and stakeholders that the company had kept up with the times.

In one our discussions, Krishna declared, 'I'm adamant about the name change.'

I was still unsure and expressed my reservations. 'I'm not sure if it's the right move,' I cautioned.

'It's got to be now or never,' he asserted.

I stood my ground and then proceeded to dismiss the matter from my mind.

That evening I went to a party. A senior IAS officer with a lively interest in the IT industry got into conversation with me. He made general inquiries about the business health of the firm and concluded our discussion with an optimistic observation that was discomfiting in the extreme. 'As long as you are associated with Infosys, Mohan, the company will do well.'

I was aghast at his slip—if that was what it was—because for him, there appeared to be no distinction between Infosys and Infotech! It was my first alert! They were such close homophones that people often used the names interchangeably.

'Perhaps Krishna is right, after all,' I thought. But I still dithered and decided to sleep on the decision.

I was struck by another ominous sign the very next day. When I opened the newspaper the following morning, a news item caught my attention—the director of a company bearing the word 'infotech' as part of its name had been arrested. It was one of those hole-in-the-wall type of firms and the police had nabbed the said individual for committing some kind of fraud. I groaned inwardly, knowing that I would be spending the rest of the day fielding calls and trying to ward off well-wishers inquiring about the scam that had hit our company. I was right. I spent the day explaining to all and sundry that the said racket had taken place in a different company. These red flags had become too frequent to ignore. I could not stand by and allow our brand name to drag the brand itself into the gutter. We needed to create a differentiated brand image. It was definitely time to switch names.

We engaged Wolff Olins (who had developed our brand promise: 'Designing Tomorrow Together') and Lexicon to create a new brand name for us. A name is a brand's calling card. It appears front and centre at every touchpoint within the stakeholder ecosystem. We needed a name that truly represented our character. Both agencies conducted a series of focused group meetings with our associates, customers and investors and arrived at the word 'Cyient'. The sound and spelling of 'Cyient' resonated at many levels. It was a fusion of 'science' and 'client', two cornerstones of our business. The 'ent' represented engineering and technology, our bread and butter. Companies often embark on rebranding exercises because they want to disengage from their past and start afresh. But we were proud of our heritage and wanted to tie our legacy, people and values with the future. So, we appended our stock exchange ticker symbol— IENT—to enrich the name.

Before adopting it, we took care to find out if the word Cyient meant anything offensive in any language or country where we had a business presence, but found none. Cyient is a coined name and is not always pronounced correctly, but it is an apt representation of our ethos. We then invested in developing the brand profile and our value proposition. Eight years after rebranding the company, our brand recall has touched new heights.

It must be mentioned here that there are a few well-meaning customers who refuse to call us Cyient even after the name change.

Loyal to Infotech, they stick to our old name to commemorate the good work we have done for them in the past. But on the whole, Cyient resonates a lot more with people because of its uniqueness.

Evangelizing IT Industry

As an entrepreneur, I believe that contributing to the industry ecosystem is as much a responsibility and a prerogative as building the enterprise because an industry is all about collective responsibilities and shared benefits.

Within a year of Infotech's founding, we started associating with NASSCOM (National Association of Software and Service Companies) and subsequently CII. NASSCOM amplified the industry's voice, evangelizing IT and developing a broad support base for the nascent industry from all the stakeholders, particularly the government. NASSCOM's international lobbying helped build the brand equity of Indian IT companies in new markets and stimulated the industry's rapid growth. It helped Infotech to become part of these industry bodies and have its voice heard.

My engagement with the NASSCOM Executive Council and advocacy for ER&D services led to the founding of an engineering services council (ER&D Forum) and launch of several initiatives to accelerate the growth of the engineering services market. Yet, the segment did not attract enough leadership attention at NASSCOM as the technology industry landscape transformed rapidly, stakeholder expectations changed and engineering services became the fastest-growing segment of the IT industry. When an opportunity came in the form of the chairmanship of NASSCOM in 2015–16, along with the larger interests of the body, I ensured that there was enough visibility and representation for the concerns of the ER&D services segment.

Even as I associated with NASSCOM, I made sure Infotech had representation in CII as well. I served as chairman of CII's AP Council in 2002–03 and supported the campaign to promote Andhra Pradesh as a priority investment destination in India. It caught the attention of many global companies, and resulted in large investment inflows and several global centres were set up in the state. Subsequently, I served as chairman of CII Southern region, chairman of CII Education Council, member of CII National Committee on Defence and CII National Committee on IT & ITeS.

In the post-Liberalization era, economic development was largely driven by the private sector. There is a high positive correlation between the effectiveness of national trade associations and their role in developing socioeconomic structures, strengthening cross-border relationships and globalization. Mature and democratic associations such as NASSCOM and CII make positive contributions to their members, the industry and the nation.

We, at Infotech, were sharply aware of the interdependencies that were inherent in the partner and industry ecosystem to strengthen the value proposition, expand the business and build an enduring institution. For me, it was important to be a proactive contributor to this ecosystem to create a future of which Infotech would be an integral part.

Giving Back to Society

An enterprise stands on four pillars. The three essential pillars of an enterprise—customers, investors, and associates—contribute to it in tangible ways. The fourth pillar of a company—society— supports it through numerous unseen methods. Consequently, it is the organization's responsibility to step forward and support the unknown faces of society. For profit-making organizations, social responsibility strategies are often borne out of a sense of obligation. But I never saw social responsibility as an 'add-on'. It was always an extension of my beliefs, an expression of who I am and how I do business.

In the early years of Infotech, we carried out several random acts of charity. We supported Project Krushi, an initiative by the alumni of Sainik School, for children in difficult circumstances. In 1998, when Krushi adopted a school, Infotech decided to build its infrastructure. This was much before the government-mandated social responsibility activity for corporations (2013). Within a short period, Krushi and its children became integral to the Infotech family. Our customers, who initially had reservations, slowly started viewing our engagement with Krushi as an organizational virtue.

We signed an MoU with the state government and it allowed us to adopt state-run schools in Hyderabad to develop their infrastructure, faculty, technology and provide student support. Soon after, we started adopting schools in the vicinity of our offices in Bangalore (now Bengaluru), Mysore, Kakinada, and Noida.

The Cyient Digital Centres (CDCs) set up in these schools imparted digital literacy with employable skills to the neighbourhood community. To support unemployed youth with employable skills, we built urban micro skill centres as per the National Skill Development Corporation (NSDC) guidelines and started imparting vocational skills in tailoring, baking, confectionery, beautician and bedside assistance services.

Our baseline in every CSR initiative is that it should have a multiplier effect. With the same intent, we adopted a village in Andhra Pradesh and introduced initiatives to convert it into a smart village by upgrading infrastructure such as roads, sanitation, drinking water, a school and a public health centre. Our partnership with LV Prasad Eye Institute led us to develop new and low-cost products for disease management, therapy and the rehabilitation of vision-impaired patients.

More than our investments and board committee directives, Cyient's CSR initiatives certainly owe their success to the contributions of 1000+ associates pan-India, who generously give their time to support the causes they believe in. This passion and commitment towards social responsibility created a differentiated image of Infotech/Cyient in the minds of stakeholders and became a competitive advantage over the years. While we certainly didn't rationalize our CSR strategy on this premise, it became a happy consequence, expanding the company's brand equity and becoming a cornerstone for building the institution that Cyient is today.

Choosing the Next CEO

Maintaining momentum in a business is as essential as having a vision and a strategy for a company and this must include succession planning. Making a conscious transition from one generation of leadership, ownership and governance to the next is essential.

At Cyient, we insist that every senior leader identify at least two teammates/associates as his/her successors and nurture them. In a competitive environment, survival depends partly on having identified replacements for key positions and preparing them for expanded organizational responsibilities. This ensures that there is never a leadership void in the company at any level.

Even for the coveted top job, I intended to have a successor. The institutional view of business made me deeply conscious that if I wished to see Cyient as a lasting enterprise, we needed to be ready for unforeseen situations. More than an emergency, once an organization attains a specific size, it needs a second-in-command to ensure stability and sustainability.

It was not easy for a founder like me, who was deeply vested in the company, to leave the game. Not when I enjoyed it so thoroughly. Yet, five years after founding Infotech, when I turned forty-five, I voiced my thoughts on retirement at an off-site meeting. I was clear that I would not be the chairman and managing director (CMD) of the company at sixty-five and would give up all executive positions when I turn seventy. My aim was to make the organization outgrow me. And that entailed a plan.

When the company went public in 1997, the first person I considered as my right-hand man was Rajan Babu Kasetty. Rajan had kept a close watch on the company right from its inception as a director on the board. But as Infotech started witnessing the next phase of growth at the turn of the century, we needed someone who had the experience of running a much larger enterprise. We then experimented with a lateral entrant, but he left the organization after a short stint.

I wanted my successor to rise from the ranks of Infotech. By this time, John Renard, who had come to us through the acquisition of Dataview Solutions in the UK, began leading our geospatial business worldwide. John had a good business acumen and was a respected senior executive. At around the same time, Krishna returned to Infotech, after completing his MBA from Kellogg's School of Management at Northwestern University in the US. He started taking lead roles in many functions, including marketing, strategy, sales and the engineering services division. I eyed John, Krishna and a few other leaders as potential candidates. I kept a close watch on them but kept my options open. I then looked for sager counsel and turned to senior board members. Since the engineering business was larger than geospatial and was expanding rapidly, they favoured training Krishna as my successor.

Choosing the next CEO is one of the most significant decisions in the life of an organization. It is critical to find the right fit. In a promoter-led company like Infotech, choosing the next CEO may appear straightforward. But we recognized that succession was a dynamic process and not a predetermined affair. It is not limited to a mere handing over of the baton, but an actual team effort, with a game plan drawn up and implemented over time.

Murugappan, who had known Krishna since he was a child and had watched him grow into a business leader, had the following advice for me. 'Mohan, I want all senior executives in the company to see Krishna as a competent leader in his own right and not because he is Mohan Reddy's son. He should get to the top post only when people respect him. That's my recommendation.'

We gave Krishna challenging roles, including a position as president of Engineering, COO and board member. He sized up to every challenge. Krishna's business vision is expansive. He brings a sense of purpose to his role and is an embodiment of that purpose. Within a short time, he developed a deep understanding of the business and the markets we operated in and built strong connections with several customers. He is a man of his word and goal-driven. He is not flashy and is something of an introvert. I have seen him empowering his team and allowing them to take complete ownership. We let him move linearly up the ranks over the years and saw him evolving as a competent and well-respected business leader.

Krishna had Ravi Bhoothalingam, former CEO of VST Industries and Oberoi Hotels, as his mentor. While Ravi coached Krishna, he also counselled me. 'Mohan, successions are successful only if predecessors find another job for themselves. Even if founders retire from work, they typically do not retire from life. Letting go is not easy for founder-entrepreneurs. They have to plan their next chapter of life, find other vocations and move on.'

I took this advice to heart and started involving myself in a bouquet of off-company activities I was passionate about. These included education, entrepreneur-mentoring, start-ups and industry engagement.

Succession is not a one-day decision. Part of succession planning for an entrepreneur is to exit from a business and let a new leader take over. It takes years of planning. I always kept that option open. I was simultaneously mindful that there was every possibility that the plan would get rejected or fail. So, I always had a backup plan even as I groomed Krishna. It took time. The one deadline I had set for myself was to have a successor in place when I turned sixty.

We had a series of conversations to gauge Krishna's interest in running the business. I was transparent with him on what the expectations would be. Once I was convinced the company could chart a growth path under his leadership, I proposed Krishna's name to the board. I decided to remain as the executive chairman of the company. In April 2014, the board unanimously accepted my proposal.

It was a hard decision. Removing myself from the operations of the company was not easy. We had evolved a clear set of guidelines limiting my involvement. I had to be disciplined and refrain from interfering in the business.

To this end, I apprised executives what the change in leadership would mean. 'I'll be serving the company only as the executive chairman. You can seek my counsel on anything any day, and I'll guide you. I'll ask you questions only once a week during staff meetings or at board meetings. You are not answerable to me, but you are answerable to the stakeholders.'

I kept my word and kept myself busy outside the company and, over time, adapted to the situation.

Years ago, when I first started toying with the idea of succession and shortlisted John and Krishna as possible successors, had I made a public announcement, it would not have gone down well within the organization. I wanted it to be a professional exercise so that the transition was smooth, without any fallouts. In fact, there were none. No one resigned when Krishna became the CEO. Prof. Kavil Ramachandran of the Indian School of Business (ISB) regards the transition at Cyient as one of the best in the country, from a first-generation entrepreneur to the second generation. Its key elements were transparency and clarity—with both parties getting what they wanted. This made the passage of leadership from one set of hands into the other a smooth affair, with none of the bloodletting that normally accompanies a changeover.

Eight years have passed since the transition and I am happy with my decision. Krishna has measured up to my expectations and the company's performance speaks for itself. There were mistakes and I had my moments of concern. But I allowed Krishna and his team to make their own errors and outgrow them.

And I? How would I feel if a bus ran into me now? Unconcerned. I have come a long way from the small boy who counted bogeys, the teenager who tried to hide his report card, the young man who chased his dreams, the middle-aged CEO who tossed a high-end job to begin a start-up from his dining table, the husband who convinced his wife that we would not lose and the seasoned entrepreneur who built a billion-dollar global enterprise. I have achieved what I set out to do, reached heights I never imagined and I am content, although there's always the next milestone to walk to and then the next.

Epilogue

Co-creating the Future

'Mohan, how's the business? Where are you spending your time these days?' Kapil Sibal, then Union minister for human resources development, inquired during a chance encounter at a luncheon.

Sibal was in town for the convocation of BITS Pilani (Hyderabad campus) in mid-2012. I met him at lunch after the ceremony. He knew me well; we had interacted several times during his previous stint as Union minister for science and technology.

'I'm slowing down, Mr Sibal,' I confessed with a candid air. 'The company now has a capable leadership team in place and I'll be naming my successor quite soon. So, I've started withdrawing from all the executive functions. I've decided to invest my time in giving back to society instead, in any way I can.'

I could see that my admission took him by surprise.

'Oh, I didn't know that,' he said looking thoroughly taken aback.

'Not many people do, outside the company,' I said. 'I'm looking for avenues where I can contribute actively, and I've more or less decided to focus on the education sector. I owe my success to the education this country provided me, and I believe it can make remarkable contributions to the development of the country,' I averred.

'Ah!' he said, visibly interested. 'Why don't you come to Delhi and meet me in my office?' he suggested.

I had no clue what was in store for me, and I blithely walked into the minister's home office the following week. I reiterated my ideas during the course of the meeting.

He heard me out patiently, without interruption, and then said, 'Mohan, IIT Hyderabad is a brand-new institution, a second-generation IIT. It's just a four-year-old baby and it needs active engagement so that it can be nurtured into an institution of excellence. Why don't you take over as chairman of its board?' Mr Sibal offered.

'Ah, that would be a dream come true and it would be such a great way to participate in nation-building!' I exclaimed. I couldn't conceal my enthusiasm. 'IIT itself is a brand, and the mere idea of being able to foster IIT Hyderabad and bring it up to par with the older IITs is such an exciting thought,' I said eagerly.

There was only one possible answer to his proposal. It was a big yes.

And thus began a new chapter in my lifelong love affair with IIT in October 2012. It had started with my stint as a graduate student at IIT Kanpur way back in the early 1970s and had continued to blossom through the years as an alumnus and later as a distinguished alumnus of this prestigious institution.

University education typically prepares students for careers defined by governments and corporates. But today, millennials are willing to shape their own careers and that of the nation. Higher educational institutions, especially technical institutes, can easily facilitate it by imparting the necessary knowledge and skills. I realized this was my opportunity to change the dynamics of technical education in the country by helping our graduates transform into job creators, and IIT Hyderabad could become the change agent. With this intent, I dived head-first into the institute's affairs.

IIT Hyderabad rapidly became a trendsetter by introducing a 'Minor in Entrepreneurship' in the BTech programme, for third- and fourth-year students. The Department of Entrepreneurship and Management was established in 2019, and all the courses are being delivered by industry leaders, leading entrepreneurs and faculty.

The 'Minor' became popular among students. It equipped them with the nuances of starting a venture and fuelled them to leverage research, funding and incubation facilities the institute offered. This led to the launch of several deep-tech, health-tech and semiconductor start-ups at the institute in a short period of time.

Further, I oversaw the establishment of the IITH Technology Research Park (TRP). The Park offers infrastructure and facilities for industry partners to co-locate their research and technology development centres within the campus and develop products and services through collaborations.

Besides TRP, an independent Technology Incubation Park (TIP) was also established recently. TIP acts as a nerve centre of all incubation and start-up activities and can host 200 entrepreneurs working on deep-tech themes. It acts as a platform for open innovation and organizes activities such as skill development workshops, industry-oriented hackathons and sensitization events around rural technology needs.

More recently, the BVR Mohan Reddy School of Innovation and Entrepreneurship (BVR SCIENT) held its ground-breaking ceremony at IIT Hyderabad. The School aims to augment the activities of TRP and TIP and envisages giving wings to the latent talent of youngsters, spurring innovation and nurturing their business instincts. Simultaneously, it aspires to facilitate new venture creation, finance, IP creation, and negotiation. This will amplify the efforts of IIT Hyderabad in creating a thriving entrepreneurial ecosystem.

Over 100 start-ups have been supported by IIT Hyderabad till date, generating more than Rs 100 crore in revenue and creating over 800 jobs. Once the dedicated facilities of TIP and the School of Entrepreneurship are fully operational, these numbers are expected to see an exponential rise.

Hyderabad Angels

In early 2010, I began evaluating start-ups with an intent to invest and started exploring platforms that created awareness and built momentum for investments. While ad hoc mechanisms and metro-based networks were many, there were no organized means for investors to come together to promote the entrepreneurial ecosystem in the undivided state of Andhra Pradesh.

I started having conversations with early-stage entrepreneurs, especially tech start-ups, to understand their funding needs and the ease of access to private capital. They apprised me that high-net-worth individuals (HNIs) invested and offered mentorship, but such avenues were few and far between.

Simultaneously, I engaged in friendly dialogue with like-minded people such as Srini Raju, Chairman of iLabs Venture Capital Fund, J.A. Chowdary, founding director of STPI Hyderabad, and D. Suresh Babu, Managing Director of Suresh Productions, to gauge their appetite for investments. Their views matched mine and they were quite enthusiastic about creating a start-up ecosystem but had hitherto found no regional platforms committed to the cause. I foresaw great synergies and win-win opportunities in bringing these two stakeholders to partner and co-create a meaningful and rewarding future.

These conversations culminated in the launch of the Hyderabad Angels Forum for Entrepreneurship Development in 2010 to 'bring value beyond capital'. After the initial momentum, the group wanted to create a more organized structure. Encouraged by the success of Indian Angel Network (Delhi) and Mumbai Angels, the group created a Section 8 company and launched Hyderabad Angels (HA) in 2012.

Leading venture capitalists, entrepreneurs, and business leaders with ample financial, business and operational acumen committed to investing money and time to support eligible Indian and global early stage start-ups. HA began collaborating with other angel networks, incubators, accelerators and academic institutes from all corners of the country and overseas to discuss, ideate, co-invest and bring the wisdom of collective investment to its members. It began mentoring and handholding the start-ups wherever and whenever needed.

As a founder and advisory board member of HA, I began investing in promising tech start-ups—Indian and global—and mentoring the founders to create tangible and intangible value for the investee companies. About fifty-two early-stage start-ups from various sectors fulfilled their capital needs through HA to the tune of $10 million, a portfolio value of $20 million and a total employment of 3500+ in India till date, returning an average 3.5X to the investors.

T-Hub

The next golden opportunity to make a difference came in the form of K.T. Rama Rao (popularly known as KTR), the young, dynamic, forward-looking politician and the IT, industry and urban development minister in the newly formed state of Telangana.

In 2014, the Telangana Rashtra Samithi (TRS) swept the polls, riding high on the plank of a separate state of Telangana with Hyderabad as its capital. As the new government was being formed, I received a call from KTR's office. I was told that he wanted to meet me. I had met KTR twice previously for television debates on the need to carve out a new state. Though our views were divergent on both occasions, I was impressed with his deep conviction, excellent articulation and controlled aggression which at the same time never lost sight of opposing views. I readily agreed, and he visited me at my home in May 2014.

After the usual round of pleasantries punctuated on my side with a string of congratulatory words, we settled down to talk business.

'Sir, this is a new state,' KTR began. 'People have a lot of apprehensions about our ability to govern but we have assured people that we will provide a clean government and are committed to the rapid development of the state. Our agenda for growth is simple— *neellu* (water), *nidhulu* (finances) and *niyamakalu* (jobs). The IT industry has witnessed considerable growth in the past. We see a tremendous future in this area and would like to hear your thoughts on the subject,' he stated, coming to the heart of the matter.

'Ram,' I reciprocated warmly. 'If you look at the profile of the IT industry in Telangana, it is largely in and around Hyderabad. Large multinationals, which saw the benefits of being in Hyderabad, have already arrived and created development centres, and others have chosen locations elsewhere in the country. While I am sure you will charm them into expanding in Hyderabad, the future growth will come from two new streams—the new-age technology industry comprising companies such as Apple and Google, and from start-ups.'

Sharp on the uptake and quick-witted in the extreme, KTR, I observed, was listening keenly to every word I uttered.

'The new-age industry requires a fair amount of marketing and enabling policies, and I leave that to you,' I paused. 'But there is one area where I can work alongside you. Around 60 per cent of the new jobs the world over are being created by start-ups and SMEs. If you wish to see Telangana as a developed state, it is critical to promote innovation and entrepreneurship, and in this you have my full support,' I offered.

KTR took to my suggestion and tasked his IT secretary and a few other like-minded individuals to create an entity in public-private partnership (PPP) mode to promote entrepreneurship in the state. We incorporated the new entity as a Section 8 company with four government-nominated directors and five directors from the corporate sector or individuals who pledged Rs 1 crore to demonstrate their commitment. On the other side, the government promised to support all capex and even provide bridge funding of opex, if required. This gave birth to the T-Hub (short for Telangana Hub or Technology Hub) on 15 April 2015. I signed off as one of the founding directors and contributed to the corpus to become the first director on the board.

T-Hub leased 70,000 sq. ft of an under-construction building on IIIT Hyderabad campus and transformed it into an uber-modern, state-of-the-art 'CatalysT' edifice, symbolizing Telangana's ambition to become one of the world's leading innovation hubs. With a huge central atrium, fully open office spaces, a huge cafeteria and facilities for meetings, conferences, networking and collaboration, T-Hub houses entrepreneurs, corporates, investors, mentors and service providers under one roof. With numerous mentoring programmes, boot camps, periodic incubation and accelerator cohorts, T-Hub fast became a one-stop destination for innovators and start-ups in various stages to learn, grow and build lasting relationships with key stakeholders of industry, academia and the public sector.

T-Hub is an outstanding example of how local business leaders can support the start-up ecosystem along with unwavering commitment and support from the local government. In the eight years since its founding, T-Hub has acted as a co-creative engagement platform, learning directly from the experiences of its stakeholders, generating fresh ideas quickly, experimenting with new offerings, building deeper relationships and trust with the community, all the while creating a unique brand of its own globally. As a nucleus of start-up activity, the Hub provided over 1800 national and international start-ups to date with access to better technology, talent, mentors, customers, corporates, investors and government agencies.[*]

Several national and international angel and incubator/accelerator networks, PE and venture capital firms started leveraging T-Hub's network and infrastructure. It quickly became a critical constituent of Telangana Innovation Network along with We Hub (for women entrepreneurs), T Works (tinkering lab), TASK (Telangana Academy for Skills and Knowledge), RISC (Research and Innovation Circle of Hyderabad) and TSIC (Telangana State Innovation Cell).

These disparate engagement platforms began drawing on each other's experiences in a continuous cycle of value discovery. While enhancing network economics, this created a virtuous cycle of benefits for all stakeholders—an ecosystem in itself.

At the time of writing this epilogue, T-Hub 2.0 was inaugurated with an estimated cost of Rs 300 crore. With room to house over 4000 start-ups, T-Hub 2.0 is expected to give a huge fillip to Hyderabad's innovation ecosystem.

---

[*] https://t-hub.co/about-us/

These enabling organizations are transforming Telangana into a favoured investment destination in India. Several lead indicators point out that Hyderabad will become the innovation capital of the country.

Entrepreneurs and private enterprises have rarely been perceived as agents of social change in the past. Yet, it is a fairly accepted concept today that business success brings economic development and social well-being. Further, embracing such a democratic approach to build an ecosystem that creates shared value—pursue financial success in a way that yields societal benefits—is imperative in today's tech-led business world. Such ecosystems have a long-term orientation and make complex interdependencies between co-evolving stakeholders; yet they are the most advanced forms of innovation and dependable routes to a nation's prosperity. I chose to walk this path to perpetuate the learnings I had internalized as an entrepreneur and attempt to bring about the required mindset shift and socio-economic change during my lifetime.

Acknowledgements

'Your beliefs become your thoughts,
Your thoughts become your words,
Your words become your actions,
Your actions become your habits,
Your habits become your values,
Your values become your destiny.'

—Mahatma Gandhi

I believe in these words of the Mahatma, and so 'Values FIRST' became a lighthouse that directs Cyient in all endeavours. It provides continuous guidance on how to treat customers, make sense of our work life, and provides a framework for achieving the vision we set for ourselves while increasing the overall effectiveness of the organization.

Everything we accomplished at Cyient over the last thirty years is a result of collaborative efforts of countless people, including the senior executive team and tens of thousands of Cyientists—who, driven by values, executed with passion. I'd like to thank each of them. In the interest of space and time, I will limit the list to a handful of people without whose efforts we could not have built a successful, sustainable global business.

Rajan Kasetty, one of the founding directors and a signatory to the incorporation of Infotech Enterprises (rebranded as Cyient in 2014). In the formative years, he always had a shoulder for me to cry on whenever I faced a challenge. He helped incorporate and build the US subsidiary too.

Sucharitha Bodanapu (my wife, Suchi), who was part of the founding team and served as a director on the board till 2014. Suchi skilfully shouldered the family responsibilities all along while continuing to be a pillar of strength for the company.

Sunil Kumar, our first hire, who continues to be with us after thirty years. He made invaluable contributions to building the digitization business. The management team of Sunil for operations, N. Lakshmipathy for accounts and Pravin Kumar for HR were of immense support in the formative years.

Every time we added a new service offering or a geography or product line, we brought new leaders—old connections of mine who had my trust. They acted as talent magnets and attracted the best people in the industry. When we decided to start CAD software development, it was Srinivas Uppuluri and Dr G.D. Rao. Our overseas acquisitions brought extraordinary local talent. We onboarded John Renard, Martin Trostel and Greg Tilly in executive positions to head operations in the UK, Germany and the USA respectively. They played pivotal roles in aligning the culture of the acquired entity with that of the parent company and facilitated rapid business ramp-up.

When we launched ourselves into engineering services with all earnestness, we recruited Rajendra Velagapudi, who further attracted terrific people like Rajendra Kumar Patro. Their contribution to building the engineering practice was extraordinary.

When operations started scaling, we brought senior talent into the company. Ashok Reddy joined as head of human resources and spent over fifteen years. We could not have run the company smoothly without him, especially with large-scale recruitments year after year. S.A. Lakshminarayan (SAL), with his process vigour and unceasing focus on quality, scaled our geospatial/GIS business dramatically.

Ashok Kumar, who had a great passion for engineering, was ideal to head our engineering services business. Rajeev Lal joined at a time the company was scaling the commercial software business. He subsequently grew to head engineering services and software delivery. It was gratifying to have Rajeev, Ashok Kumar, SAL and Ashok Reddy serve the company till their superannuation.

N.J. Joseph started a dedicated marketing department but became my strategic partner working on all the acquisitions and their integration into the company. He currently serves as the chief strategy officer (CSO). Anand Parameswaran came with a strong delivery background but played many business roles, led HR function and now serves as president and global head of technology delivery organization. Prabhakar Atla, who joined as marketing manager, grew to become the president of three critical verticals. His vision, comprehension and attention to detail brought a new dimension to the company's thinking. When the Pratt & Whitney account grew and we needed somebody to handle it independently, we found an amazing asset in Tom Edwards. Katie Cook, apart from efficiently handling the P&L of a business line, had the wisdom to lead the diversity and inclusion efforts.

The company had the benefit of having three outstanding CFOs during my tenure—Mohan Krishna Reddy, Nataraja and Ajay Aggarwal. Their financial discipline, perspectives on financial planning and their strategic financial acumen brought a lot of value at different times of growth. Without them, we couldn't have come this far.

Krishna Bodanapu's induction into the company fulfilled many a dream of mine. He helped building the engineering business from ground zero and transformed himself as an outstanding thinker and solid executioner. As the CEO of the company, Krishna has built an impressive track record.

The addition of P.N.S.V. Narasimham as head of human resources brought in technology and transformation into HR function. His enormous wisdom and ability to command respect make him unique. Karthik Natarajan as COO brought tremendous aggressiveness to the company. His deft handling of the operations during and after COVID-19 has been outstanding.

Deep gratitude to many members of Cyient/ Infotech board of directors, notably M.M. Murugappan, Alain De Taeye, Paul Adams and Som Mittal. Thanks to all the fifty directors who served on the board since inception. Successful companies share one thing in common—a strong partnership between management and their boards. In our case, too, it is the board's support, advice and encouragement that made us perform so well.

I have been the chairman and CEO of the company for twenty-four long years. Thereafter, I served as the executive chairman and now function as a member of the board. Throughout this journey, the stakeholders—customers, investors and partners—were very supportive. They trusted the company and joined us on this exhilarating journey.

I will fail in my duty if I do not acknowledge the support of government, industry bodies, especially NASSCOM and CII, and civil society, who helped in seen and unseen ways in building and transforming Cyient into a successful multinational.

Engineered in India is a labour of love to serve the future generations with my entrepreneurial experiences and insights, and to prod them to partake in nation-building. And I owe this to scores of former and current associates mentioned above, industry colleagues and customers who came forward to share their experiences of working along with me and validated or augmented my recollections of over four decades.

A hearty shout-out to my colleague BhanuRekha, for being the connecting tissue from the word go until the book was released. N.J. Joseph, for carefully reading through the early draft and suggesting valuable improvements. Prof. Kavil Ramachandran of ISB and G.V. Prasad of Dr. Reddy's Laboratories, for patiently going through version 1.0 and giving extremely constructive feedback and thoughtful suggestions.

I am much obliged to Namita Kala and Bhavdeep Kang for providing an excellent editorial review and enhancing the narrative with qualitative refinements. I appreciate Richa Vijayavargiya for providing research support. I acknowledge my colleague Navroze Palekar, for bringing meticulous legal counsel so the memoir was ready for publication.

I would also like to appreciate Radhika Marwah and Vineet Gill at Penguin Random House India, for their seamless support in bringing the story of my life to the world and to readers like you!

Notes

Chapter 2: Thinking like an Entrepreneur, Acting like a CEO

1. Jason Dedrick and Kenneth L. Kraemer, *Globalization of Personal Computer Industry: Trends and Implications*, Center for Research on Information Technology and Organizations (CRITO), University of California, Irvine.
2. B. Dhar, R.K. Joseph, *India's Information Technology Industry: A Tale of Two Halves*, 2019, in: K.C. Liu and U. Racherla (eds), *Innovation, Economic Development, and Intellectual Property in India and China*, ARCIALA Series on Intellectual Assets and Law in Asia, Springer, Singapore https://link.springer.com/chapter/10.1007/978-981-13-8102-7_5
3. V. Rajaraman, *History of Computing in India (1955-2010)*, IEEE Computer Society, http://www.cbi.umn.edu/hostedpublications/pdf/Rajaraman_HistComputingIndia.pdf
4. https://bit.ly/3jawLIB
5. https://www.javatpoint.com/sun-microsystems
6. Dinesh C. Sharma, *The Outsourcer: The Story of India's IT Revolution*, MIT Press, 2015.
7. http://www.cbi.umn.edu/hostedpublications/pdf/Rajaraman_HistComputingIndia.pdf
8. *The Outsourcer: The Story of India's IT Revolution.*

Chapter 3: Birth of a Dream

1. *The Outsourcer: The Story of India's IT Revolution.*
2. T.N. Srinivasan, 'Economic Liberalization and Economic Development: India', *Journal of Asian Economics*, 10490078, Summer 96, vol. 7, issue 2.
3. *History of Computing in India (1955-2010).*
4. *History of Computing in India (1955-2010).*

Chapter 4: Growing Pains

1. https://www.encyclopedia.com/books/politics-and-business-magazines/analytical-surveys-inc

Chapter 7: Driving Growth: Aerospace Engineering

1. Albert Einstein, 'On the Methods of Theoretical Physics', Herbert Spencer Lecture at the University of Oxford, 10 June 1933, published in *Philosophy of Science*, April 1934.
2. Muhammad Ali as co-author with Richard Durham, *The Greatest: My Own Story*, 1975, p. 365.

Chapter 8: Riding High with New Verticals

1. G.K. Chesterton, *Orthodoxy*, Chapter 2, 'The Maniac', John Lane, 1909, p 27.
2. Kiran Karnik, *The Coalition of Competitors: The Story of Nasscom and the IT Industry*, HarperCollins, 2012.

Chapter 15: In Times of Crises

1. https://h2o.law.harvard.edu/collages/42157
2. https://law.justia.com/cases/federal/district-courts/FSupp/946/1079/2097296/
3. https://www.bbc.com/news/uk-scotland-40416026